Horns of the Moon

HORNS *of the* MOON
*Techniques in
Traditional Magical Arts*

Kerry Wisner

TROY BOOKS

First printing in paperback
October 2021

ISBN 978-1-909602-44-1

Published by Troy Books
www.troybooks.co.uk

Troy Books Publishing
BM Box 8003
London WC1N 3XX

Cover art: Kerry Wisner
Cover design: Gemma Gary

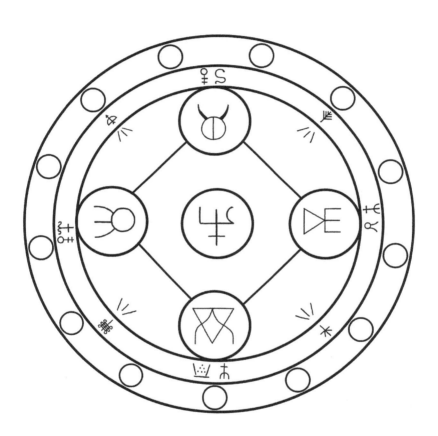

Contents

Photoplates
between pages 144-145

❧ PREFACE ❧

In nature there exists an underlying current; a continuity of wisdom moving as a subtle force within all that is. This can be termed *The Geassa*: a sacred bond of transcendent awareness that lies at the core of existence. And, as discussed in the first book of this series, the Geassa can best be understood as a living consciousness finding expression in the animistic magical practices of indigenous people the world over.

The west is no exception. While, to all appearances this connection to the land has been lost, the reality is that within certain magical arts essential elements of a living system still exist. These serve as a vehicle that allows one to experience different states of being, different dimensions of reality, and to reconnect with deeper forces hidden in nature.

This is the second in *The Geassa* series: a set of books that presents principles and techniques of the magical arts as I have come to understand and practice these. One of my first teachers called this *The Willow Path*: a term that is directly related to the Middle English word "Wiche" and later to "Witch". This is a clear reference to the use of the term for that which is "pliable" and "bendable", just as Willow osiers can be easily bent and used in weaving, tying and binding. Similarly, those of the Art bend and shape reality.

As explained in the first book, the procedures described represent a blend of three important strands of wisdom that have contributed to the Western Mysteries:

- Traditional Witchcraft, 'folklore' and with it a certain amount of information drawn from ancient pagan

11

sources including Celtic and pre-Celtic teachings;
- Hermeticism and ritual magic stripped of much of the influence that crept into this from Abrahamic sources;
- And, Ancient Egyptian teachings drawn from accredited sources and texts.

In my experience I have found these strands are largely compatible and, in fact, complement each other. Together they form the fountainhead of most western occult sciences. Yet, in saying this, it is important to understand that the foundation of the system that I am presenting rests firmly in the natural, animistic practices of Traditional Witchcraft. In particular, this involves building a relationship with one's locale: the environment in which one lives. From understanding the various seasonal tides of power, to forming alliances with otherworld beings, this forms the basis on which much of our practice rests. Within this, though, can be found universal concepts and techniques that are indicative of all magical arts reaching beyond locale, region or even periods of time.

While the first book discusses the foundational practices of this system, this second volume builds on this. As such, it is advisable that one reads *The Willow Path* before setting out to understand the concepts which will be discussed here. Without a thorough understanding of the teachings found in the first book the information presented here, while useful, will not convey the deeper meaning that is intended.

This adjunct readily applies to those who may consider themselves adepts within other traditions. Precisely because the teachings regarding the nature of reality described in *The Willow Path* reflect a paradigm drawn from ancient sources which are rarely understood or discussed in more contemporary esoteric schools. This is particularly so of those occult Orders that draw heavily from Qabalistic sources. In presenting the Art, I will do my best to draw clear comparisons when possible. Yet some of these concepts are, to my knowledge, unique to a very limited number of initiates.

In this series I present the magical arts as I learned these. In no way should the reader assume that this is the only way to view the traditions inherent in western esoteric circles. On the contrary, this system represents just one approach to the overall practices and teachings. I am certain that there will be those who will take exception to some of the concepts presented in this series. That is as it should be.

As mentioned in the first book, there are many facets and by-ways within the wisdom that is the bond of the Geassa. Various traditions kept different aspects of the wisdom alive that others may have forgotten or not know about. Yet other groups focused on developing new approaches while using the older teachings as their foundation. My goal in writing these books is to preserve the teachings and techniques that I have been taught while helping to carry these forward for others to follow should they find these of value.

As noted in the first book these teachings are drawn, in large part, from notes I had taken throughout my training. As such, in some places information overlaps with references to subjects discussed elsewhere. This has been done chiefly because these books are a melding of the notes and teachings I've received over decades of practice. Please keep in mind that much of this training came in the form of private one on one sessions with no systematic format intended. Rather, much of this was drawn through conversations with my teachers, while other information came in the form of in-depth study and research. I have done my best to blend these together in a readable format, giving them structure here. In doing so, it is my hope that the reader will get a sense of how the teachings were passed to me and how I have built upon these with further study and application.

Chapter One

✤ To Travel the Willow Path ✤

In the Art there are a number of practices that form the foundation of much of what we do. As such, one needs to develop these as much as possible. These include the techniques of *Merging* or *Becoming*, the ability to *Travel in Spirit*, recovery of past-life memories, the ability to influence others and change circumstances through the Art, as well as the ability to communicate with spirits and otherworld beings. Much of this will involve the use of spell-crafting, 'charms', enchantments or words of power, talismans, amulets and sigils, divination, as well as an extensive knowledge of herbal lore. With this comes a measure of intensive training in occult correspondence and philosophy.

In considering all of this it soon becomes clear that the Willow Path is a way of living, of thinking and being. Traveling this path brings with it the means by which consciousness is changed while one's world view expands in ways that one could never have imagined. It is through this process that those of the Art learn to ultimately change reality itself. This only comes from study, daily practice and commitment. Yet it is through this effort that the Art brings real and lasting results.

Having said this some people do have certain 'natural abilities' and a predilection toward the Art that others may not. One of my first teachers, Grandma Julie,[1] felt that this

---

1. Julie was the matriarch of a family practicing Traditional Witchcraft with roots reaching to the Basque region of Europe. As discussed in the first book, *The Willow Path*, I had been led to her through correspondence with Sybil Leek. Julie, in turn, took it upon herself to work with me until her passing.

difference was a direct result of experiences lived through previous incarnations in which one had been part of the Art before. Julie went on to explain that those so endowed have natural, innate abilities which predispose them to the Art. These people will frequently be drawn to the path early on in age with the doors to initiation opening sooner than for those who may not have had a similar past. In her words, such individuals are 'natural Witches' possessing strong magical powers.

In her book *The Complete Art of Witchcraft* Sybil Leek was careful to describe the difference between a 'natural' Witch and a sorcerer:

> "A sorcerer, says the modern anthropologist, is one who uses medicines, plant roots, nail, hair and such things to create a magical influence. The Witch, on the other hand, possesses strong magical power within her and by concentration alone on a person or an object can cause changes in its condition. Anyone who can take the time to practice and study can become a sorcerer, but not too many have the innate power of a Witch."[2]

Despite this, everyone has the ability to develop skill in the Art. Just as there are those who have 'natural' musical talent and go on to be great musicians, the rest of us still have the ability to make music. And, with practice, many people can go on to be truly accomplished musicians. The same holds true for the Art. With practice and training anyone can learn to apply practical magic in their life.

I want to emphasize that whether one has 'natural' talent or not, to be consistently successful in the Art takes dedication and practice. Because of this some may find that it is not the system for them. Further, it needs to be understood that by its very nature this tradition is essentially a journey of self-discovery and personal development.

---

2. Leek, Sybil. *The Complete Art of Witchcraft*, p.75.

To travel the Willow Path is, for the most part, to make this journey alone, or if one is lucky, with a few trusted companions. Even for those involved in Covens, Clans or Orders, the majority of their Art remains solitary in nature.

Yet, in my experience, at some point each person who sincerely aspires to practice the Trade will come in contact with a teacher or teachers. In my opinion one-on-one training is essential. And with this, the transformative effects of the rituals associated with initiation serve to awaken the Witch to the deeper essence of these practices.[3]

I know that this is a subject which has become controversial in recent decades. There are many who will state that being self-taught, along with claimed 'self-initiation' is a valid method for becoming a Witch. In regards to this, I can only speak from my own experience. In my opinion, while much can and should be gained through private study and practice, the finer points of procedure, specific rituals and many of the deeper concepts of the Art are best understood and experienced through the tutelage of one who has received these from others before them. The reason for this is simply that the Art really is a living tradition that has evolved and grown. At times it can be eclectic in form, drawing as it does from the rich historical tapestry of its roots. Nevertheless there are real techniques that have come down through the teachings of others that can't be expressed through the written word alone, hence the need for a teacher in the Art.

Further, it is important to know that the role of the teacher is much more complex than the simple passing of information to another. The relationship between teacher and student ideally should be dynamic with each contributing to the process itself.

---

3. See Chapter Thirteen of *The Willow Path*, "The Distaff and the Woven Thread" for an in-depth discussion on the meaning and purpose of initiation in the Art.

In the first book we examined the principle of polarity, explaining that this is best understood through the interaction that occurs between the sexes. As it has been taught to me, much of the Art hinges on experiencing and using these dynamic complementary energies.

In the Art, as Julie and others had practiced it with me, women train men and men train women. Exceptions to this were fairly rare. When exceptions did occur they were usually because a suitable teacher of the opposite sex wasn't available, or in the case of family lineage, a parent or grandparent of the same sex could teach the younger family member introducing them to some of the concepts involved. However, even in these instances, the training was not complete until a member of the opposite sex finished the student's development.

Perhaps Sybil Leek's own training sheds some light on this. In her books she frequently spoke of the training her grandmother gave her. Yet, along with her grandmother, Sybil went on to discuss at length the exchange of ideas and training her father also provided. She went into a fair amount of detail regarding this in her books *Diary of a Witch*, *Telepathy* and *ESP: The Magic within You*.

I find it important to note that when it came time for her initiation it wasn't her grandmother who conducted this. Rather, Sybil explained that she was initiated by a man who was part of a Coven that her family had ties to in Nice, France. Thus, in Sybil's case we see both scenarios occurring. That is, a member of her family of the same gender introducing her to the Art, yet her training culminated in initiation through the agency of a male elder of a known Coven.[4]

The reason for this training model is that, in the vast majority of cases, normally only a seasoned teacher of the opposite sex can awaken the apprentice to the divinity inherent within them. I know this sounds controversial.

---

4. See Sybil's book *Diary of a Witch* for more information on how she received her training and initiation.

17

However, in practice the reasons are clear. In the case of a man, he is brought to *recognize* the masculine aspect of the divine residing within himself by *experiencing* the divine feminine within his teacher. The same holds true of a woman, awakened by her teacher to her own connection to the divine feminine while coming to experience the divine masculine in him.

This is such a subtle and unique process that it usually occurs over time. In many cases it isn't recognized for what it is until some time has passed. Nevertheless, in my experience, the effect is vital to the student's psychological, magical and spiritual development. Even simple acts, such as discussing techniques, relating inner feelings regarding life, and careful scrutiny of one's motives or desires, all of these can serve to awaken deeper levels of awareness. This can also include introducing the student to many of the more esoteric concepts and ritual techniques.

On a more profound level, there are occasions when the energy flowing between teacher and student can be palpable and is easily exchanged. This can best be seen in ritual activities. In these situations the affect can be quite intense and immediate. In all cases, when this connection is made, the student changes, grows and learns. They will never be the same, having evolved a richer understanding of their own true nature. What the student does with this new self-awareness determines the direction they will follow on the Willow Path.

During various stages of one's life it is common for the student to have different teachers. Often these will be of varying ages and hold different roles in one's life, mirroring specific characteristics of a particular Goddess or God within the system one is involved with. When this does happen it is usually quite spontaneous rather than by design, though there are exceptions to this. In most cases the teacher will enter the person's life just when they are needed.

Having said this, in Hermetic expressions of the Art, the rule of opposite sexes training the other is not as obvious. In many Orders members of the same sex frequently do train the same. This was also seen in some of the ancient Pagan practices, with women forming their own sects for training, as well as male wizards and shamans taking on apprentices of the same sex.

Even in these situations when members of the same gender train each other it is my experience that at some point a member of the opposite sex almost always enters the student's life at a key moment in their apprenticeship. If the neophyte is to be successful, an exchange of polar 'magnetism' (for lack of a better word) – the 'experiencing' of the other – will then take place. The point is that it has always been recognized that the polarity embodied within the sexes is a vital component of the Art, and the dynamic exchange of energies between them is essential for spiritual and magical success.

One could almost use the analogy of how electricity is generated. Essentially copper wire is spun between two magnets with their poles reversed. The force of the two causes the electrons in the copper to start flowing, becoming a source of power. While this is somewhat basic, the concept is essentially the same when considering magic.

In the cases just noted, if no 'exchange' and 'experiencing' occurs between the sexes during training the student may become polarized, cut off from their opposite. When this happens an imbalance occurs. This can only be corrected by finding a working partner of the opposite sex; someone whom the Magician or Witch can balance their energy with.

I need to point out that the relationship with a working partner is different from that of teacher and apprentice. The teacher acts as a guide and mentor. The working partner, on the other hand, is more or less equal in ability and skill. They will almost certainly have different talents and knowledge yet, ideally, these will complement and balance each other.

Beyond this though, the relationship with one's working partner sets in motion the exchange of dynamic energy in new and multifaceted patterns. This exchange will inevitably occur through ritual activity. However, it may also take on a more intimate and complex arrangement, though this is far from necessary. No matter the situation an exchange of energies must occur. Of course with polarity comes the realization that gender is the expression of two extremes on a single scale and that their union produces the fruitfulness of all that is.

It is important to understand that I am not saying that one can't work magic with other members of the same sex. Of course one can do so, on a consistent and regular basis. However, at some point one almost certainly needs to form a dynamic balance with a person of the opposite sex, even if on an occasional basis, to form that exchange of energy on a subtle occult level.

I saw a good example of this early in my training. Grandma Julie was married. However, her magical working partner was a gentleman ten years her junior. While there was admiration, there was no romantic involvement or sexual contact between them. Yet in ritual, the dynamic energy that passed between them was very real and powerful.

This, of course, raises the question of the homosexual student. In the Art one's sexual orientation has little to do with the need to experience and exchange energy with the opposite sex. I have known several powerful and highly talented homosexual members of the Art. Each of them did, at different points in their magical training, invariably have teachers of the opposite sex through which the transfer of creative energy took place during ritual. In the same vein I have known many who went on to form active magical partnerships with members of the opposite sex which lasted many years.

Please understand that in no way am I implying that sexual intercourse occurred between these partners; it didn't. Rather through ritual the dynamic interplay of energies balanced each other well, forming the creative link that lead to a successful magical partnership. This didn't inhibit or change either person's sexual orientation. If anything, it helped each to understand their own identity of who they are in this incarnation, as they developed on the Willow Path. Beyond this, these partnerships also provided the magnetic energy of creative opposites for each to use in an occult relationship.

Ultimately, if the evidence from past life memories are an indication, we all embody these different polarities at different times as we move through the cycles of rebirth. In different lives we experience the material realm as both sexes, along with the joys and challenges each brings. It would appear that for many of us one gender tends to be expressed more than another through the progression of lives. Yet, in my case, I have found that the balance of these tends to swing back and forth between the two. That is, it appears that over a long succession of lives we tend to find a close balance in the number of lives spent as women and as men. As such, it becomes easy to understand how, in one's current life, one could relate to and even identify with the gender opposite that in which they are housed. Nevertheless, I am convinced that forming a creative dynamic relationship, on an occult level, with a member of the opposite sex can be very powerful and, in fact, is vital to any who practice the Art no matter one's orientation. In this regard, working in a small group, whether it be a Clan, Coven, Grove or Order can afford the opportunity for this type of exchange for magical purposes.

Again, I want to emphasize that this model involving the interplay of energies between student, teacher and ultimately magical partner is that which was taught to me. As such, I am passing this along as part of the Art as I know it. Please understand that I don't doubt that there may be other methods which I may not have had access to.

At this junction it is important to understand that I am not advocating that one must join a Coven or Order to follow the Willow Path. On the contrary, such a relationship brings with it responsibilities and obligations that the individual Witch may not want to take on. However, there are several advantages to working in small esoteric groups. Some of these were discussed in the first book. Perhaps the most obvious is that frequently there are those in the Coven who are more experienced in different areas or specialties within the Art. As such, this can afford the opportunity to learn from other members directly.

If the group is run well, a sense of bonding, unique to the members involved, can be formed that ideally reaches beyond friendship. With this, trust and commitment form the foundation of the group. Without these no real work can be accomplished. Yet if this is maintained on a genuine level the group can manifest magical feats beyond those that a single individual can typically achieve. And it is in this regard that the dynamic exchange of energy between members within the group forms the nexus from which the Coven's power derives.[5]

Returning to the subject of magical training, tradition dictates that students should practice with their teacher for no less than a year and a day before initiation be considered. This is very much an apprentice style relationship during which careful scrutiny of the candidate takes place.

This period of time really affords both the teacher and apprentice the opportunity to assess whether the Willow Path is meant for them. Or, in particular, whether the teacher or group involved is the right venue for the individual. My advice to any would-be student is to take your time when considering training in any Order, Coven or with a particular teacher. There are many different strands and by-ways in the Geassa that one can follow. Meditate long, listening to your intuition, before committing to train

---

5. See Chapter Thirteen of *The Willow Path* for a detailed discussion on the links forged with forces and otherworld influences that a Coven engenders.

in any one system. If you have any concerns at all it is best to hold off.

It can be difficult to find a teacher or group that is suitable to your needs. And to be honest there are a tremendous amount of 'wanna-be' teachers, particularly here in the U.S.A. These tend to be pseudo 'gurus' who have collected an odd mix of new age lore, mixing this with some elements of ritual magic gathered from the latest 'white light' texts produced solely to sell to the masses. It takes time to sort through the morass of misinformation and ego driven groups or teachers today. In our experience the best way to find a suitable teacher is to listen to your intuition, practice what you can on your own and let the teacher come to you. Another option would be to write to someone you respect in the Art and ask them if they are aware of any suitable groups or teachers in your area.

Don't get discouraged. There are many fine teachers of the Art, perhaps more so today than at any other time since the forceful closing of the Mysteries at the beginning of the Abrahamic era. All I am saying is to use good judgement in selecting the right teacher for you.

Keep in mind that once you have begun training there will be times when your teacher will have to be very honest with you, sometimes shining light onto areas of your inner self that you'd rather not face. This is normal and healthy. However, there should always be a sense of mutual respect between the student and teacher. This needs to go both ways. Should you find that at any time the individual becomes controlling, demanding, or implies that you must act in a way that is against your core values you need to get out of the situation as quickly as possible and reassess whether this person or group is right for you. Ultimately you have to do what is right for you.

In considering this, please realize though that any good teacher will challenge their student's current view of reality. There are concepts and teachings that will be completely beyond the paradigm that most students will have when they first set foot on this path. It is inevitable that students will on occasion feel disoriented and even uncomfortable simply because long held views of the world and of oneself are being tested. This is as it should be. In fact, I would venture to say that if this doesn't happen fairly early in the relationship then something is wrong. However, the teachings can and should be delivered with respect and care. A good teacher knows how to introduce these changes without seeking dominance over their students.

During training, if at any time the student or teacher decides that the arrangement isn't right for all involved, no matter the reason, the relationship should be ended. It is no reflection on either party if this happens. On the contrary, we each need to find our own path. However, keep in mind that a long held occult law states that anything that was taught to the student in confidence needs to remain secret. To break that trust is to break the sacred bond that is the Geassa itself, and the repercussions of such a breach will be felt throughout the person's life with very serious consequences.

So think carefully before deciding to pursue the Willow Path. For once begun changes will occur that can't be undone. The Geassa is experienced and lived. And once one crosses the threshold of initiation one will never view the world the same again.

Earlier we discussed the difference between the Witch and the sorcerer. I think it is also important to draw a distinction between the Witch and the Magician. While there are many similarities, in my experience the difference between the two is in their approach to ritual, or rather, their *state of consciousness* during ritual itself.

In both the preparation for ritual and the way she actually performs the rite itself, the Witch works to place herself in a progressively altered state of mind. This frequently can be recognized as stepping just across the threshold between normal waking awareness and that of light stages of trance. This isn't to say that the Witch is not aware and functioning

24

on a material level. On the contrary, she is very aware. However, the Witch's attention shifts to one in which she opens herself to the perception and experience of occult forces present in the locale and in the ritual itself.

Ritual Magicians, on the other hand, tend to approach ritual from a more critical state of mind. For them, their attention is focused on the details of the rite itself. From the specifics of proper colored robes, the consecration of tools, calling on a very specific hierarchy of spirits, to the exact moment that certain gestures are to be used, the Magician is much more centered on the formula and tasks involved in the rite itself. This isn't to say that the Magician, too, doesn't enter into altered states as well. Rather, it is not something that is necessarily sought unless he or she is working specifically with scrying work or with traveling in spirit. Rather, the change in consciousness occurs in the Magician precisely because he allows his mind to be so focused on the tasks of ritual itself. This singular concentration pushes the mind to become aware of the force that the ritual is seeking to breach.

It for this reason that many Magicians prefer to have clairvoyants present in the circle. In these cases it is the psychic who slips into altered states. They, in turn, may perform the scrying, or are present generally to perceive any messages that may come from the spirit evoked.

Having worked in both settings I can say that the difference between Witch and Magician is subtle. In my experience the Witch begins to slip into a state of becoming or merging (discussed further in this book) even before the rite begins. Like the Magician, in the initial stages of the ritual her focus is on getting the details right; ensuring the proper incenses, oils, taglocks and tools are in place. Yet, once she is satisfied that all is prepared she will quickly slip across the threshold into deeper levels of perception. Some Witches are extremely adapt at making this transition. The Mistress of our group can slip into this state very quickly when she has decided to work a spell.

The line between these two approaches does get blurred, and both are very effective. Much depends on the purpose of the rite itself and if one has others present who can perform different roles in the ritual. If so, one or two may slip into trance while others perform the technical aspects of the rite. However, for the solitary Witch this can pose a problem. I have had many occasions when I have worked alone. In these cases, frequently the ritual required that I be focused on specific procedures and yet, to achieve the success desired, I had to place myself into deep levels of awareness.

This is where, in my opinion, Traditional Witchcraft has an advantage. For rather than relying solely on long evocations and very specific gestures, the Witch uses rhythmic chant and frequently movement such as dance or circumambulation. She may purposely stare into the flames of the hearth or candle, or trace her finger over the pattern of the maze while letting herself slip deeper into a state of altered awareness. In these moments there comes a point at which the energy of the rite itself takes over and the Witch loses herself, if only for that brief time, to the deeper connection she has formed with the forces involved. This doesn't necessarily mean that she allows entities to possess her (though in some rituals this is desired). Rather she succumbs to the flow of energy and passion the rite engenders, the same energy that forms the connection to the goal sought.

The ritual Magician's approach is one in which he seeks to summon the forces to his circle and then either persuade these, or failing that, command the entities involved to perform the task at hand. This is particularly so in Solomonic or Goetic magic.

One can argue which technique is better. Again, much depends on the type of magic being performed. There are techniques within Hermetic circles in which the Magician also welcomes the entity to merge with him. Known as *assuming the god form* this is generally only done in situations involving highly complex deities under very controlled circumstances.

26

Thus, while the Magician is using the set formula of the exact prescribed image to draw the deity into himself, rarely does he allow himself to 'succumb' to the passion that the rite brings on as a Witch might do.

For our part, generally in ritual we seek to find a balance between the two approaches. That is, from the beginning we purposely seek to enter altered states and yet, at the same time, we follow fairly standard procedures in the rituals themselves. We try to keep our rituals simple in form, yet involving specific symbolism and gestures to aid in the work. Also, as much as possible of the rite is memorized beforehand. In this way, once we do begin the ritual, invariably we will find ourselves slipping deeper into the *becoming*, merging with the forces involved. We find that the deeper we can *merge* the more effective the rite will be.

Chapter Two

❖ BETWEEN THE HORNS ❖
MERGING & BECOMING

The cold winter winds battered the side of the cabin, buffeting it with snow and ice. Lying in bed next to my wife, I awoke to the sound of the windows rattling. The small one room structure was cold, despite the woodstove that was struggling to keep up with the extreme bitter temperature that the January storm was bringing to the top of the mountain. Yet it wasn't the wind or the cold that woke me. It was the whispering, almost like voices that seemed to come from the wind itself.

For weeks I had found that deep in the night images would come in my sleep. Powerful images . . . symbols and objects. A Stang – the wooden staff with two horns rising to either side of its apex; circles of light and energy; worlds within worlds. All these came as images and sounds, words and symbols that flowed in my dreams at a feverish rate. Increasingly I found myself jarred awake as I scrambled for my notebook and pen, frantically writing everything down. But it was the voices that were the most profound. Did I hear them, or was it something else . . . somehow perceived or sensed rather than heard?

For months both I and my wife had been hearing a very high pitch tone, almost like music, that seemed to be just on the threshold of normal human hearing, yet it was there. We both had heard it deep in the woods. Where it came from we still aren't sure. Consistently it had the same quality and vibration, reminding us of Tibetan singing bowls. Yet somehow this seemed different; even richer or more pure then those made by material means.

I had heard this before, many years ago, but only after performing high ritual invocations to ancient deities in an attic temple that had been dedicated to the Art. Now, here in the forest, atop a mountain of quartz and granite, this same tone regularly made its presence known to both of us. Some evenings it would be stronger than others. But no matter how hard we tried, we have never been able to determine its origin, if in fact it has a physical source.

On other occasions, both together and separately, we each heard clear voices seeming to come from the forest. Often these were actual words, greetings spoken as if one were welcoming someone to their home. When they occurred they always seemed to come from the edge of the forest just feet from our cabin. On one occasion they seemed to come from the tops of a group of tall pines. Most of these incidents occurred in the winter well beyond the normal hunting season. So it was doubtful that we were overhearing conversations of hunters who may have strayed on to our property, and our nearest neighbors are close to two miles away. Despite the clarity of the voices we are convinced these didn't come from any mortal being.

However, this particular night seemed different than these other incidents. Something compelled me to get up. It wasn't because of the now normal, frantic need to write down the images of dreams. In fact I don't recall that I had the intense visions that previously were so pervasive. Rather there was a sense of calm wonder, or perhaps a feeling of 'opening' that seemed present in the room, and the whispered voices that seemed to flow from the winter wind.

So, I crept out of the bed trying not to disturb my wife as I moved to the woodstove. There I placed another log on the fire and sat staring into the flames through the glass door. In a drawer nearby I had kept a small glass ball, approximately two inches around. It had been a gift from my father many years before. Like me, he too, had a deep interest in the Arts, studying many facets of the occult sciences. He had a keen mind and a craving to learn all he could. While I was a child he saw the same budding interests in me. So it was that he would pass me books and tools related to the Art. This small crystal ball was one of those objects.

Sitting before the fire I felt the need to pull the ball from its keep and then settle once again in front of the fire. There was no effort to my actions as I began looking into the crystal ... no thought of trying to see or experience anything. Rather I just found myself gazing gently into the glass. I recall seeing the firelight from woodstove dancing through the orb, while the winter storm continued to batter the cabin walls as the sound of the wind rushed through the bare trees outside.

The scene was clearly hypnotic as I felt a shift in consciousness. It wasn't a sudden 'revelation'. The only way to describe this is that I remained fully aware of the crystal and yet my mind seemed to gradually 'move' or expand. My awareness seemed to ride with the wind over the wintery landscape outside, through the trees and over the land itself. Despite the harsh bitterness of the night, everything was alive . . . alive with energy, consciousness, spirit.

It was then that the 'interaction' came: a sense of the Lady in the Land. Words really can't express the essence of what I was feeling. Perhaps it can best be thought of as a sense of experiencing Her; experiencing the joy, beauty and simple majesty of the Queen. Despite the fact that this wasn't the first time I had made this deep connection with Her, in this moment a deeper understanding of the forces in nature, the essence of Her came flooding through. She was as wild as the storm that ranged outside and yet there was a calm inalterable presence to Her as an essential force of nature itself.

In the first book I explained that the Lady is the *center*; the power *within* the land. She is creative desire, the timeless essence of nature who speaks to, and lays deep within each of us. We find Her in the land, the oceans, in the light of the Moon, in fact anywhere where we can merge with the essence of nature itself. Despite the vastness in which She is experienced, She is a living consciousness; a sentient being who relates to each in personal, meaningful and powerful ways. This is no 'archetypal image' or 'symbolic representation' of some subconscious underpinnings of the mind. Rather She is a vibrant, living, sentient being who is at once beyond our realm and yet within it.

Still, on this cold winter night, deep in the New Hampshire forests, scrying in a simple crystal ball, it wasn't only the Lady who came through the veil. For within the wind itself, the wild rider could be felt. His strength and passion filled the air. While She is the power within the land, He is 'of' the land. He is the force that moves through the trees and over the fields, and tonight He was the wild force of the wind high atop the granite mountain. All of this came flooding through on this dark winter night.

In the Art it is essential that one gains the ability to move between worlds, shifting one's state of consciousness, allowing one to become aware of other realities, other states of being, and with this, otherworld beings. In Traditional Witchcraft this ability is frequently called "the Mystery of Becoming", a phrase used by pre-industrial British cunning folk. Sources who have trained with Sybil Leek explain that she, too, had taught this discipline, using the same phrase.[6] We prefer to call this "Moving Between the Horns". Explaining how to achieve this state in writing is difficult to do. As such the following may seem obscure and esoteric. It isn't meant to be.

Early in my training one of my first teachers constantly stressed the need to develop the skill of 'merging.' She described this as the ability to drop the ego and let yourself

---

6. Having said this, I am not aware of her using this specific term in any of her writings. However, she clearly describes this state of mind in several works, most notably her book *Reincarnation: The Second Chance.*

become one with nature, the universe, and in particular, merge with the object of one's spell. In all forms of Traditional Witchcraft that I am aware the ability to open oneself to the subtle energies of one's surroundings is essential. With this comes a sense of connectedness and oneness to the psychic and spiritual energies of the cycles at play in the various realms or 'Worlds'.

Moving between the Horns occurs when one is able to relax, letting the mind gently free itself from worry and from focusing too much on tedious tasks. This allows one to simply slip into a calm state of mind where the surrounding energies gently flow through you. It is then that this sense of connectedness occurs. This is best achieved in remote places of nature were the flow of energy is steady and apparent.

This is the music of nature – the energy of the land, of water, the sky, the Gods. And in this relaxed state one's awareness expands and the 'tune' – the forces – merge with the Witch. Gemma Gary describes this process well:

"However, by far the best way to achieve the states of mind and natural wisdom useful to the Witch is to simply be in the land, to walk, find a place to settle, maybe in a place of liminality – 'places between' seen by the Wise as useful intersections between the worlds; such as a break in a hedge, a stile, upon a cliff or beside a stream, and simply sit, watch, feel and listen, but try not to think too much! One must become quiet in body and in thought to be receptive to the wisdom that deep observation of the comings and goings of nature can bring, and the potent forces of the landscape so vital to the working of the Craft."[7]

Some traditional methods of entering into this state also include walking slowly in a Moonwise, tuathal or

7. Gary, Gemma. *Traditional Witchcraft: A Cornish Book of Ways*, p.41.

widdershins circle while simply relaxing the mind and letting the concerns of the day slip away. Spinning wool on a distaff or spinning wheel have long been means used in Witchcraft to slip Between the Horns. Chanting, singing, slow rhythmic breathing, as well as gently looking into a fire, a pool of water, a mirror or a crystal, all are means that can be used.

In a ritual setting we find it helpful to chant the following while circumambulating or dancing. We call this "Stirring the Cauldron":

"Round and Round
Throughout and about,
The wheel weaves in and the thread spins out.
By Stang, By Besom, By Cauldron deep,
We meet together in the Lady's keep."

This can be surprisingly hypnotic and very effective. This can be performed by members of the group *while* the Master and Mistress ritually create the Roth Fail around the assembly. It can also be done immediately after the Roth Fail is evoked, particularly if one is working solo. I have also used this as a preliminary to the actual casting of spells. In this way it is meant to help the Witch move between the horns, as well as awaken energies in the working space that will be used in the spell itself. This latter point is important and it is in this capacity that we call this *Stirring the Cauldron* as a means of raising power.

It may be important to note that we prefer not to use terms such as 'raising energy' or 'charging' when describing ritual work. In our opinion, we feel that that this gives an incomplete and, thus, an inaccurate portrayal of what is actually occurring in ritual. Rather, *Stirring the Cauldron* is a very effective means of entering into the state of mind while also evoking forces that are essential to magical practice. Or, as some in Hermetic circles call it "string the astral light". We will be looking closer at the subject of 'raising energy' further in the book.

As Gemma Gary noted above, I too have found that the simplest means for attaining a state of becoming is to go into nature and gently experience the flow of energy through meditation, reverie and peaceful contemplation. In particular I find meditation under the Full Moon to be exceptionally conducive.

In our practice, one of the simplest methods we use on the Full Moon is called the Lunar Rite of Union. This has its roots in certain Strega techniques I have access to. However, I have included "Words" or "Charms of Power" drawn from Gaelic and Egyptian sources, finding these to be exceptionally helpful in this technique. If you feel more comfortable not using these terms, by all means feel free to leave them out. While this will seem relatively simple in form, in practice I have found it to be very effective.

The Lunar Rite of Union
Facing the Full Moon raise your hands above your head and touch the thumb and forefinger of each hand, forming a triangle just over the crown of your head. Clear your mind and allow the light of the Moon to gently flood your awareness, streaming in through the triangle. When ready enchant:

"Banu, Great Queen! Goddess!
Source of Illumination.
I open my Akh to you,
And ask, may you impart your wisdom to me!"

Lower the triangle directly in front of your forehead, again, allowing the light of the Moon to fill your consciousness through the triangle. When ready recite:

"Enlighten my Ba
That I may perceive clearly
All things I seek."

Continue by lowering the triangle in front of the Solar Plexus, with the apex remaining pointed upward. Take some time to envision the light of the Moon filling your torso as you intone:

"Illumine my Ka,
Imparting your essence of wonder!"

Now turn your hands over forming a downward pointing triangle, lowering this in front of your genitals. As before, envision the power of the Moon gently filling this area of your body as the seat of your creative power while in material form. When ready chant:

"Empower my Sekhem[8]
With your essence of life,
That I shall know you through all worlds."

Finally, spread your arms wide, while envisioning yourself as a great falcon, crow or raven.[9] Allow yourself to bathe in the light of the Moon as you enchant:

"I reveal my true self to you,
That I may follow in your ways!
Bandia (pronounced BAHN-JEE-uh), Great Queen!"

Once a state of Becoming begins to emerge the power in nature becomes accessible and tangible. It is then that

---

8. The meaning and use of each of these Egyptian terms is discussed chapter six.

9. This may vary depending on the ritual work being done. The crow and raven are strong totem animals in Traditional Witchcraft bringing wisdom, cunning, and opening the paths to other realms. The falcon has strong spiritual connotations across both Celtic and Egyptian beliefs. Several ancient texts refer to the initiate as changing form and "rising as a falcon to be one with the Gods."

those of the Art gather this energy, almost as if drinking it in. As such the Witch opens herself up to these energies, collecting this both within herself and her tools. The Fe or wand is very useful for this. I will also bring my Alraun familiar root out during the Full Moon to expose her to its light and power as well.

In particular the staff, including the Stang, is a powerful ally in summoning, gathering and storing this energy. It is not uncommon for this power to be referred to as Serpent force, the Serpent's Breath, or Dragon energy, and the Witch quickly becomes aware of the places in nature where this tends to collect, pool, and flow.

Some of the best places to experience this energy are in clearings of forests on Full Moon nights. In a hypnotically induced session, Sybil Leek explained that during Full Moon rites with her Coven, the energy inherent in the land reaches upward, while the subtle power of the Full Moon flows down. She explained that the trees in the forest act as a conduit between these two forces, with roots in the ground and branches reaching toward the sky. Thus a connection is made between the two in very tangible and yet spiritual ways.[10] The Witch then acts as a vehicle to channel this energy using it as she needs and desires.

Other areas where this energy can readily be found include running water such as clear mountain streams and rivers. Lakes and sea shores are powerful sources of energy. Mountains and rocky hills are often gateways between worlds allowing the energy of the different realms to cross over and transcend each other. In New England some of the most potent places to experience this are in the White Mountains of New Hampshire. In particular, Franconia Notch is exceptionally powerful.

Clefts and caves are also unique portals affording natural paths between worlds. Similarly hollow trees with openings in these can be excellent sources of power. The source of

---

10. Holzer, Hans. *The Truth About Witchcraft*, 1969.

this power comes from the fact that these are areas where the different realms and worlds merge, both coalescing and transcending each other; blending as it were.

Beyond the staff and Fe other objects are used to store the Serpent's Breath. In particular, quartz crystals and granite rock can be used quite well for this. Our outdoor ritual site is set in a circle of granite rocks, laid in a typical New England stonewall arrangement. Being made completely from the natural granite and quartz of the mountain, this acts as a collector drawing the Serpent's Breath to, and through, it.

The Mystery of Becoming is vital to almost all practices of the Art. For it is in this state that one is able to easily effect changes. Astral workings, known in Traditional Witchcraft as *Crossing the Hedge*, or *Traveling in Spirit*, as well as trance induction and spirit communication are best accomplished once the Becoming has been made.

Beyond its use in magic I can't think of anything more moving and pleasurable then entering this state mind while in nature and spending the time to simply experience the forces and intelligences inherent in the locale. Some of the most profound spiritual experiences of my life have occurred in this manner. It is through Becoming that the Witch taps into the Geassa, experiencing the voice of nature and communing with otherworld beings – spirits, the nature folk, as well as those whom we have come to know as Goddesses and Gods, the 'Old Ones'.

Chapter Three

✤ BONES OF THE CROW ✤
THE NATURE OF MAGIC

In practicing the Art there are three distinct qualities that one needs to understand and develop in order to succeed. The first of these involves the way in which one selects goals, especially those goals which one may direct their enchantments toward. This is tied to the dual concept of prevention and pursuit. As one strives to succeed, one must avoid those obstacles that keep success from manifesting. On the surface this sounds exceptionally simple. Yet, oftentimes desire can cloud our judgement.

One needs to make clear choices using reason and intuition before following desire. As such, it is important to meditate on any goal before choosing to pursue it. In fact, those of the Geassa rely as much, if not more, on intuition and meditation than they do on reason. It is important that one does not let one's desires have total control over the choices made in life. To do so is to invite failure. And yet, desire is the engine that drives one forward. For once a goal is set, it is the passions that are employed as a powerful stimulus supplying the ambition to bring the goal to fruition.

In this way we can see that there is a real need for balance between these three parts of the self: desire, reason and intuition. Desire is the passion which fuels motivation. Too much desire can cause one to make choices that may be harmful in the long run. In such cases extreme desire can lead to obsession and even addiction. Yet, an absence of desire and passion leads one to live a life lacking in meaning and pleasure.

Reason, on the other hand, allows one to logically consider the elements of a situation and decide which path makes the most 'sense'. Reason enables one to calmly deduce possible outcomes based on the information available. However, reason is only as good as the information available. And, in the end, reason alone simply can't take in the hidden elements of a situation. The Ancient Egyptians understood this well. For them Sia, meaning intuition or literally "sign of recognition" was considered *more* important than Rekh, the Ancient Egyptian word for reason and logic.

Intuition is the ability to be still and know. This is the art of listening to the inner self. For those who follow the Willow Path, intuition is superior to reason and desire as it is our connection to all else. Because of this, much of the training and daily practice in the Art is designed to open oneself to this inner perception. The more one uses these techniques the greater one's awareness becomes.

Yet, it is important to know that for those of the Art all three components are critical. We have to have our desires, passions and pleasures to drive us forward giving us joy and purpose in all we do. Reason helps to plan the logical steps toward achieving those pleasures, while intuition alerts us to the deeper hidden realms and elements involved in situations. By meditating on a desired goal before making the decision to actually pursue this, we allow ourselves to perceive whether this is within our realm of possibility or if this is a desire that is best left alone for the moment. The use of Astrology can be a vital tool aiding in this decision process.

Once the goal is perceived to be one that is something we can and should strive toward, it is emotional energy, balanced with reason and intuition which is tapped into. This is especially so during ritual. When casting a spell these qualities are brought to bear, directing one's innate energies toward the realization of the goal. In fact, passion for life, passion in doing and being, is an essential quality of those who practice the Art. Early in my training, Julie explained that in magic you must have an intense desire to succeed and have total emotional, even passionate involvement in the ritual itself. Or, as Sybil Leek stated when discussing her Grandmother's teachings:

> "Anything one ardently desires, sincerely believes in, vividly imagines and enthusiastically acts upon must, inevitably, come to pass."[11]

The second quality to consider involves always seeking balance in all that we do. Enjoy life, seek pleasure, but never do anything in excess. Excess can lead to imbalance which, in turn, is the root cause of disease, strife and chaos. I discussed this at length in the first book when we looked at the *Counsels of the Wise*. For this discussion on magic it bears bringing up again. Once the goal is decided upon and the procedures for achieving this have been set in place, it is vital that one keeps a proper perspective or balance, as one proceeds. Further, one should strive to keep her personal life orderly with nothing done heedlessly.

The third quality revolves around the need to seek security from self-deception and fear. One should be sure of herself in all that she does. This includes both her personal and professional life. This extends to being secure and sure in all interpersonal relationships. To do this one must have a healthy sense of self, acting in confidence, with an understanding of one's true self as opposed to being a victim of one's conditioned ego, or falling victim to the manipulations of others.

This can be difficult for it is very easy to get caught up in the persona one creates as we go through life. Rather, in the Art it is essential that one keeps a clear understanding of one's true self – strengths and weaknesses. In doing so, keep in mind that those weaknesses present areas of opportunity

---

11. Leek, Sybil. *Diary of a Witch*, 1969.

for growth. It is for this reason that during the early stages of training any apprenticeship to the Art begins with an in depth look at oneself. Whether this training be with an elder within a group or the training is begun alone. Inevitably the forces involved bring the apprentice into a close examination of one's own strengths and flaws.

In my own training Julie was at once kind in her approach toward me, yet she was very direct. She never failed to point out my flaws when needed and yet she would just as easily respond with advice and encouragement as I advanced on the path. She was very wise, using keen wit and humor while also being direct in her approach. She knew how much she could push without breaking the student and yet still make the impact needed. I can't say the same of all of my teachers. However, they too were important if only to teach me how not to approach my own students.

Returning to the qualities needed to be successful in the Art, one of the key points that Grandma Julie had emphasized involved four essential components:

• A firm faith – a belief that you can do the task at hand.
• A strong will – a powerful desire to accomplish that which you have undertaken.
• A good imagination – you must be able to vividly imagine the successful outcome of anything you are about to undertake. Remember that all that we do is first imagined before it can be put into reality.
• Secrecy – In Julie's words, "Not necessarily hiding away in a 'broom closet'. Rather secrecy means using discretion when concerned with others."

These, of course, are the much discussed four corners of magic found in so many occult books. However, I find Julie's interpretation of these give an added dimension. Julie went on to say:

"Remember nature abhors a vacuum. If you don't have faith you have doubt, if you don't have will you have weakness."[12]

Another teacher whom I trained with used to have her students cultivate their imagination by reading richly descriptive novels. I recall that I was somewhat skeptical when she suggested this. However, after sometime I found this did increase my ability to visualize easily, or more importantly, to think in highly descriptive terms. In doing so I found that my ability to place myself into a desired situation and envision my ultimate goal during spell casting increased over time. With this came the ability to focus more intently on the goal and perhaps more importantly to involve my emotions far more easily. For in those moments of performing the rites I could engage all of my inner senses in the reality of the goal happening.

Of course, this use of reading novels to enrich the imagination can be seen as similar to the ancient tradition of storytelling that would have taken place before the hearth or around the camp fire. Much lore today comes from the oral traditions of the pre-industrial era. In most of the Celtic countries it was common for Bards to memorize countless stories and legends which they would recite to groups to entertain and educate. One can easily see this tradition as promoting the art of thinking in descriptive terms.

While it may sound simple, keeping focus can be quite challenging. As such, regular disciplined visualization also forms an essential aspect of the Art. A simple but highly effective technique that I learned early in my magical training was to sit each day in a quiet place and begin with simple, slow rhythmic breathing. Once a feeling relaxation began to take hold, I envisioned an object, something simple. One of

---

12. Any quoted texts drawn from Julie's teachings are taken directly from my personal notes made at the time I was training with her (1979–1980) and which I still have in my possession.

my favorites was an apple. But rather then holding this as a static picture in the mind I envisioned this from all angles. It was almost as if I saw this while walking around the apple. I would picture its rich color, the shine of light on its skin. I could smell the wonderful sent of its fruit, and even try to sense what it must feel like to hold the apple in my hand, or taste its flesh.

Another simple trick to visualization is to envision the object resting still, yet behind this imagine the background as if moving. Think of it as if the object were sitting on the windowsill of a train while the scenery outsides slides by. This can be highly effective, giving the imagination something to think about while envisioning the object at hand.

In spell casting this technique can prove effective. For in those instances one may see the person or desired goal in a scene in which movement is apparent. For example, one could envision the person's hair gently blowing in the wind, or envision them as they walk down a street. All of this is meant to keep the conscious mind engaged in the process while desire and emotion begin to generate the needed force to be directed toward the task.

It is essential to employ all of your senses in the Art of magic. See your goal, feel your goal, be your goal. For the one moment that the spell is cast throw yourself completely into the reality of the goal. While there are any number of techniques used by Witches to add power to their rites, this ability to have a total sensory and emotional involvement with the goal is fundamental to all successful magic. As stressed in the previous book, 'change your state of consciousness to change you state of being'. For as Hermetic Orders frequently teach, imagination is not the same as fantasy. In the Art we understand that imagination is the mind's ability to perceive energies, forming patterns from these, as well as to create a matrix for these energies to manifest in our realm. As such, 'force follows will'. Fantasy, on the other hand, is simply self-generated storytelling for personal entertainment. As such, there is a distinct difference between the two.

It is important that the Witch understands these differences because the creative use of imagination in magic serves to form patterns through which the currents of power flow. The clearer the patterns are, the easier it is for these currents to bring the desired goal into one's life. Conversely, in the Art, imagination is also understood to be one's ability to perceive 'astral' or 'psychic' energies, forming patterns out of these. These patterns aren't 'made up' fantasies. Rather they are the mind's attempt to understand the energies presented to it, just as one's eyes perceive waves of light which the mind then translates into understandable patterns. As such, it is important to think of imagination as a vital tool used to alter consciousness and perceive alternative realities.

This leads us to consider the use of drama, story and sacred legend in ritual. These are extremely common in all forms of the Art, from Shamanic cultures, Ancient Egyptian magic, to Traditional Witchcraft. In looking at ritual drama one could easily argue that this is, in a sense, the use of fantasy. However, if one draws this conclusion one misses a key component of ritual practice. In magical drama and sacred narrative, while it can and should be entertaining, its primary function is that of being a *formula*. There is no other way to look at it. Ritual drama serves to introduce symbols in a steady flow of patterns that are meant to both alter consciousness and help form the matrix through which the currents of force can manifest. This is why rituals frequently incorporate portions of legends and with this the enactment of specific magical 'story telling' and more. In contemporary Hermetic schools this is demonstrated in the common practice of 'path working' or 'guided meditation'.

In Traditional Witchcraft we find portions of sacred drama in the ritual identification of the Witch with different deities, totems, or otherworld beings. This is very common. It is for this reason that masks are frequently employed. Whether it be that of the Green Man, Horned One, various animals such as the crow, horse, hare or other totems. In all cases the purpose is essentially the same. In doing so the participants in the ritual are, in essence, changing their 'normal' sense of self, their 'normal' state of consciousness, in an effort to resonate more closely with the forces being sought in the rite.

Resonance is a vital aspect of the Art, perhaps more so than the much celebrated 'raising of power'. For while energy can be generated or 'raised' by anyone through passion it is resonance that is the missing component in so many rituals. While I will be speaking at greater length about this concept in the next chapter I do want to discuss how, in this state, one is able to merge in consciousness with other people on a limited level. This is particularly useful when working spells meant to influence others in a specific way.

For this, essentially a connection is purposely formed between the mind of the Witch and that of the person being influenced. Once created this link becomes a channel through which information on an intuitive level travels. It is important to remember that this link will act as a two way street. Not only will you be influencing the target person with your mind, but potentially the target person could influence you as well. So you must be careful as to whom you perform this on and when. Further, it is important to sever the link after the rite has been completed. Given all of this generally the best time to 'merge' with another is while they are sleeping or in some relaxed state of mind.

To create the link you must learn as much as you can about the person, becoming as familiar with them as is possible. What do they look like? What do they sound? How do they smell? How do they normally dress? What is their character like? Are they a leader? Ambitious? A follower? Meek? Are they a nervous, high strung type? Or are they relaxed, laid-back? Are they emotional? Practical? Caring? Callous? *You must know your subject!* I have found that if I can get their birth date and full name, a quick read of their Astrological and Numerological information is excellent for

45

this purpose. This will also give me the correct colors to use in ritual to link with them.

In the days before performing the magic, if possible, spend some time with the person. Watch them, listen to them, see how they walk, try to observe as many different characteristics as you can. Just let yourself experience that person for a while. Get used to what it *feels* like to be around that person.

In the magical operation itself gather together any personal, physical links you may have. We call these "taglocks"; items which belonged to, or have come in contact with, the person to whom the spell is being directed. Some of the best include clothing they have worn that hasn't been washed, a sample of their hand-writing (their signature makes an excellent taglock), hair, nail clippings, blood, in fact anything that comes from that person. The more personal, or the longer the item has been in contact with them the more powerful the link will be. Also you may want to have on hand any perfumes, photographs, etc. which will serve to awaken the feel of that person in your mind.

Prior to ritual you will want to let yourself slip Between the Horns. As stated this is best done with unhurried calm in a quiet place in nature. However, if you are confined to a house or building simply allow yourself to relax. Gently and purposely go through the preparations of your ritual space. The setting up of ritual items in a quiet and purposeful state of mind can help move the deep mind, turning one's consciousness away from mundane concerns and slipping gently into an awareness of realms just beyond 'normal' perception. For me, as noted earlier, gazing into the flames of our woodstove/hearth while using steady rhythmic breathing helps me to achieve this state.

Once all is ready and you feel yourself relaxing, close your eyes and with unhurried calm recall all that you have learned about the person. See them in your mind, hear their voice, watch them move. Let yourself totally experience that person just as you had done when you were with them. Do *not* force this, just gently bring the experience to yourself. Maintain this until you feel that you are in 'contact' with that person's mind. This takes time and practice. Yet, you will receive a gentle sense of connection forming between yourself and the person. This is the moment of "merging". At this point you can begin the magical operation in earnest. The content of the spell depends entirely on the intent of the Witch. However, everything involved should have meaning. Everything should be done with unhurried calm, and above all I have found that this should be kept simple and clear. Imagine yourself as if 'inside' the person's mind gently talking to them, evoking the emotions and passions of your inner self as you envision the person thinking and doing the intended act of the spell. Throughout this remember to keep the connection by 'experiencing' the person while in this 'merged' state of mind. Yet keep your thoughts direct, simple, clear and passionate. Clear intent and the evocation of real emotional passion are vital, for it is the emotion which supplies the power that the intent rides on. This applies to any intent whether it be to gain friendship, influence your career, perform a specific function in your life, or conversely to instill the need for them to cease an activity; you want to evoke the emotional and mental response in the person intended. The procedure is essentially the same no matter the reason for the spell.

Once the rite is over it is important to close the connection immediately. This can be done by any number of ritual means depending on the purpose of the spell. The simplest is to simply feel yourself focusing more on the mundane surroundings in the room itself. Finish the rite and then do something else, anything else! Do something completely different. For the time being forget about the rite, forget about the person. Change to a different venue and activity. It is for this reason that traditionally, magical work almost always was followed by a meal and merry making. In this way the link is severed and the energy sent during the rite is allowed to go into the target person's mind to achieve the desire effect.

If you do not take actions to close the link and you continue to dwell on the subject after the rite is completed two things occur. First, there is a tendency for the energy sent during rite to have a drag on it, being called back to the Witch and lessening its effectiveness. By dwelling on the rite or the person that the spell was intended for it is almost as if one had shot an arrow toward a target yet had tied a string to this and continued to tug on the string to see if the arrow was going to hit the target. Naturally in such a situation the arrow is likely to fall short of the mark. In practical magic it is vital that, after the ceremony is completed, the Witch simply lets go.

The second thing that occurs if one fails to close the link is that the very real possibility exists for the target person to either wittingly or unwittingly influence the Witch. Many people have very strong personalities and may have latent ability that they tap into on an unconscious level. By keeping the link open one runs the very real risk of becoming the target of the other person!

It needs to be mentioned that the more often you form the link with a person the more permanent it will become. This bond can be seen among close friends, families, spouses and lovers. Also, should one repeatedly perform rites to influence a specific person, even though precautions may have been taken after each rite to close the link, with time and repetition the link can easily form a more lasting connection. In this way the other person may, over time, be able to influence the Witch.

Beyond these considerations one needs to be careful, for if the intended person is adapt in the techniques of the Art themselves, there is the real possibility that they will become aware of your attempts to influence them. If so, unless they welcome the intrusion, they will almost certainly reflect the spell back onto you. There is also the real possibility that they will have set protections in place around themselves and their homes which you may not be able to get through. If so the spell will recoil back onto the sender. My advice is to be sure of your intentions, know your target and follow the Counsels of the Wise discussed in the first book. I have found this technique to be very effective. Remember, with power comes responsibility.

Chapter Four

✤ HORNS ON THE HORIZON ✤
CIRCUITS OF POWER

In many places in these books we discussed the occult teaching that all is consciousness, all consciousness is energy and that all energy vibrates. Given this, most contemporary occult groups focus almost exclusively on one aspect of this theorem: the 'raising of energy' and with it the ability to 'charge' objects, tools, talismans, candles, potions, etc. with that energy. Without a doubt there is real validity in this. The ancient maxim so often referenced by occultists to "enflame thyself with prayer" has real merit. Without passion there is no power to ignite the engine that is ritual magic and spell working. However, it is as if these occultists would prefer to take a hammer and strike with all the force they can muster without considering the subtle nuances of the situation at hand. For them their tools, candles, amulets, etc. are little more than 'batteries' that need to be filled with energy so that these, in turn, can discharge power into the person or goal for which the rite intended. In this perspective it is as if one is trying to force one's will on to the situation at hand. However, unless one is exceptionally powerful, many times spells approached in this manner will fail. The reason for this is that the Magician didn't take into account the Hermetic principles of balance and polarity which, in turn, bring resonance.

Julie taught that the Willow Path is one in which currents of energy are bent and woven, not forced. To understand this we need to refer back to the first book in which we looked at the principle of opposites only being separated by stages or degrees. The difference between hot and cold is only a matter of degree. The same can be said of so many things in life: love and hate, prosperity and poverty, joy and sorrow. In ritual the Witch strives to find that balance between what currently may be occurring and the desired outcome. In doing so, she must find a way to swing the pendulum in the direction of her desire, rather than simply hit it with the hammer of her will alone. Certainly the Witch's will – her passion and desire – are vital to this process. But only as the fuel that powers the careful weaving of the osier of the Willow, bending the currents in the direction desired. This can be seen in practice from the most basic of spells to highly complex of ritual magic.

For example, consider what is involved in working a simple attraction or friendship spell on another. Despite the fact that you may generate a tremendous amount of passion and energy in the spell casting itself, if done properly you aren't forcing your will on the person desired. Rather you are creating the circumstances that will awaken their own longings for friendship while injecting your presence into their desire. This is such a subtle but important difference.

Those new to the Art try to 'force' the other person to be attracted to them, whereas the seasoned Witch creates a resonance with the other person, bringing the attraction between the two into focus, almost as a natural or organic act. This is somewhat like the effect that occurs in music when a vibrating string creating a tone causes another string near it to vibrate in the same tone. In music this is known as 'sympathetic vibration' or 'resonant frequency'. The energy of the original vibrating string creates a similar response in the next. A similar principle is applied in magic.

So, in the example of the friendship spell, the Witch is using the energy of her passions to create the vibration that will cause the other person to resonate with the same desire. On the surface this can appear to be the same as 'forcing your will' on another. However, the reality is that the desire for friendship already was present in the person on whom the spell was cast. The seasoned Witch simply energizes this, bringing this to the forefront while placing herself in the position of being the object of that desire. Like the tuning fork, when the energy strikes one prong, both resonate with the same tone. In this way one isn't discharging energy that constantly needs to be replaced. Rather, one is creating a channel through which energy resonates back and forth between the two creating a circuit of power.

In addition, one is helping move the pendulum along the scale of balance. For in this instance, it is assumed that the target of the spell previously hadn't expressed interest in forming a relationship with the Witch. With this spell the Witch is moving the point of desire from one of disinterest to friendship. These are essentially different degrees along the same scale of manifestation.

This resonance with another person is best achieved through the process of merging and forming the mental link as described in the previous chapter. For when forming the link, ideally one isn't forcing one's presence on the other person so much as creating a resonance with them. In doing so it is far easier to enlist that person's own ideas and desires, bending these to the Witch's goal.

This same process can be brought to bear in using magic for more abstract goals. A good example may be found in casting spells for overall prosperity and success. However, in this situation the Witch seeks to resonate herself with the forces surrounding prosperity. For this, those of the Art turn to occult teachings regarding correspondence: the concept that specific plants, scents, natural items, as well as symbols, markings, sigils, tones of music, etc. relate to and partake of specific forces.

To understand this teaching we need to return to the realization that all is consciousness which manifests as energy. These in turn form intrinsic patterns. In our example of performing a rite for prosperity the Witch seeks to identify the overall dynamics that bring prosperity. These patterns, in turn, manifest in the various Worlds or realms of the Witch. Here on the threshold between Abred and Annwn (our material world), in our little corner of space, we find these in the correspondences related to Jupiter or the Sun and all that these represent.

To resonate with these forces the Witch first moves *Between the Horns*, entering the state of *Becoming*. She then gently shifts her consciousness to merge with the energies desired. As a part of this she will use those implements, herbs, oils, sigils, colors and 'Charms' or 'Words of Power' that correspond with Jupiter or the Sun. Of course, this same technique is applied to all other goals as well.

For many new to the Art the use of correspondence can be difficult to understand or, perhaps more accurately, for their rational mind conditioned by modern society, to accept. However, the simple fact is that because all is consciousness, all partakes of patterns of power. Which pattern that an item partakes of is determined, in part, by the correspondence that it shares with larger currents of force. So, as we saw in the first book, there are specific colors, numbers, tools, herbs, etc. that we use in ritual to align our own awareness to these larger currents. This 'alignment' in essence, represents the process of the resonance. The use of specific items, whether found in nature as in herbs, or created by the Witch as in talismans and sigils, draws that resonance closer, because they too are manifestations of these same circuits of power. Because of their inherent manifestation of the forces sought, the items used serve to enhance the Witch's alignment with the same. The greater the resonance becomes, the more power there is to use.

It is only when this resonance occurs that the seasoned Witch then projects the creative vision of her goal into the Abred where it can take form so that it can manifest later on the material levels of reality. It is in this state as well that her will, driven by desire and passion, feeds into the matrix of her imaginative creation on the Abred.

Without a resonance being formed between the Witch and corresponding patterns of energy, the Witch is relying solely on her own inner power to force her will into being. As noted earlier this can be effective. However, few people have the self-discipline and inner power to sustain this for long. Thus, their magic tends to be hit or miss depending on the circumstances and the amount of passion raised.

However, when resonance is formed with the patterns of energy that affect the specific goal the circuit of force becomes complete, moving through the various worlds to the inevitable outcome. This, of course, applies not only to the use of objects, herbs, oils, sigils, etc. but also to the timing of the rite aligning to these same powerful patterns.[13]

To understand how the circuit of force moves through the various Worlds we need to return to our earlier discussions on polarity. For, no matter what realm or dimension the Witch is working with, polarity is expressed throughout all of these. Occult teachings explain that, that which is potent in one realm is latent in the next, only to become potent in the realm beyond that. This is known as the concept of 'Reversed Polarity.'[14]

Reversed Polarity provides a natural ebb and flow of energy between worlds allowing for each to affect the next in a rhythmic progression. It is for this reason that those things created on the astral,[15] given enough force, eventually manifest on the material. In the same vein, energy drawn from the realm beyond the astral and infused into the astral image causes this to have more lasting effects on the form which manifests on the material.

Whether the Witch or Magician realizes it or not this principle is used in almost all rites or procedures in the Art.

---

13. Tides of power were discussed at length in *The Willow Path*.

14. Dion Fortune has written at length on this concept in many of her books.

15. The Astral is one set of conditions which are active in the wider scope of the Abred. Please see *The Willow Path* for a more detailed account.

This can be seen in the overall construction of the Roth Fail, with its three circles and the Cauldron at its center.[16] In this process we are tapping into each of the various realms. Once created, the Roth Fail acts as a closed circuit drawing power from each realm and bringing these to bear on the point that is the center.

Each circle is connected to the energy of the realm from which it flows. This then transfers over to the next circle, changing and transforming; active and passive forces flowing into each other creating a circuit of power that meets in the center of the circle as the Cauldron which rests at the heart of the 'Castle of Glass' – the energies crystalized and ready for use in magic.

One of the greatest secrets of the Witch or Magician is the ability to understand and work with this circuit of power, manipulating this as it moves through the worlds and applying this to the goal at hand. This is a vital aspect of all true magic.

This circuit of power not only occurs as a ritual process, this also occurs within the Witch herself. For each of us are composed of multiple forms extending through several different worlds. In some realms this circuit is active and potent, in others it may lay fallow and passive. Yet, through it all the energy remains and can be manipulated simply because at the root of this lays one's own consciousness. The energy flowing from world to world and body to body does so because it follows the levels of consciousness. This is why ritual, meditation and the vast array magical techniques in the Art are so important and powerful, simply because they provide the means for consciousness to access the power of these associated Worlds/dimensions.

As part of this process, many within the Art go to great lengths to form the "Magical Personality": a persona that embodies their magical will and abilities. There is no easy

---

16. A detailed description on the symbolism, use and construction of the 'Roth Fail' is given in *The Willow Path*.

way to describe the Magical Personality or its formation. However, in essence this is the culmination of the person's highest spiritual ideals and insights, combined with the full intent, will and magical talent they possess. This is then carefully crafted into an actual form. Frequently the Witch will form an actual visual representation or image of what their inner spiritual and magical self should look like if one were to meet this as a person in the mundane world. As you will see further in this book, this is done through the projection and formation of the fetch as well as combining this with certain Ancient Egyptian concepts.

The process for doing this occurs over months, even years of steady work, self-analysis and visualization. With this process, one is aligning the personality to the deeper will of one's own spiritual 'true self' or Akh as discussed later in this book. In doing so, the goal is to form a pattern of energy that resonates across all levels of the self; from the deepest part of oneself that is immortal and beyond incarnation through to the levels of mundane awareness one takes in daily tasks. Yet, the Magical Personality is reserved solely for those times when one is performing works[17] within the Art.

In some forms of the Art the apprentice is encouraged to go into great detail into the actual appearance that the Magical Personality should be visualized as. This is exactly the same rational behind the use of 'God Forms' when one calls on specific entities. As we saw in the discussion on the Gods in *The Willow Path* these visual appearances are in fact meant to represent and characterize the qualities of the God or Goddess themselves. So too, the appearance, as visualized by the Witch, of her Magical Personality is a composite of the qualities she seeks to embody and carry through in her magical work.

---

17. 'Works' is a term frequently used by many in the Art to refer to any magical operation. It is somewhat generic, however, it does make conversation among those in the Art easier than going into great detail on the exact types of magic they may be using.

This was discussed at some length in the first book when we examined the use of rings in the Art. As noted, the form the Witch creates is projected into the Abred or astral where it takes shape. Yet, throughout it all one maintains the desire to have this as a personal link to the deeper aspects of the self. This is only achieved through steady practice, deep meditation and the regular assumption of the Magical Personality. For many the use of a special ring that is solely linked to the Magical Personality is a tremendous aid. Because of this the ring is chosen very carefully, with metals, stones and engravings that resonate directly with the forces that the Magical Personality embodies. This ring is then worn only when practicing the Art.

Once one has begun to fully build this form and personality up on the Abred, binding this to the deeper spiritual aspects of the self (again, through deep meditation and visualization) she can and should become used to assuming this personality whenever practicing the Art. In time this becomes second nature, almost as if one were slipping on an article of clothing, or in fact, a ring. Yet this isn't done lightly. For a properly formed Magical Personality is a very powerful tool for the Witch or Magician. And it is in this tradition that the taking on of a magical or 'craft' name comes into play.

Chapter Five

✤ CHARMS OF WORDS ✤
NAMES, WORDS, AND SOUNDS IN THE ART

There is power in a name. To name something is to give it identity, defining it in a manner that ultimately embraces its very nature. This is especially true in the Art. As such, to learn the name of a spirit, intelligence, or force is to gain a measure of control over it. It is for this reason that such systems as Goetic and Solomonic magic place a strong emphasis on knowing the name of the being one is calling. This concept, at least in part, comes directly from Ancient Egyptian teachings.

Many of the Gods and Goddesses of Egypt had multiple names, some of which were only used by the priesthood in temple rites. Many of the names known to the average person (and which have come down to us today) are actually titles and not the secret names of the deities. As an example consider the Goddess Hathor. This is a Greek derivative of the Ancient Egyptian title Hwt-Hrw. The word 'Hwt' means 'house', while 'Hrw' means 'Horus', the Greek name for the falcon Sun God 'Heru'. Thus, the name Hathor is actually a title meaning the *House of Horus*. This title has several meanings. First, Hathor was a sky Goddess. As such, the falcon Sun God belonged in the sky. But 'hwt' or 'house' was also one word the Egyptians used to refer to the womb. Hathor and Horus were considered lovers in the ancient texts. So the title of House of Horus is also a reference to this Goddess as the lover of the Sun God. Having consider all of this, the question remains; what was this Goddess' actual name? There are many clues inscribed in the temples dedicated to Her. But that is a subject for another time.

A legend from Egypt also speaks of the Goddess Isis (Egyptian spelling 'Aset') seeking to learn the secret name of the Sun God Ra. In doing so She wanted to have power over Him; to be able to control Him if She needed to. The legend explains that despite asking Ra for His secret name, He would not reveal this.

Isis decided to gather spittle that fell from the ageing Sun God. With this taglock She was able to fashion a snake which then bit Him. With Ra in agony Isis offered to heal Him. However, to do so She needed His name. He proceeded to repeat a number of titles that were commonly known. However, Isis persisted, stating that to perform the magic She must have His secret name. Reluctantly, He whispered this to Her under the condition that she only reveal it to Her son Horus.

This legend, along with the secrecy surrounding the names of other deities, illustrates just how vital names as Words of Power were to the Egyptians. Not only were they important in understanding, defining and controlling otherworld beings, the Egyptians themselves often had more than one name. This was particularly true of royalty and of the temple priesthood. From the Old Kingdom on, the Pharaohs traditionally had five known names, as well as at least one secret name. The three most frequently known to the public were the Horus name, the Praenomen name and the Nomen name.

The Horus name is that which equates the king with Horus. The Praenomen name was given at the king's ascension to the throne, while the Nomen name is the king's birth name. It is this latter name which scholars use when referring to the various kings. The other two names, which were generally secret, are the 'Two-Ladies' name which is a reference to the twin sisters Isis and Nephthys (Egyptian spelling 'Neb Het'), and the Golden Horus name.[18] In the same respect initiates had both public names

18. Collier & Manley. *How to Read and Write Egyptian Hieroglyphs*, p.20.

and at least one secret name. This secret name, or 'Ren' as the Egyptians called it, was meant to embody the spiritual essence of the individual.

Given this legacy it is no wonder that many occult schools, orders and Covens today require that their members take on a new name at initiation. This is particularly true of Hermetic orders. In fact, I am not aware of any Hermetic magical group that doesn't ask this of its initiates. As for Traditional Witchcraft, I believe this varies from group to group.

There is the distinct possibility that during the persecutions Coven names were used as a safety precaution. During that time magical groups would have been kept small with great lengths being taken to preserve members' identities. It is likely that when not at a gathering members seldom, if ever, interacted with each other. Should one encounter a member while in public only the most casual politeness would be exchanged if any acknowledgement at all. It was best to act as if one didn't know the other.

Under these circumstances ideally, during Coven meetings, only the magical names would be used. Members' public or 'Christian' names normally would not be part of any conversation. If possible each person's public name was kept secret. This practice ensured a measure of anonymity, and could be particularly effective if the members came from different towns or rural areas, or if the Coven drew from the larger cities. In these cases there was every chance that the members would seldom encounter others except at the gatherings.

Of course, in smaller communities this almost certainly would not have been the case. Small towns would have been too close-knit for one to remain anonymous. However, for those groups that did draw from different villages this could be the case.

In many groups, ideally, only the Master, Mistress and the Summoner would know the individual's public names. The exception to this would also be the sponsor who would have trained, spoken for and introduced the candidate to initiation. I am aware of some traditions in which the leaders apparently kept lists of member's names in a book or some other document. This, in turn, was kept secret. There were several purposes for this. The first is simply for the sake of historical records. But more importantly it would serve as a record should a member decide to go to Christian authorities to turn in fellow members, because their name would be listed along with those they accused in the Coven records.

At first it would seem very risky for a group to keep such records. Yet, should the Master or Mistress be in a position where they ran a business, I can see situations in which they may keep registers and lists of vendors, customers, etc. It would be very easy to hide a roster of Coven members disguised among lists of other 'business' documents. It seems likely that it was from this practice that the Christian belief that Witches sold their soul to the devil by signing their names to his book came from.

The custom of keeping lists of member's names continues in many magical groups today. Sybil Leek alluded to this in her book "Diary of a Witch". And, in fact, the Hermetic Order in which I had trained, also kept a similar record reaching back many years. In this, they recorded the initiate's public name, as well as the name taken at their Adeptus initiation.

Without a doubt, not all Covens took these precautions. And I strongly suspect that many would not have kept a written record of members out of the obvious concerns of this being discovered.

It is also important to note that all of this is drawn from my own conclusions based on various strands of lore that I have gathered coupled with my own experience in groups today. It could very well be that during the persecutions members of some Covens had full knowledge of each other's public persona as well as their magical workings. This would seem to be very risky, yet when working in a close knit magical group a bond of deep fellowship and trust does develop. Nevertheless, the remnants of careful precautions along with the repercussions of betraying the group remain today in various strands of Traditional Witchcraft; from oaths of secrecy, to alternative names, the signing of a document, to the taking of taglocks during initiation.

Having said this, when it comes to family traditions they simply kept their secrets within their clan. I have to state that in my time with Julie she never discussed the use of a magical name. I suspect this was because hers was a family tradition, and thus there was no need to keep identities hidden. Or it may have been that because I wasn't part of her family I was never told of her or her family members' secret names.

As time went on the persecutions began to subside. With this many of the practices meant to keep groups secret weren't necessarily needed. Yet, many of these have survived as part of the Art, evolving in meaning and purpose. Like the Egyptian 'Ren', individual's Coven names now take on a richer purpose than solely to hide one's identity. They have come to form links to one's true self and spiritual aspirations. The oaths of secrecy have taken on the purpose of linking one to the spiritual teachings and otherworld beings that guide the Coven, instead of being solely a guard against exposing others in the group.

Returning to our conversation surrounding the Magical Personality from the previous chapter, it is here that the name one takes in the Art becomes very important. For the name chosen should reflect the highest aspirations of the Witch or Magician. As such, great care needs to be taken when making a final choice for this. In doing so you will want to consider any mythological or historical ties to the name. This is important as, without fail, I have found that the characteristics, temperament, strengths *and* flaws portrayed in myth will, inevitably manifest in the Witch once she begins to identify with the name.

I have seen this happen time after time. On more than one occasion I, as leader of the Coven, had to go to aspiring initiates and have them chose different names prior to being accepted because of this reason. In these cases they chose names which had backgrounds in myth which were not in the best interest of the apprentice under my charge.

In addition, it is important to consider numerological influences. This can be critical. Choose the spelling well. Consider what qualities, talents and skills you wish to have as you advance on the Willow Path. Numerology can be a tremendous asset here. One's name of Art forms the foundation on which future progress proceeds.

It should be noted that it is also very common to have more than one magical name. Usually additional names develop years later as one advances in knowledge. These in no way invalidate the power of the previous names. Rather, they form layers within the self, with each successive name revealing a deeper, richer aspect of the individual. Most people will find that they have a Coven name used in the Art for work with others, or in the casting of spells related to mundane goals. However, they will also come to possess a secret name that is only used in works related to deeply spiritual endeavors. This may include rites of invocation of Gods or Goddesses, as well as works related to becoming more aware of one's true spiritual self, or the 'akh' as Egyptians termed this. I find that I only use this name when the full force of who I am is needed.

In the final analysis, one's Name of Art comes to form the matrix around which the Magical Personality is built. I can say that assuming one's Magical Personality, as one places the ring of Art on the middle finger of the dominate hand while intoning one's Name of Art is a powerful act of magic in itself.

From this discussion it now becomes easy to understand that the names of Goddesses and Gods can and do act as magical formulae through which the deity called is able to manifest. If spoken in the proper way, with the correct intent, and while the Witch is in the appropriate state of mind, the names of Goddesses and Gods become Words of Power.

With this realization, Words of Power can be understood to be key words spoken during ritual or in spells that are intended to arouse currents of power within the 'astral light' as Hermetic orders like to term this. In essence these are emotional keys which, in many cases, have built up within them symbolic meaning over thousands of years of use. They carry energy becaus. of their relationship to, and resonance with, the forces they represent and because of the 'egregore'[19] that is associated with them. With the right use they are meant to carry the will of the Witch while stirring the forces or beings which they correspond to.

In Egyptian magic the spoken word in ritual is exceptionally important. Egyptologist, Dr. Assmann, explains that for the Egyptians, "the radiant power of speech made the divine realm, in all its otherworldliness, capable of being approached, conceptualized, and represented, and speech was thus a dimension of divine presence".[20]

As can be seen Words of Power, or *Charms of Words* as they were frequently called, have been used from very ancient times. That these were an aspect of European Traditional Witchcraft is noted by Historian Alan Macfarlane when he stated that 'cunning folk' "prescribed Charms of Words to be used over the victim, herbs, bags of seeds, or holy writings".[21]

It is best to use Words of Power which are not part of one's daily vocabulary. For our purposes we prefer to use either Gaelic or Ancient Egyptian words depending on

---

19. A term used to describe the inherent meaning of a word, symbol, image, etc., carried through in the various worlds that have been generated through centuries of use.

20. Assmann, Jann. *The Search for God in Ancient Egypt*, 2001.

21. Macfarlane, Alan. *Cunning Folk and Wizards in Early Modern England*, 2010.

the type of ritual being performed.[22] Having said this, it is common for some Magicians to 'create' Words of Power, drawing from key magical symbolism related to specific powers, Gods and currents.[23]

When spoken these are meant to be intoned or 'vibrated' more than simply 'said'. When intoned one feels the force of the word vibrate through their body while the will is carried out into the astral creating the desired effect. As with so much in the Art, this takes practice to achieve well. Nonetheless, a strongly intoned Word of Power can be a tremendous tool. Perhaps Aleister Crowley's comments on the subject can shed some insight:

> "With all such words it is of the utmost importance that they should never be spoken until the supreme moment, and even then they should burst from the Magician almost despite of himself – so great should be his reluctance to utter them. In fact, they should be the utterance of the God in him at the first onset of divine possession."[24]

The Word of Power then is meant to be an organic release of intention, passion and power manifest through a single word or series of words. It shouldn't be forced. Rather, the word or words become the means by which the raw passion and desire of the occultist takes form. And, yet, when combined in an incantation or chant, such words act to drive passion as well as open the consciousness of the Witch to the forces in play.

---

22. Our use of Words of Power with a listing of many of these will be presented in the third book of the Geassa Series *The Art*.

23. This latter technique is highly advanced and should only be attempted once one has a solid grasp of the language and occult system being employed.

24. Crowley, Aleister. *Magick in the Theory and Practice*, p.70.

There is nothing quite as heady as standing before the hearth on a dark night with only the glow of fire light, the faint swirl of incense wafting by, as one chants a rhyming spell or invocation that uses specific Words of Power to stir the astral energies. For that one moment the Witch becomes lost in her work, focused solely on the ritual and the goal for which the spell is being cast.

Please be aware that if you use the names of Goddesses, Gods or specific spirits in your incantations be very careful of the context. Given the right setting and emotional drive these otherworld beings will come, whether you are clairvoyant enough to perceive them or not.

A key factor that is seldom mentioned is that, when one intones Words of Power, visualization is absolutely critical to enhancing the effectiveness of the words spoken. Just before you begin to utter the phrase, envision brilliant light welling up within you being pulled up through the land and filling your body. Let this gather in the solar plexus. The color will depend on the type of work you are performing. It may be helpful for the reader to refer to the first book in this series with its in depth discussion on color. If no specific color is to be used I often fall back to a vivid white light, or more often a sun like radiant gold. Whatever the color, allow this to build in power and brilliance. When the light has reached its peak, utter the word with as much intention as you can while 'seeing' the light you built in your body rushing out as the word itself into the planes of the Abred. Then take a moment and envision the goal of the spell clearly, as if it was already happening. In your mind let the light you had sent in the Charm of Words merge with the goal, becoming the goal, breathing life into the goal.

This brings us to the subject of 'correct' pronunciation of these words. This can be difficult at best. If the Word of Power is from a known, living language then one should make every effort to find the pronunciation of this. However, keep in mind that these will be different depending on region, dialect and even time period. Gaelic can be particularly challenging, as all of these factors come into play. My advice is to do the best you can and be consistent.

In using dead languages, such as Ancient Egyptian, the problem is compounded as vowels were seldom written. Thus, we really only have educated guesses on how the language was spoken. Nevertheless, experience has shown that use of the words as we have them today, when spoken with meaning and the correct visualization do produce the desired magical results.

It may be important to note that in Ancient Egypt, individual cults and temples dedicated to a particular Goddess or God also used words that were specific to their practices. This has proven to be very challenging for Egyptologists in their attempts to translate texts. However, this illustrates an additional factor related to the practical application of the Art. Magicians and Witches have, in the past as well as today, used words specific to their own practices and groups. These then become almost a form of secret language. Nevertheless, the power of such words is apparent.

Generally, there are two different distinct reasons for this. The first was simply to hide key components or ingredients that go into a spell or potion. Thus we see older records calling for obscure ingredients such as 'bat wings' or the like. In fact, bat wings was a Craft term for Holly Leaves.

On a different level, Witches and Magicians will use their own Words of Power as a means of transmitting the intention of the Witch. As one teacher whom I had worked with explained,[25] these are frequently employed to avoid the use of words that often have two meanings. He explained that the subconscious is very literal in its thinking. In order to tap the deepest levels words that might confuse the deep mind are best avoided, replaced by words that are secret and more specific to the goal at hand.

---

25. Robert Moser, Samhain 1980.

Ideally incantations should be memorized in advance of the actual ritual. The more you have memorized the easier it will be to slip into a deeper state of mind, merging with the purpose of the spell itself. This is where rhyme aids in tremendous ways. The deep mind responds well to prose, pace and rhythm. This doesn't mean your chants need to be great pieces of poetry. Few of us have that talent. Nevertheless I have found that the better a chant rhymes, the greater the ease in losing myself to the moment allowing my mind to focus on the goal.

This can frequently be accompanied with movement, specific gestures and even dance. Believe me, I am no great dancer. However, movement joined with a solid rhyming incantation that incorporates Words of Power while one is mentally visualizing the goal sought is a very potent combination. It can become almost hypnotic in its effects. One tends to lose all awareness of the material world. Time and space disappear and all that remains is a merging with the forces called, coalescing in the goal that is the spell's purpose.

In Sybil Leek's book, *Cast your own Spell*, she briefly mentions that a well-guarded secret in certain traditional forms of Witchcraft is the use of musical tones. Unfortunately she doesn't elaborate on this. However, the use of tone has been an important part of some forms of Hermetic practices as well, particularly those drawn from Greco-Egyptian influences. In some groups this includes a direct correlation between the seven tones of the musical scale and the seven known planets of the ancients. These are as listed here:

Planet	Tone
Sun	G
Moon	D
Mars	A
Mercury	E

Jupiter	B
Venus	F
Saturn	C

Traditionally Low C is used for the more mundane practical matters related to Saturn, as well as some of this planet's darker aspects. High C, on the other hand, stimulates deeper states of awareness, acting as a vibration or gateway to spiritual realms, worlds and states of being. It is important to keep this in mind when working with this tone.

It can be very easy to incorporate tone into ritual, especially when using specific planetary energies. Like Words of Power, tone should be sounded at key moments in the rite. And they should never be a distraction. Rather, they should come almost naturally as if there was the organic need for the tone to be released.

For any important ritual it is always best to run through a basic practice session of the rite to ensure you have the right equipment, are familiar with the incantations, and know the correct tone to be used at the correct time. There is nothing more distracting in a ritual then fumbling to find the note needed. Practice is key to this. In my personal magical workings I use a simple pitch pipe, finding it to be an easy and reliable way to produce the tone desired.

Beyond the seven planets, in our work with the traditional Worlds of the Witch we have found that specific tones resonate well to each of these realms:

Annwn – Low C
Abred – D
Gwynfyd – G
Caer Wydyr – High C

These work very well when seeking to move into or through these realms. They can be used to open passages to these realms, and to call otherworld beings to the Roth

Fail from the realm which they normally inhabit. In personal workings I use these as well to alter my awareness and state of being, as well as to explore these different realms through light trance and meditation. In such cases I will intone the appropriate note while in the Roth Fail. These can be used as well in some of the procedures for traveling in spirit. In this way the fetch or ka double can be eased into the realm desired with the aid of the tone involved.

Chapter Six

✤ CORN AND BARLEY ✤
THE 'BODIES'

In the Art we recognize that as living beings we partake of the consciousness that is all on a very deep and profound level. In order to find expression in the various realms, consciousness sheaths itself in the elements of the realm which it seeks to experience. As such we possess a series of 'bodies' or 'vessels' which we slip in and out of depending on the dimension we seek. Sometimes those 'bodies' deteriorate returning to the raw elements of the realm in which they primarily function (such as our physical body), while other bodies can move more freely within a limited set of realms.

In different branches of the Art there exist extensive teachings on the various bodies. From Traditional Witchcraft to Hermetic circles, this lore gives vital clues into the nature of the vehicles we all possess. Some of the most profound and clear descriptions come from the secret traditions of Ancient Egypt. As such I would like to begin this discussion with teachings drawn from Egyptian texts.

While alive, the Egyptians referred to the physical body as the *ht* or the *jrw*, both terms meaning "form" "appearance" or "house." After death, however, the body was referred to as the *Khat*, as well as the *Sha* or *Shat*, meaning that which is corruptible, similar to our use of the word corpse. These terms clearly imply that the physical body is both a receptacle for higher energies, and yet subject to the forces of impending aging and decay.[26]

---

26. Naydler, Jeremy. *Temple of the Cosmos*. Copyright, p.188-189.

Closely allied with the physical body, Egyptian teachings explain that each of us possess a *Swt*; a hidden 'shadow' self. Yet, this is very different from the concept applied by many contemporary magical orders for the 'shadow.' In these groups the shadow is frequently viewed as one's baser or negative self; almost as a psychological aberration. This almost certainly came into vogue with the advent of Jungian psychology in the early twentieth century.

In contrast the ancient Egyptians, as well as traditional European Witches, saw the shadow as being an essential part of the living person. In these systems the Swt, or shadow, was seen as being a protective guardian, an aspect of the self with the power to preserve one from adversity. Further, the Swt was able to provide hidden knowledge not normally experienced through the five senses. In this way the Swt acts in many respects independent of the person, gathering knowledge that is later communicated through dreams and intuition.[27]

After death, the Swt of an individual was frequently perceived as being similar to our understanding of a 'ghost.' This could literally be seen as the faint but visible form of the deceased. This was sometimes also known as the *Khaibit* by the Egyptians.

It is important to know that the Egyptians taught that the shadow also acted as a bridge uniting the physical needs and desires of the material body with the 'Ka'. As we will see, the Ka in many ways can be understood as corresponding to the 'astral body' described by contemporary Magicians.[28] Thus, the shadow functions similarly in nature to Victorian era Occultists' views of the etheric body. For them the etheric body was seen as a link between the physical body and the astral self.

In traditional European Witchcraft the equivalent of the Swt or shadow is frequently referred to as a 'fetch' or

---

27. Lurker, Manfred. *An Illustrated Dictionary of the Gods and Symbols of Ancient Egypt*, p.110.

28. West, John Anthony. *The Traveler's Key to Ancient Egypt*, p.65.

one's 'second skin'. The second skin is generally thought of as replicating the physical body yet it can be molded into different shapes as desired.[29] This is exceptionally similar to Egyptian teachings on the Swt. For they too felt that the Swt could take on different forms.

In Egyptian magical practices the two most common forms for the Swt to take were that of a dark silhouette, or else a globe or ball. In these shapes the Swt would gather information and then return this to the Magician later. In Traditional Witchcraft the fetch is used in a similar fashion; that is it will be sent to gather information or to visit the intended target of a spell.[30]

The teachings surrounding the actual projection and molding of the Swt, fetch or "second skin" are an important part of practical magic. This involves steady practice, focusing the will on the form desired and empowering this with the passion, and if desired, the consciousness of the self. This vehicle is then able to move independently to perform tasks on its own.

Traditionally the Witch will form the fetch into the shape of animals which she then uses to travel 'in'. However, there is a cautionary aspect to this practice. If one chooses the form of an animal there is the real possibility that the overriding 'tribal' spirit or natural impulses of that species can take over the form. Further, the influence of this animal 'impulse' can begin to affect the Witch herself once the Swt or fetch is integrated back into the self.

This then forms the basis of the stories of shape shifters and skin walkers. The legend of the werewolf almost certainly has its foundation in this simple occult practice. It is for this reason that some esoteric orders strictly forbid its members from engaging in the shaping of astral images into

---

29. Morgan, Lee. *A Deed Without A Name: Unearthing the Legacy of Traditional Witchcraft*, 2012.

30. The Fetch is a highly complex concept in Traditional Witchcraft. As such, I will be discussing this further in this text.

animal forms, largely out of concern that the Magician will be overcome by the 'animal impulses' of the species chosen.

Having said this, shamanic practices the world over do incorporate the visualization and projection of animal forms on many levels. For them this is a vital practice that is central to their Art. Celtic tradition abounds with detailed accounts of enchantresses, sorcerers, druids, Gods and Goddesses shape shifting into a variety of animal forms. Undoubtedly some of these refer to the use of animal hides and masks in a ritual setting. Yet others are clear references to the ability to shape the fetch in different forms.[31]

Ironically the very esoteric orders who have strict taboos against such practices frequently employ the same technique in certain rituals meant to draw the spiritual essence surrounding the image into the Magician. In many ways this seems hypocritical to me. I tend to think that their moratorium on individuals using animal forms shows a lack of understanding about the nature of the different 'bodies' involved, and the energies they are drawing on.

For our part, we are very careful which animals we choose to merge with. Still, with care, we do use this technique, drawing from totem animals tied directly to the tradition, the individual's spiritual goals, or those animals that possess characteristics which we relate to easily. Thus, it is common in the Willow Path for the Witch to assume an animal form through her fetch. After the Swt has been projected and it eventually returns to the Witch, it needs to be reabsorbed so that the information it received can be perceived.

It is important that the student understands that if the form is not reabsorbed back into the Magician or Witch, this same energy can take on a life of its own. In such cases these can become autonomous thought forms feeding off the energy and emotion of other living beings. It is from

31. Spence, Lewis. *The Magic Arts in Celtic Britain*, p16-20. This book gives a detailed overview of the lore surrounding Celtic uses of shape shifting.

this technique that, as mentioned before, the legends of the werewolf, as well as the vampire, incubus and succubus, glaistig and other entities likely come from.

For those who are natural 'materialization mediums' these forms can take on an almost physical presence, drawing from the vital essence of the Witch. In such cases the fetch can become almost tangible in form. When this happens these beings may become vulnerable to injury, and this injury will oftentimes manifest in the physical body of the Witch once it is absorbed,[32] usually in the form of bruising. Because of these reasons the methods of projecting the fetch have been carefully guarded secrets, confined to the inner workings of occult Orders and Covens.

The techniques themselves vary, yet they are surprisingly simple in method. The challenge is in obtaining a state of consciousness between intense concentration while remaining relaxed, and then learning to project the 'substance' that makes up the Swt. I will be examining some of these techniques in the next chapter.

In darker forms of the Art it has been known that some will draw out the 'second skin' or etheric substance of another person and use this to form a vehicle in which to "ride". This is a very subtle and negative use of another person's Swt. In essence the Witch uses the energy of another, shaping this into the desired form, just as she would her own fetch. She then possesses this for a time while traveling in this form.

Legends abound describing the intensity, exhaustion and oftentimes fear that the victim will feel during such encounters. The advantage to the Witch is that she does not have to use her own vitality for this process, instead relying on that of the other person. This, of course, is a very dark form of magic and something only be done under dire circumstances. This method is particularly employed by older Witches whose own vitality may be waning. As

---

32. See *Mastering Witchcraft* by Paul Huson, 1970 for information on this in his chapter of protection.

such, the subtle essence of a younger person is sought, if only temporarily, giving the older Witch the power to move easily in a vibrant form. This in turn accounts for the many legends of Witches 'sucking' the youth out of people in order to make themselves young. These, of course, are an over exaggeration. Yet, given the practice described here, it is easy to see this as the origin behind such stories.

Following the Swt we come to the Egyptian *Ka*. The Ka is perhaps one of the most difficult concepts to describe for there is no clear modern translation for this word. Essentially it appears that the term means "double" or "vital force" and is a clear reference to a part of the individual that transcends the death of the physical body. Egyptologist Richard Wilkinson explains that "in all periods [of Ancient Egypt] it is used as a term for the creative and sustaining power of life".[33] The Ka also can be seen as the vitality and energy inherit in all living things. The hieroglyph for the Ka is two arms raised as if mirroring each other. This glyph, used as an amulet, was worn to preserve the life force of the wearer.[34] John Anthony West states that the "Ka is the power that fixes and makes individual the animating spirit".[35] In this context we can see that the Ka is very much like the contemporary understanding of the astral body.

Taken a step further, the teachings surrounding the Ka shed light on astral realms, or those which we of the Willow Path equate with the Abred. As such, we can see that the energies of the Abred are vital to sustaining life, spiritual continuity and development. In essence the Abred, as Ka 'energy', acts as a vitalizing force.

From the Ka we move on to the closely related doctrine of the 'Ba'. Most Egyptologists refer to the Ba as being similar in meaning to the modern concept of the soul. However,

---

33. Wilkinson, Richard H. *Reading Egyptian Art*, p.49.

34. Lurker, Manfred. *An Illustrated Dictionary of The Gods and Symbols of Ancient Egypt*, p.73.

35. West, John Anthony. *The Traveler's Key to Ancient Egypt*, p.64.

this is an understatement. In fact, it is best understood as meaning "spiritual manifestation." In early Egyptian texts the term Ba was used to signify the hidden essence of the Gods themselves.[36]

In relation to the human experience Richard Wilkinson explains that, "the Ba was a spiritual aspect of the human being which survived death, and which was imbued with the fullness of a person's individuality".[37] In this regard the Ba of an individual is portrayed in Ancient Egyptian religion as having the head of a human and the body of a bird, usually a falcon. In magical practice it is this form, this spiritual body of the individual, which traveled between the different worlds or realms.

In many ways it would appear that the Ba holds similar characteristics to that of the contemporary esoteric teachings of some Hermetic Orders regarding the 'mental body'. The Egyptian representation of the human headed falcon as the Ba would suggest the mind as governing a body fashioned for movement into higher realms of understanding and existence. This would seem to be an apt image to describe the idea of the mental body of Hermetics.

In addition, a reoccurring theme emerges in many of the Ancient Egyptian texts: the realization that the uniting of one's Ka with one's Ba are essential for the being's effectiveness.[38] Egyptologist A. Lloyd explains that "essentially, the Ka is the individual's vitality, the Ba is the capacity for movement and effectiveness".[39]

This union of the Ka with the Ba is extremely reminiscent of certain Hermetic teachings regarding the union of the Nephesh (a Hermetic term derived from

---

36. Lurker, Manfred. *An Illustrated Dictionary of The Gods and Symbols of Ancient Egypt*, p.31

37. Wilkinson, Richard H. *Reading Egyptian Art*, p.99

38. West, John Anthony. *The Traveler's Key to Ancient Egypt*, p.64.

39. Yale Egyptological Studies. *Religion and Philosophy in Ancient Egypt*, 1989.

Hebrew) or astral self with the Rauch (similarly, a Hermetic term borrowed from Hebrew) or mental self. In their classic work on the Hermetic 'Ogdoadic' tradition, *The Magical Philosophy*, Melita Denning and Osborne Phillips explain that the "Rauch [mental body], then is bounded at its extremity by the Nephesh [astral body] which it to some degree interpenetrates, and at the other extremity by the domain of the higher faculties to which it should be receptive." They go on to state that the Rauch (mental body) "must both control the Nephesh [astral body], and work with it".[40]

It is important that one keeps these concepts in mind as we examine the vehicles available to the Witch. Essentially what the teachings are saying is that the vital force of the individual, contained in the Ka and forming the astral, needs to merge with the awareness of the individual as their consciousness or Ba. In this way the Witch has the ability to move freely, traveling in spirit, through the worlds. These worlds include our own physical realm as well as the many different realms that populate the Abred, Annwn and to some extent the threshold that rests at the entrance to the Gywnfyd.

Beyond the Ba, the Egyptians were aware of the *Akh*, sometimes referred to as the *Khu*. These terms best translate into "transfigured spirit," the "shining one" or "luminous one." This body is one's 'true' self, the immortal spirit or, as the Ancient Egyptians explained, that part of the person that is "imperishable".[41] Egyptologist A. Lloyd explains that the Akh "differs in character from all the other entities as it represents the total person in a state of beautitude and power beyond the grave, i.e., nothing less than the deceased

---

40. Denning and Phillips. *The Magical Philosophy*, 1975, 1988.Vol II, 209 – while complex and coached in esoteric language this work (all five volumes in the set) are an excellent source of magical teaching for those with a leaning toward complex ritual practice, especially within the Ogdoadic Hermetic system and Hermetic Qabalah.
41. West, John Anthony. *The Traveler's Key to Ancient Egypt*, p.65.

reconstituted and placed in all respects in a position where he can function according to the Egyptian concept of the blessed dead".[42]

For the Egyptian initiate, awareness of one's Akh was exceedingly important. The Akh is that part of us that transcends time, space and incarnation in the temporal world. Renowned Egyptologist, Dr. Jan Assmann, explains that the root meaning of the word Akh is to "blaze, be radiant"; thus the Akh "designates the usefulness and efficacy of those human actions that are able to reach out into the sphere of heavenly eternity".[43]

The final stage in Egyptian spiritual transformation can be considered that of the *Sahu*. The Sahu, in essence, represents a union of the individual with the Neteru, the Gods. Thus it was seen as a merging with the divine, and the means through which the divine becomes manifest to the person on an individual and intimate level. Perhaps a better way to view this is in the way in which the pyramid texts speak of this. Repeatedly they discuss the deceased, as a Sahu, being welcomed as an equal to and among the company of the Gods. This can almost be thought of as a process in which the immortal self of the Akh transforms into the state of a Sahu.

By understanding the true self, we open the doors to communication with the divine, the Gods. So the first step of anyone who walks the path of the Art is always one of self-discovery which is meant to lead one to an eventual spiritual metamorphosis while learning to move into other realms of being.

The Egyptian texts which I am referring to come largely from traditional 'funerary' sources. However, Egyptologist Walter Federn argues that, while these certainly were used

---

42. A. Lloyd: *Psychology and Society in the Ancient Egyptian Cult of the Dead*, p.117-133.

43. Assmann, Jan. *The Mind of Egypt: History and Meaning in the Time of the Pharaohs*, p.61.

in this context, they also reflect actual ritual activities conducted by living initiates in the temples to bring about spiritual transformation *during* life! It is likely that these are texts accompanying ritual acts designed to carry the Ba-Ka (mental and astral bodies) of the initiate through different forms, connecting the self with various modes of divine expression. In this way the initiate rises to the awareness of the true self in the Akh so that ultimate union with the spiritualized self of the Sahu could occur.

These ritual procedures were the means by which the Ancient Egyptians explored the various worlds which they describe so vividly in their underworld texts, the Book of the Dead, and numerous pyramid and coffin texts.

The following table, while very simplistic, may serve the reader in helping to understand some of the possible correspondences between these systems:

Contemporary Occult Terms	Hermetic Qabbalistic Terms	Ancient Egyptian Terms	Celtic Gaelic Terms	Popular Terms
True Self	Yechidah/ Chiah/ Neshamah	Sahu/Akh	Realtch	Spirit
Mental Body	Ruach	Ba	Spiorad	Soul
Astral Body	Nephesh	Ka	Anam Coimimeadh	Soul
Gross Astral, or Etheric Body	Nephesh	Swt/ Khaibit	Taibhse/ Taise Coimimeadh	Ghost (fetch, shadow, & second skin in Traditional Witchcraft)
Physical Body	Guph	Ht/Khat	Colann	Body

As with our examination of the worlds in *The Willow Path*, it is important not to look at any of these bodies as being lesser, or somehow evil when compared to any other. Each has its own function and is important in order to experience the dimension which it best functions in. It is also important to understand that this is far from being a definitive description of the bodies that consciousness may take. Rather this is meant to be an overview of the major modes through which we experience certain realities.

You'll notice that the table above includes Celtic/Gaelic terms. Upon comparison with the other terms, it is clear that parallels exist. In Gaelic the term Colann refers to the physical body and flesh. The Taibhse can be described as a ghost or phantom while the Taise is equated with the same as well as with the shadow.

Another Gaelic term that can be equated to the Swt or shadow is the Coimimeadh, the 'co-walker.' In his book from 1692, Robert Kirk discusses this in detail explaining that the Coimimeadh is from Scottish folk tradition representing one's double.[44] It is easy to see a connection between these and the contemporary concept of the etheric body or "gross astral".

The Anam has been equated with both the soul and one's life force. This is exceptionally similar to the Egyptian concept of the Ka, as well as current occult teachings on the astral body. This can be understood to be followed by the Spiorad: a word meaning 'spirit' as well as 'life'. While this is not conclusive it is tempting to compare this with the Egyptian Ba, Hermetic Ruach and the contemporary occult view of the mental body. Lastly we come to 'Realtch'. This is a word meaning 'starry' 'sidereal' or 'celestial'. One could easily draw parallels between Realtch and the Egyptian Akh and Sahu, though I am not aware of this term being used directly in relation to an aspect of the person.[45]

---

44. Kirk, Robert. *The Secret Commonwealth of Elves, Fauns & Fairies.* 1692. Reprint with commentary as *Robert Kirk: Walker Between the Worlds*, edited and commentary by R.J. Stewart, p.24.

45. I need to mention that my understanding of the Gaelic terms used here is limited. Others with more proficiency may be able to clarify these better. Having said this it does seem clear that parallels do appear to exist between these systems of thought.

Please understand that this was a very quick and overly simple comparison between these different traditions. Nevertheless it isn't too difficult to see similar characteristics running through these. Again we are brought back to the concept of the Geassa and the common spiritual teachings coming through despite the differences in time, locale and culture. It would be tempting to ascribe this similarity to an exchange of ideas over time and between these different peoples. In fact, this is exactly what had happened on a limited scale. Yet, I don't believe that this alone explains the similarities. Rather, the thesis of the Geassa as a vital living consciousness implies that these people all had tapped into the underlying current of the Mysteries. They had tapped into the Geassa and gave it expression in their own way.

Within the Hermetic Order in which I have been trained there exists the teaching that as living human beings we possess all of these bodies at once, each existing in the realm which it best functions. It is only our awareness at the time which determines which body we are most cognizant of. Ceremonial Magician Dion Fortune makes an interesting observation concerning this:

> "Just as the physical body builds itself up out of the inert substances of the physical plane, so each of the subtler bodies renews its substance from the corresponding level of the subtler planes, there is a constant subtle psychic metabolism going on; a constant in-breathing and out-breathing on every plane. If this is impeded the corresponding level of being becomes unhealthy. If it is entirely cut off, that level dies, and the levels below it are cut off from the central directing guidance."

> She goes on to state that, "this in-breathing and out-breathing appears to be readily susceptible to regulation by the mind; it is in fact normally controlled by the mental attitude."[46]

---

46. Fortune, Dion and Gareth Knight. *The Circuit of Force*, p.20. Thoth Books, U.K.

As the death of the physical body approaches consciousness starts to shift away from the material realm. The physical body then dies, eventually returning to the natural elements of this world. For a time one may then be aware of this world through the vehicle of the Swt, shadow or etheric body. Normally this is limited in duration as the Swt, too, remains close to the material realm. In the event of a person dying who has strong emotional ties to events in this world one may remain conscious within the Swt for an extended time. Incidents such as this often give rise to reports of ghosts and hauntings.

This can be unfortunate for both the deceased and any observer. In both cases the Swt may be strongly tied to the condition and appearance of the physical body. As such after death this will frequently, though not always, begin to appear in the form of the corpse. Thus, as the corpse decays the appearance of the Swt can appear the same. This, of course, has been the source of so many reports of ghastly appearing spirits through the ages.

This, too, is strongly linked to the 'revenant' discussed in some Traditional Witchcraft teachings. As Lee Morgan explains, the revenant is a "potent ghost" that draws its energy from the corpse and will often take on a life of its own.[47] Eventually, as consciousness withdraws from the Swt, the deceased will become aware of the Ka or astral form moving into the Abred. There the individual is drawn to the aspect or world within the Abred which she or he has the strongest affinity. Like the material realm there are countless 'places' or worlds which one may experience. It is here that one will encounter the various 'afterlife paradises' or conversely, 'hells' found in many of our world religions. Each of these are real in the sense that the individual will experience them as objective

47. Morgan, Lee. *A Deed Without A Name: Unearthing the Legacy of Traditional Witchcraft*, p.26.

and yet, being astral in nature they can be transitory and are easily changed and shaped by strong thoughts and emotions. Further, unless weak willed, the individual is not 'stuck' or 'condemned' to anyone one of these astral worlds. Once again the occult axiom "change your state of consciousness to change your state of being" needs to be recalled.

As consciousness moves into the astral body, the Swt or etheric body will frequently continue to hover near the material realm as it continues to degrade, eventually returning to the raw elements of the lower astral plane. As it does this the grosser astral shell, as some contemporary Orders refer to it, will hold basic impulses and memories of the material life, yet at this point it is acting more or less as a robot in a somatic state. In some of the darker aspects of the Art, necromantic magic frequently calls on these forms. Many new comers to the Art will mistakenly believe that they have summoned the spirit of the person, when in reality all they have attracted is the decaying shell of the former person. This may easily explain many of the accounts of 'undead' and 'zombie' appearances. These decaying astral shells are frequently attracted to strong emotions, and other sources of psychic energy. From these many will draw power allowing them to exist longer. As discussed earlier in this chapter, in this regard they can drain vitality away from the living. Thus the abandoned Swt can become vampiric in nature.[48] It is in this guise that it becomes a revenant as noted in Mr. Morgan's research. Nevertheless, these forms will, in time, return to the raw elements of the lower astral, just as the physical body returns to the physical elements.[49]

---

48. As noted earlier, undoubtedly, the decaying and abandoned etheric body or Swt is the source of the legend of the vampire.

49. Ritual techniques exist protecting against the debilitating effects of these 'vampiric' beings, and which aid in the removal of such entities.

If the deceased individual is sufficiently evolved to understand how to merge the Ka with the Ba, or the astral body with the mental body, they can begin to move into some of the realms further on in the Abred which border on the threshold of the Gywnfyd. In the Art there are specific techniques designed to help the initiate attain this ability during material life. This is done through meditation, as well as trance and ritual, all of which have been a vital part of most shamanic traditions the world over.

Behind each of these 'bodies' though, lays consciousness. Looking to our model, one has to wonder where consciousness falls on this scale. The inhabiting force of life, consciousness, is best related to the Akh or Sahu itself. This is ever present, though in a state of evolution as it experiences the worlds through the bodies provided. Most people, in their daily lives, have no knowledge of this deeper part of themselves. Rather they are bound by the egocentric conditioning which has formed their personality in this life. Yet who we are is directly related to the experiences we have had in the past, both in this life and all of our previous incarnations. Through these, consciousness, and ultimately our Akh or 'true self', grows – becoming fuller and richer, reaching deeper into the ultimate which we are all seeking.

In the Art we are taught that eventually consciousness cycles through the worlds, drawn back into various forms and bodies. In so doing we reincarnate, pulled into the tides and circumstances best suited to our development. Once we return to material form, sheathed in a new Swt and physical body, we go through new experiences, yet these are experiences that are shaped by past actions as we continue to learn.

Some final thoughts before we leave the subject of 'bodies'; the physical body can be thought of as being similar to a radio, both receiving and sending information. Our true self, Akh or consciousness is ever existent. In this analogy we can think of the Akh as 'sending a program' to the body. The material body is nothing more than a receiver set to a frequency or rate of vibration which the individual's consciousness can manifest through. Picking up the 'frequency' of the individual, the body responds and one's consciousness becomes aware of its surroundings through the vehicle of the body.

The body not only receives the information from the Akh, it also sends information in the form of stimuli back to the 'true self'. It is no wonder that we identify so closely with the body given the amount of information, as well as the constant input of physical and emotional sensations that passes to the true self. Should the body be damaged in anyway, like a radio, consciousness can only come through as good as the receiver. Thus a radio program can come through on a damaged radio as scratchy, out of tune, missing information. While on a well maintained radio the signal comes through strong and clear. So it is with the body. When the body dies, like an old radio that has worn out, the program doesn't die with it. Rather it can manifest through another new 'radio'.

While this is a somewhat crude analogy it does help explain a number of phenomena including reincarnation. This too can explain spirit possession. By opening oneself up and changing the 'frequency' of oneself, the body can become aligned to other 'programs'. In such cases an affinity is formed allowing other spirits to enter. Once again I must emphasize, change your state of consciousness to change your state of being. At these times one's normal consciousness steps aside allowing another being to enter. Only when the person's normal state of consciousness begins to return will the frequency of the body created for that person respond, forcing the other spirit out and back to the realm from which it came. In some cases, if the original consciousness is weaker than the presence, the invader may remain a dominant influence in the person for a very long time. When this happens specific ritual techniques may be needed to help remove the unwanted spirit.

There are times though when possession is a welcomed and even sought after experience. Some examples include trance mediumship. However, a well-trained medium knows how to enter into these states in a controlled manner, allowing entities to possess the body for a limited time only. Then the medium is able to regain control with very few negative side effects.

In high magic possession by otherworld beings of a more complex order is often experienced. When this occurs it is almost always only after the Magician has actively sought this, altering their consciousness to attune themselves with the deity sought. This is done by surrounding themselves with symbols and images while also employing ritual actions to directly invoke the being. This is usually done, in part out of devotion to the being, and in part, to gain a measure of the being's characteristics and power. A third, very valid reason for seeking this experience is simply to let the being manifest in corporeal form for the duration of a ritual as an act of supplication. In these incidents many Gods actively seek the experience of material manifestation for limited periods, if only to enjoy the sensations this presents. They also seek this in order to speak to and directly interact with human beings. We see this in various forms of the Geassa. Ancient Egyptian texts relate a number of accounts in which the Gods or Goddesses will inhabit members of the priesthood to conceive children who will be part divine. An excellent example of this can be found in the texts surrounding the conception of Queen Hatshepsut. In Voudon rites, possession by the Gods represent a central aspect of this religion. In these situations the Loa will manifest in ritual to enjoy the foods, rituals and dancing that their tradition engenders.[50]

In the final analysis ultimately each of us is unique. At our center lays the spark of spirit, a highly complex being

---

50. I will be discussing the subject of spirit possession and the invocation of deities as this relates to Traditional Witchcraft in greater detail later in this book. See the chapter "Mare to the Gods".

that is part of the ultimate consciousness, the Geassa itself. The various bodies are simply the vehicles through which we move and become aware of the worlds or realms in which we are most focused. These bodies fall away as we transition from world to world not unlike the way we shed clothing in this life.

Yet the tides of power cycle through, calling us back into different realms, picking up where we left off while we continue to grow and learn in the realms we visit. So too, new bodies emerge from the elements of the various realms, clothing the consciousness of the Akh as we continue on in the grand adventure that is the spiral of life and reincarnation.

Chapter Seven

✤ WHISKEY IN THE GLASS ✤
"TRAVELING IN SPIRIT"

In the old English ballad of John Barleycorn, grain is harvested, ground, made into bread or beverage, and even buried in the earth. Yet no matter the form or 'body' he takes John Barleycorn returns, his spirit contained in Whiskey and Ale. The analogy couldn't be clearer. Despite the metamorphosis between forms, the essence remains, carried forward as the intoxicating elixir, spirit, which directly affects consciousness.

Our inner 'true self', the essence of who we are beyond the many forms and bodies we may clothe ourselves in, remains. Like the spirit of alcohol found in John Barleycorn our spirit, too, is refined through the process of this change from form to form. So like whiskey in the glass, spirit can be 'poured' into different forms and shapes. We examined some of these forms and their relationship to the self in the previous chapter. In this chapter I would like to present different techniques used to allow one to 'travel in spirit' or to 'pour the whiskey.'

To achieve success with traveling in spirit it is best to work in a series of graduated procedures or formulae, each of which builds on the success of the exercise before it. As such, consistent practice is needed. There are multiple reasons for this. First, just as an athlete needs to train before testing herself in competition, the Witch needs to condition her abilities so that when needed these skills are available. In addition, I have found that the state of awareness that occurs in projection is quite different from normal consciousness.

Unless one becomes accustomed to these altered states, when projection does occur it can be unnerving. Progressive steps and steady practice help the Witch to ease into these states, recognizing them when they occur and learning how to function in other realms.

"Flying" Ointment
Before beginning there are some aids that the Witch can prepare in advance. The first of these is a traditional "flying ointment" or oil. There are several recipes one can use drawing from medieval sources, however, many of these are highly toxic. As such, caution is recommended. The two recipes that I am presenting here have proven to be effective and are relatively safe.

For the first of these, make an infusion of three parts Wormwood and one part Vervain in either mineral oil or Olive oil. Olive oil tends to go rancid over time, as such you may want to use mineral oil instead. The herbs should be freshly dried so that they retain their full potency.[51]

The best method I have found to create this is to use a double boiler on the stove placing the herbs in the pan and covering these with the oil. Set this on a low heat and don't let the oil boil. Rather keep this on a low simmer allowing the herbs to gently release their natural properties into the oil.

Once the oil has become a deep emerald green remove the pan from the heat and let it cool. You will then want to strain the spent herbs out. The oil is then bottled, sealed, labeled and stored in a cool, dark, dry place until one is ready to use this.

A more complex, yet very effective recipe calls for the use of equal parts of Vervain, Wormwood, Poplar, Cinquefoil and Mugwort. Like the previous recipe these are placed in

---

51. Fresh herbs are more likely to mold due to moisture content. Fresh herbs should only be used when not stored for a long time. Dried herbs are more potent so use less than you would of the fresh.

a double boiler pan and covered with either mineral oil or Olive oil. This is then heated slowly until the oil is deep green. Once cool the herbs are strained out of this. The oil is then bottled and stored until needed.

Normally the oil is applied just before any type of 'Crossing the Hedge'- traveling in spirit – is attempted. Generally the ointment is only used when in the Roth Fail (Circle or Maze), or when working in the Chamber of Art (a separate room dedicated solely to your practice) after it has been sealed. When anointing oneself traditionally thirteen key points of the body are addressed:

- The soles of the feet;
- The knees, front and back;
- Genitals;
- Base of the spine and buttocks;
- Navel or solar plexus;
- Breasts;
- Wrists and hands;
- Nape of the neck or under the chin;
- Forehead.

Some Witches insist that it is best that the oil is placed on or *inside* the body in such a way that it can be readily absorbed into the blood stream. This comes from the realization that such herbs as Wormwood and Mugwort have a mild but real intoxicating effect. Looking to our list of portions of the body anointed there are only two points noted that would allow for relatively quick absorption. In fact, there is some debate among Traditional Witches today on whether the Besom handle was used for this function. In such cases, they argue that the handle would be lubricated with the Flying Ointment and then inserted into the appropriate orifice. I leave it to the reader to decide if they want to experiment with this suggestion.

It may be worth noting that records from the persecutions show that some Witches also applied the ointments in the armpits. This would have the desired effect of being absorbed into the blood stream as well.

Incenses for "Traveling in Spirit"

Another aid that can be prepared in advance of the actual working is the making of incense to be burned during these processes. There are a number of local herbs and resins available which, when combined, help to create effective incenses that aid with traveling in spirit. There are multiple reasons for this. The Art teaches that everything possesses power. The essence in every plant resonates with certain fundamental energies. These energies, in turn are released when burned as incense. As such, the smoke from certain incenses lends itself to adding substance and form to the energies projected when forming the bodies the Witch seeks to travel in.

When burning these there is no need to have this billowing in order to aid with the work at hand. On the contrary, I find that excessive smoke is a distraction rather than an aid. In practical astral workings it is best to have the overall scent of the incense present in ritual. The scent itself released through burning provides more than enough of the essential elements needed. Keep in mind that the use of the oils and incenses brings the principle of resonance into play. Their use in ritual sets the correct 'tone' aligning the energies within one to those associated with this type of work. So it isn't necessarily about quantity so much as the right use of the substances to help bring the results desired.

Whenever possible we prefer to use ingredients grown locally. This is done in part because our system of magic draws heavily from the power inherent in the locale we live in. As such, the plants and resins found here will have the greatest links to the Covenstead itself. I have little doubt that, except for the very wealthy, Magicians and Witches in the past would have been limited to those items they could find in their surrounding natural settings.

I personally get pleasure in walking through the forests and fields gathering herbs, resins, barks, roots and berries for use in the Art. The shear act of meditatively hiking through the mountains while seeking items of power is, in itself, a great way of gathering energy while slipping into a state of Becoming. In this state one can mix the ingredients into the desired incense while infusing this with the intention of the rite for which it will be used. For us, living in New England, such herbs as Wormwood, Mugwort, Blue Vervain, Poplar, Arrow Root, Solomon Seal, Bay Berry, Birch, Cherry, Pine, Cedar, Juniper, Elder, May Apple, Bloodroot and many other plants grow wild. Other herbs which are useful can easily be grown by the Witch. We have successfully cultivated Marjoram, Dill, Orris Root, Valerian, Coriander, Jasmine, Rosemary, Lavender, St. John's wort, European Vervain and many others.

Having said this, I have to acknowledge that we do live in very different times now, and many of the more exotic ingredients found in recipes from medieval grimoires are much more readily available. If you feel that your ritual work will be more effective using some of these ingredients by all means do so. I frequently make use of Sandalwood, Frankincense, Myrrh, Gum Mastic and many others. The following are some recipes for incense used to aid one with traveling in spirit. It should be noted that each of these can also be used in rites for summoning spirits. I find it interesting that the two are linked.

Wormwood and Vervain Incense
Like the first ointment noted earlier I have found that a combination three parts Wormwood with one part Vervain (either European or Blue) burned as an incense can be highly effective. However, you may find that the bitter scent of the Wormwood is not to your liking. In such cases you may want to add Rosemary, Frankincense or Gum Mastic. These latter ingredients are frequently used to give additional essence for the manifestation of spirits or 'astral' forms.

Wormwood and Vervain 'Compound'

Beyond the combination of three parts Wormwood with one part Vervain described above, the Witch may add ½ part Olive oil, ½ part red wine, and a ½ part Honey. Tradition dictates that putting a few drops of one's own sexual fluids released during orgasm into the mix gives this incense additional power. This is done because these fluids carry within them the energies and essence of life itself. Barring this one may add a few drops of one's own blood.[52]

This combination is mixed well and then left to set under the light of the Full Moon. If the mixture appears to be too moist, add more powdered Wormwood, Vervain or, if desired, Rosemary. The next day this should be fairly solid and will crumble to the touch.

Mugwort and Dill Incense

During the waxing Moon, on the night of Mercury, combine equal portions of Mugwort and Dill. If Mugwort isn't available use Wormwood. As with the others, if the Witch finds this too bitter of a scent she can add Rosemary, Frankincense or Gum Mastic to offset this while enhancing the power of the incense itself.

Incense to increase the sight

This is a traditional compound of herbs used in divination. As such, it can also be used in works related to traveling in spirit. For this combine equal parts of Valerian Root, St. John's wort and Mugwort. To this add a pinch of Saffron if available. If not Rosemary can be substituted.

Rosemary and Mastic Incense

A combination of Rosemary and Mastic helps give the Fetch

---

52. The use of one's own sexual fluids in these types of incenses is a common practice in Strega, traditional Italian Witchcraft. Keep in mind that once you have added your own fluids the incense is then strongly linked to you. As such I would not recommend letting others use this.

or 'spirit body' form. It is also used to increase 'the sight' – one's clairvoyant abilities.

"Astral" Incense

This recipe is drawn from Hermetic sources and is used in rituals intended to bring about astral projection. On a Monday during the waxing Moon, mix equal portions of Benzoin, Dittany of Crete (or Marjoram if Dittany is not available), Sandalwood and Vanilla Bean.

It isn't essential that the Witch make an ointment or incense in order to be successful in any of these techniques. However, their use does help the process significantly. As an additional aid the Witch may make a sachet of Mugwort and Arrow Root. If desired Sandalwood and Cinnamon can be added as well. This is then placed in the chamber or carried by the Witch while performing the formulas.

Breathing

While spontaneous 'projection' can and does happen to many people at some point in their lives, to be able to Cross the Hedge at will requires steady practice. This first exercise is meant to condition oneself over a period of time in preparation for the more advanced techniques that follow.

The breath has long been recognized as a means of moving energy and with it, one's intention. Learning to regulate breathing enables one to both increase and retain energy on many levels. Physically, breathing controls the amount of oxygen available to the body. On a more esoteric level the breath is used to gather 'psychic' energy or what the Egyptians called Sekhem.

The ritual act of exhalation onto an object is meant to move this Sekhem into the item. This is seen in both ritual magic and in Traditional Witchcraft with the act of 'breathing life' into poppets, amulets and talismans. Further, as noted in *The Willow Path*, accounts from medieval Witch trials of kissing the devil's ass are, in fact, a Christian debasement of an actual magical practice. This was, and still is, a part of some initiation rites in which Sekhem, in the form of the Witch's breath is directed into the initiate at different points on their body. It is not a physical 'kiss', nor is it directed at the backside. Rather, the Witch directs her will into her breath and then exhales gently onto the base of the lower spine at the small of the back (among other places) of the person she is initiating. When this is done by one experienced in the technique the effect can be quite profound. I still recall the rush of energy that this created during my own initiation. It was an almost intoxicating effect that lasted for hours. In the process my own awareness of the energies and otherworld beings present in the rite increased dramatically.[53] What was particularly interesting is that, at the time, I had no idea that the process was being done. All I knew was that the person involved walked around behind me. We were both robed during the rite and I had no physical sensation of feeling the 'breath' on my body. Nevertheless, the effect was psychically very intense. I mention this here to demonstrate the reasons those of the Art learn to control their breathing. For this same energy can be employed in the projection of the bodies that one uses to travel in.

Begin by choosing a place and time that you can be alone and undisturbed. Ideally this should be the same each day. For this you will want to stand, placing your feet slightly apart and facing forward. Push your hips slightly forward, keeping your spine straight. Your arms should be at your sides. Tip your head forward slightly as you imagine holding an apple between your chin the base of your neck. This posture ensures that your spine is straight. Practice this posture regularly until it feels natural to you.

When ready slowly and gently breathe in through your nose as you physically feel your abdomen push out. At first this may not seem natural. Most people only fill the upper portions of their lungs when breathing. However, for these

---

53. The actual technique for directing this "kiss" will be discussed in the third volume of the Geassa series, *The Art*.

exercises you want to form the habit of breathing while gently distending the abdomen.

Breathe in through the nose to the count of four. Then hold this to the count of two. Follow this with a gentle exhale through the mouth to the count of four. Hold your breath again to the count of two and then slowly, through the nose, breathe in again to the count of four. Continue this pattern for several minutes.

It takes some time to get used to but this is a very relaxing exercise that helps to open the inner senses while conditioning the natural gateways of the bodies to the flow of energy on multiple levels. In addition, breathing with the abdomen fills much more of the lungs, providing more oxygen to the body. It for this reason that this technique is also used in many martial arts schools.

This procedure can also be done while seated or while lying down. The key is to keep the spine straight and to breathe rhythmically with the abdomen. This should be practiced daily until it becomes natural. In time you will find that you breathe this way normally.

Shades in the Triangle: The formulae of the Swt

The energy that is the Swt or Shadow comes from the Second Skin, Gross Astral or what Victorian occultist had referred to as etheric or even ectoplasmic material. In Hermetic Orders this is often referred to by the Hebrew term of 'nephesh'. In essence, this is a substance that is almost tangible in form, existing as it does on the level of the Abred closest to the material. This energy is easily malleable.

Once you feel you have gotten to a point that you are comfortable with rhythmic breathing you will want to proceed with this next step. While not essential, ideally this should be done after fasting for four to six hours. In your chamber, or normal place of working, lay out a triangle. Traditionally this should be laid using your ritual cord (as described in *The Willow Path*) or by placing three Stangs so that the base or 'male' end of each rests between the horns or 'female' end of the next creating a circuit of energy that easily flows throughout. Barring either of these one may trace a triangle of Art in chalk, flour or herbs (preferably Vervain and Wormwood).

At this point you may want to anoint yourself with the ointment and light a small portion of incense. Then sit or stand facing the triangle. Allow yourself to relax as you perform the breathing technique for several moments. With your arms at you side, or if sitting, resting these on your lap with palms on your thighs, gently envision a stream of energy start to flow out from your abdomen. Allow this to begin slowly and evenly as a silvery grey substance. Don't be afraid to use your imagination to its full extent. Again, I want to emphasize that, in the Art, force follows will, or as one teacher used to tell me "what the mind can imagine the will can create".

Spend some time envisioning this. As you become more involved in the process you may soon feel a sense of tugging or pulling coming from the abdomen. This is quite normal. Don't try to force it, simply relax and let the energy slowly slide out in a stream into the triangle. In your mind imagine the energy forming into the shape of a silvery grey ball or globe connected to you by the stream that extends from your abdomen. Spend some time envisioning this, allowing it to form and take shape. No matter how much you may feel that it is "all in your imagination" suspend any disbelief you may be feeling and simply let it happen.

After several minutes reverse the process. Gently feel yourself pull the energy from the fetch, the Shadow, back through the stream into you abdomen. Envision this as slowly being sucked back into yourself as if through a straw. Once complete continue the rhythmic breathing for a few minutes longer. Then conclude the exercise by picking up the triangle and then proceeding to do something completely different and mundane. It is often best to have light meal. This in effect closes the centers of the body and allows the energy projected to return to the self.

Ideally this step in the formulae should be performed several times over a waxing moon period. This allows you to become familiar with the technique while also building up the Swt, the fetch, on a regular basis.

Once you feel you are proficient at this it is time to begin to shape this form into different images. Again, I want to explain that some occultist are very resistant to this next process. However, it is not only traditional in Witchcraft. Cultures around the world have used this technique as part of their magical practice. Personally I find it quite invigorating to allow the fetch to change forms and take on characteristics which, in turn, give this added power.

To do this go through the same steps as before; that is, begin with the rhythmic breathing, followed by projecting the Swt energy from the abdomen into the triangle while forming a globe. Then, at this point, allow the ball to grow in size and shape forming a shadow of yourself. This should be life size and made of the same substance that the globe had been. In these early stages there doesn't need to be any real detail to it. This is your shadow-self, made from the etheric energy that comes from you. When formed simply allow this to stand before you as you become used to the sensation of having your own shade existing on its own, yet connected to you in thought and deed.

As with the previous steps I strongly suggest that this be practiced repeatedly over a period of time. You will find that as the Full Moon draws near the shade or fetch becomes more visible taking form more easily. This is because 'etheric' or 'nephesh' energy flows more readily during this period in the month. As such, the Witch takes advantage of this tide of power when forming her shadow.

It is at this point that the fetch can be given a specific task to perform. Traditionally this has been anything from gathering information, visiting a person, delivering a spell, protecting a place, and much more.

When sending the fetch it is best to set a time at which it is to return. Ideally this should be tied to a celestial event.

For example, midnight the next evening, or the rising of the Sun, etc. I am reluctant to give a specific number of minutes or hours as the fetch is governed more by tides of power. At the appointed time return to your chamber and face the triangle. Then mentally call the shadow back. This is easier than it sounds for essentially the shadow is a part of the self, given form and mobility. Once you feel the form has returned, it is important to thank it for its help and recognize it as an important aid in your Art. Then gently pull the energy back into yourself.

You can do this through one of two ways. You can either slowly pull the energy through the stream that you had formed, into your abdomen as you had done when projecting the globe earlier. Or, if desired, simply allow the form to move toward you merging with your entire body. I have used both techniques successfully. The latter method is very helpful as it begins the process of getting used to re-entering the body during the projection of the Ka and Ba in more advanced techniques.

Once the shadow has merged with you, be aware of any sensations or impressions that come to you. I suggest that you write these down as soon as possible. You will find that frequently these images will correspond to actual events and places which the fetch had been sent to and experienced. If you are recalling the shadow just before sleeping, be aware of your dreams, writing these down upon awakening.

In the tradition of European Witchcraft, the fetch can also be shaped into the likeness of different animals. It is through this custom that the accounts of Witches changing into hares, crows, cats, stags and other animals come from. Undoubtedly those with the 'sight' would very likely have been able to see these shadow forms. If desired feel free to experiment with this process. However, I recommend that you work only with one animal form at a time and that the animal chosen has qualities you can relate to well. Again, keep in mind the concerns of some occultists that the overall characteristics of the animal can begin to influence the Witch. As with so much in the Art, care and common sense are essential ingredients. If you find that working with a particular form is causing problems, by all means stop using that form returning to a more human shape.

Basque Witches have a wonderfully simple, traditional technique they use to send forth the fetch. For this the Witch stands naked with her hair down in her chamber at night with a lit candle set behind her, facing the wall so that she can see her own shadow which she addresses. In doing so she then recites her request for the fetch to visit the intended person or place, giving it instructions on what to do once there. No matter the purpose the Witch envisions her passion and intent flowing from herself into the shadow filling this with energy. Frequently a time for which the fetch is to return will be set. Or, if this isn't specifically stated, the shadow is normally expected to return to the Witch while she sleeps. Once the Witch feels the intention and power have been conveyed, the candle is extinguished and the Witch retires to bed. The similarities between this simple spell and the techniques described earlier are obvious.

There is one final step to consider when working with the shadow or fetch. In Traditional European Witchcraft oftentimes the Witch would use the fetch as a vehicle through which her consciousness could travel. In this regard it was often seen as a 'second skin' and referred to as a 'mare'; the horse one rode in nightly journeys. Because the shadow is made primarily of substance that is very near to the physical realm this form will be limited in its ability to travel. As such it is excellent for moving about in the physical world, affecting objects, animals and people. However, travel to realms *beyond* those regions that immediately border the physical, such as the deeper regions of the Abred or Annwn, generally isn't possible in the form of the shadow alone. For this you will need to work with some of the other bodies more suited for these other realms. This, in turn, requires transferring your consciousness into the shadow.

101

Transferring one's consciousness into the shadow requires that prior to projecting the stream of energy into the triangle you will need to lay down. I have found that lying on a thin cushion or mat with a small pillow works best. Records show that frequently Celtic magic employed the use of an animal hide on which the Druid or Magician would lie or wrap themselves with. In some Covens today a type of 'trance mat' may be used in a similar fashion. No matter the means, the purpose is that you want to be entirely relaxed and able to slip into a light trance state without falling to sleep.

Lying before the triangle, begin with the breathing technique already given. Then project the silver grey energy from the abdomen into the triangle. Even though you are lying on your back this energy can easily bend and move, transferring from your prone body to the triangle. When you reach a point at which you feel that the shadow has been created imagine what it must be like to be the form itself. What does it see? What does it feel? As one of the teachers whom I respected greatly stated, use your imagination enthusiastically! Let yourself engage with, and be, that form. Allow the shadow to turn, looking about the room. Take in everything it experiences. It has been found that if one concentrates on the eyes of the form, frequently consciousness will transfer more readily.

At first you will almost certainly find that your awareness is centered mostly on your physical body. You may feel an itch, or have the need to readjust yourself to be comfortable. This is perfectly normal. Go ahead and make any needed adjustments. You want to be comfortable throughout this exercise.

As you become more involved in experiencing the shadow, 'imagining' what it is seeing and feeling, you are going to find that little by little your awareness shifts more and more to that reality and sensory input, while shifting away from your physical body. Just relax and let it happen. Don't try to analyze the reality, or lack thereof, of the experience. Rather, simply let this happen. Again, there is a real difference between imagination and fantasy. By allowing your 'imagination' to slip into this form, your will follows this.

In my experience there will come a moment when you are aware of the sensations of both bodies simultaneously. The mind is a wonderfully complex thing, and is fully capable of being aware of sensations in more than one part of the self. Just as at any given moment you are aware of the feelings in your feet and other extremities while also focusing on other tasks physically. So too, in this exercise, you will find you are aware of the sensations in both your physical body lying prone on the floor, and yourself as the fetch standing in the triangle.

It is at this point that, as the fetch, you may now will yourself to go to the person or place you seek to visit. It really is quite simple. In this form movement follows will. Focus on the goal and the fetch will begin traveling. When this happens almost certainly your awareness of your physical self will decrease dramatically. Yet in the earlier stages of this working you will still feel the floor beneath your body, and if there are any sudden movements or sounds in the room your attention will be brought back quickly to the physical form.

As for the shadow itself the clarity of your experience will vary. In the early stages you may find that fleeting images are all you receive. However, with practice these will grow in vividness. As with everything in the Art this takes time and lots of practice. When you are ready to return simply will yourself back to your physical body.

Re-entering the body properly is important. For failure to do so can leave one with a very disjointed and tired feeling that can last for hours. Further, there is the real possibility of leaving excess energy on the threshold between the Abred and our world. There, it can tend to wander on its own creating a certain amount of psychic havoc. Or worse yet, this energy could be used by other entities for their own purposes.

As noted earlier, this can be re-absorbed by willing the substance into the physical body through the abdomen. Or, the method I prefer, is to let the shadow hover over the physical body and then gently settle into this. This is similar to slipping into a coat, glove or pair of pants. In this way the two bodies merge as one.

Once you have returned take a few moments to become accustom to the physical body. Allow yourself to return to 'normal' consciousness. Then get up, close out the ritual space, write your notes regarding the experience in a private journal and then have a light meal.

As already noted your success in these exercises will vary. When you first begin these you may doubt that anything happens at all. Yet every time you perform this you are conditioning yourself to go further into these other realms, even if incrementally. Whatever happens never berate or criticize yourself if you don't get the result you expected. Instead you want to give your subconscious encouragement. Repeated practice and patience will gain success. You want to keep these workings fun and exciting.

When I first began working with these techniques I often chose locations to send the fetch which I had not been to, but were close enough that I could go to physically afterward. In this way I could compare my notes from the exercise immediately after with what was physically there. This was a great way to build success, for invariably I would find that the impressions received closely matched the features of the location I had chosen. With each successful journey my ability also grew. With this, too, my confidence in sending the fetch further and to do more complex tasks also grew.

Chapter Eight

❧ HEARTH AND MIRROR ❧

Wood and fire the hearth requires
To feed golden embers burning bright.
The cauldron bubbles and the potion boils,
Rise Witch into the night!
Over the hedge, in Full Moon's light,
To secret circles, in sacred flight.
The Great Queen calls;
Fly, fly – the time is at hand!
For the wheel weaves and thread spins.
Rise, rise into the night!
Between the horns lays the path we keep!
The Lady calls,
Fly into the night!

In the Art the ability to alter one's consciousness *combined with* the systematic presentation of specific symbols is an essential tool that is employed on all levels. In the practice of traveling in spirit this becomes *the* main venue through which success is achieved. For the right use of symbols presented when one is in a meditative state creates the means through which the Witch can transcend physical awareness and move into other realms. In this sense the correct string of occult images become a magical formula of immense power. The order in which the symbols are presented, as well as the specific images themselves determine the realm in which the Witch can gain access. Keep in mind that in the Art occult sigils and images are *not* representations of specific forces or entities. Rather the sigil itself is a material manifestation and extension of the power involved. Just as in this incarnation, your physical body is the manifestation of your spiritual self in this place and time.

In this chapter I would like to talk about some of the items and techniques that the Witch or Magician uses to travel in spirit beyond the use of the fetch alone. The two most popular items for attaining this are the hearth and the mirror. The hearth was the most common as, prior to central heating, some form of a hearth existed in every home. On the other hand, until the early nineteenth century, mirrors were relatively rare and expensive to own. As such the country Witch of the 1600s would have been lucky indeed to have a large mirror available for spirit travel.

As such, in Traditional Witchcraft, one of the central images used to travel in spirit is the hearth itself. Living deep in the forest, to my mind, there is nothing quite as soothing or hypnotic as watching the warm glow of a fire. Its gold red flames rising from the brilliant embers while the scent of burning oak, ash, birch and beech rise up the chimney. Staring into the flames one can see why our ancestors focused so much of their life around this important part of the home. This was not simply because it gave heat and cooked their food. The hearth was a place where all worlds and realms converged. It is perfect for spirit travel simply because of its ability to draw one's deeper perception into its satisfying warmth and mesmerizing glow.

If you have an actual hearth, whether this be a fireplace or a woodstove with a glass door, build a good lasting fire that has a solid bed of glowing embers in this. Ideally you should set a comfortable chair near this. Or, if desired, lay a mat or cloth on the floor that you can recline on. The important point is that you need to feel comfortable and yet, not so comfortable as to fall asleep during the process.

If you don't have an actual hearth, place the chair so that you are facing north. If you are using a mat, place this in the center of the area you are working in such a way as to have your head toward the north when lying down on this.

As with all other magical workings, you will want to choose a time when you will be undisturbed. Ideally the nearer in the month to the Full Moon the better. Tradition also states that Saturday or Monday lend themselves well to this process. If you have fashioned an Alraun root as described in *The Willow Path* you will want this present with you.

You should be wearing loose clothing or nothing at all. Make sure that the area is a comfortable temperature as well. You don't want to be too tired, nor overly excited. In addition, you should not have eaten any solid food, or had any dairy products for at least four hours prior to this ritual. You will also want to ensure that the area is magically secure. For this we set the Roth Fail as described in *The Willow Path*. Those working in different systems can use the methods adhered to in those schools accordingly.

If available feel free to burn an incense conducive to this. In addition, the use of one of the oils described in the previous chapter can be applied. But please don't think that these are required. Rather these are tools meant to enhance the experience. However, you will want to place your Besom either on the floor in front of the hearth, or have this standing next to the hearth. Ideally the Stang should be standing to the other side of the hearth. If working outdoors the Stang should be standing in the north of the circle and the Besom laid next to you in front of the place where you will be resting during the actual projection. Once the area is secure, gently relax and then address the Besom:

"O Besom, standing by hearth and Stang,
Let your shaft be strong
Your brush be fine.
Hark, O hark my horse!
Hark, O hark my mare!
Hark, O hark my horse!
Carry me into the night!
Like the winds that the Lady rides,
To the lands of Annwn we now fly.

Below and above, in the skies of the Abred.
Sweep along as the wind,
To the fields of fair Gwynfyd.
Besom, O my mare,
To the Castle of the Lady we go.
O Besom, Horse, my Mare
Carry me to and fro!

In some cases it may be helpful physically 'ride' the Besom while reciting the incantation above. In doing so the intention is to aid in entering the state of becoming. Let this unfold naturally as you continue the chant. If room allows, it is sometimes helpful to actually circumambulate the Roth Fail as the merging increases. Be careful though as, if the circle is too small, the Besom can easily knock over candles and other items. When you feel you have begun entering the desired state move on to the next phase in the ritual.

For this next step begin with the breathing technique discussed in the previous chapter. In doing so allow the very essence of nature itself to fill your body. With each breath allow yourself to experience the living pulse of the land or locale in which you are performing this rite. Take this in almost as if you were drinking in the satisfying waters of a mountain spring, feeling this fill every part of your being. Take your time with this. For, with each breath, you are pulling in power that will be used when traveling in spirit.

If you haven't done so already either sit in the chair or lie on the mat. Then take a few moments to adjust yourself so that you are comfortable. As with the previous practices involving the projection of the fetch, at first it you may be almost overly aware of your physical body, feeling every itch and distracting pain. Don't worry about this. Rather, go ahead and take care of these as you would in any normal situation. Eventually you will begin to relax. Continue the rhythmic breathing as you allow yourself to envision projecting the Swt energy from your body, just as you had before. This can be done through the abdomen as described, or if desired simply envision the Swt as a duplicate of yourself slowly slipping out of your physical body.

Keep in mind that in the early stages of performing this it is common for the critical mind to try to state that this is all "imagination" and, at first it is. Remember force follows will, and imagination is the faculty of the mind that is used to perceive energies and forces in other realms. It is important that during the rite itself you suspend critical disbelief and let yourself simply go with the images and processes involved. There will be plenty of time to analyze the experience later. Rather, for this one moment, use your imagination to the fullest. Let yourself picture Swt energy forming into a double of yourself fully and completely. Take your time as you delight in creating this image.

Unlike the fetch you will want to form this body in great detail. Envision this as much as possible taking shape, becoming a double of your physical body in every way. If you are sitting in a chair allow the form to build up, standing directly in front of you. If you are lying on the mat simply allow the form to take shape above you.

Once you are satisfied with the image, if you haven't done so already, close your physical eyes and gently begin to feel yourself slipping into the form, just as if you were removing one piece of clothing and slipping into another. Again, let your imagination do the work here. Just let yourself 'imagine' the sensation of moving into the other body. Don't be too critical in this process. With practice you will find this is rather easy.

Then, keeping your physical eyes closed, in the form of this double, imagine opening 'its' eyes and looking around. Just as you had when working with the fetch, allow yourself to see what the double sees. Let yourself see the room from its perspective.

As an aid to feeling more comfortable in this body I have found that recreating the magical space *while in this form* is exceptionally helpful. For my part I go through the actual steps of retracing the Roth Fail in this spirit form. Take your time with this and involve all of your senses. See what it sees, feel what it feels – hear, smell and sense as it would. As you go through this process you are going to find that your attention is drawn more and more into the experience of the spirit body while your awareness of your physical body diminishes significantly.

Keep in mind that even as you function more in this other body you will still have a part of your awareness that remains with the physical. It is a very unusual feeling and difficult to explain in writing. It is as if your consciousness shifts from focusing solely on the physical to moving more into an awareness of what the double is involved with. Yet, you will still be very aware if something happens physically that needs your attention.

Allow yourself to go through the entire process of re-tracing the Roth Fail. By the completion of the Roth Fail you will find that much of your awareness is focused on what this double is doing with little or no real focus on the physical body that is resting in the circle. Going through this process of 'astrally' recreating the area's protections has the added benefit of enhancing these on a much more subtle level. This is important as during this procedure the physical body is potentially 'open' to the influence of outside forces or entities. By conducting this in the Roth Fail, and reinforcing this with the astral double, the body remains safe.

It is during this process that the Witch moves beyond simply working within the form of the fetch. In performing the ritual tasks in this other form, the Ka form begins to take over. This is a very subtle process that is seldom noticed at all. Yet it brings with it greater mobility than that of the fetch alone. And it is in this Ka form that Witch can now seek other realms beyond those only found on the physical level.

To do this the Witch turns her attention to the hearth itself. See the stone or brick pattern formed around this. If one is working with a wood stove be aware of the stone, tile or cement boarding that this rests upon. If the pattern is in a checkered pattern so much the better. Be aware of the red and gold embers, the flames of the fire dancing in the hearth. Feel the smoke as it rises high up the chimney. It is almost as if it pulls at your double, like a lover calling you to follow.

If you are not working with an actual hearth we have found that the mere mental image of one can work well. Keep in mind that in astral working what one envisions takes form on the Abred. The mental image of the hearth becomes a representation, and thus extension of, the reality that will be a portal through which you will travel.

Before you do, envision picking up the Fe with the double's hand tracing the sigil of *Opening the Worlds*, beginning with the horizontal line first going from right to left, followed by the vertical line and moving from top to bottom. Allow this to hover in the air as a brilliant electric blue.

Then replace the Fe. Almost immediately you will be aware of an opening, window or portal that starts to form at the entrance of the hearth. With both hands envision yourself either parting a veil, or conversely gently opening a double door. And with this, the light of the hearth becomes brighter and more enticing. This gesture of opening is very important as the reverse act at the end of this rite serves to seal the opening later.

At this point envision yourself taking your Besom and straddling this between your legs. See this in your mind, feel the wood of the shaft between your thighs as your buttocks rest on the brush. Take as long as needed to allow the sensation of actually experiencing the Besom, Hearth and circle through the sense of the fetch and Ka manifest. As this builds you will feel yourself being pulled through this opening at the hearth. In many cases you may have the sense of rising, just as the smoke of the hearth rises up the chimney. Others experiencing the sensation of moving through a tunnel, or get a sense of flashes of light or colored mist as one moves through these. Let yourself go with this.

There will be a rushing feeling and then a sense of release. It is then that you may choose to visit the goal desired.

Generally it is best to have chosen a specific location before the rite was begun. Some authorities, including Sybil Leek and Robert Moser,[54] feel it is best to state this out loud before beginning the projection itself. This is intended to give the subconscious mind a clear directive for the purpose of the work at hand. In practice I have found that this isn't necessary so long as one remains focused once passing through the opening and rising.

Be aware that it can be very easy to get caught up in the sensations and experiences that projection brings on. If this happens one may simply lack the ability to seek the location that one may have originally planned on. Practice and discipline are needed to ensure that one stays focused. Keep in mind that the more focused you are on the location, person or goal you intend to visit the clearer and faster this will occur.

In the early stages it is likely that you will get a jumble of images and impressions. Just let this happen. With practice you will find that the images will come more clearly, and with this your accuracy will improve. Oftentimes, too, the sensation of the Besom will fade away. Again, it is important to know that it was used as part of the symbols involved in the overall magical formula of the process itself, just as the hearth, sigil and other tools used are. I have found, too, that during this portion of the experience your awareness of your physical body – while still there – is very minimal. Rather, you will be largely focused on in the images and sensations that traveling in spirit involves.

In this state certain forms of practical magic can be very effective. This includes the influencing of individuals, particularly if they are very relaxed or asleep when you are

---

54. Robert Moser was a highly respected teacher of the Art who had headed a school of esoteric practices named Fountainhead in the early to mid-1970's. He was also the leader of a working coven

visiting them. I have found that setting protections around property or over people can be exceptionally powerful while traveling in spirit. In addition, communication with entities and otherworld beings associated with the locale can be very profound. We will be exploring this further in the next chapter.

When you are ready to return this is relatively easy. It is only a matter of focusing your attention back onto your physical body. When you do this you will almost immediately feel a sense of being pulled back. With this it is common to see many of the same images and symbols that had appeared when you had begun the exercise reappear in reverse order. For example, you may find yourself astride the Besom and returning back through the hearth. Just let the experience happen.

Once your awareness of your physical body starts to become more apparent and you feel yourself as if returned to the physical locale, envision the portal between the worlds close. This is best done with a specific gesture. When you have returned to the Roth Fail let the double stand before the hearth and envision oneself closing the double doors or the veil that you had opened earlier. This is important as this simple act ensures that the portal is closed and that no other entities can cross over into the Roth Fail following this exercise.

One then moves to the physical body. Whether one was sitting in a chair or lying on a mat, the return is simply a matter of aligning oneself to the body and gently settling *into* the physical form. Take your time with this. However, you will find that when you do this your awareness slowly but steadily returns to the physical body. You will find yourself more aware of your breathing. You will feel the sensations in your hands, arms and legs. Let your eyes open as you become aware of your physical surroundings.

As with the absorption of the shadow or fetch noted in the previous chapter, it is important to re-enter the body slowly and carefully. You don't want to do this too quickly as it tends to create a very unsettling feeling of disorientation, almost as if you hadn't put your clothes on right! When this happens it can take several hours for the physical body to readjust, absorbing all of the Swt and Ka material as it should have. If done in haste you will continue to feel 'out of sorts', unable to concentrate well, and generally not feeling in the moment. This too can leave both Swt and Ka energy somewhat vulnerable, as it hasn't been fully absorbed. In such cases this can tend to 'leak away', take on a life of its own, or even be energy that certain parasitic entities may use or draw energy from.

Similar to the exercises surrounding the fetch, in the early stages you will have times when you doubt that anything 'real' happened. Your conditioned, material mind will try to rationalize the experience as fantasy. Yet, without a doubt you will have success, even in these early stages. When you have finished the experience take notes of the impressions and experiences you had. You will be surprised at the accuracy of these when you check these against physically objective information regarding the places visited. Above all, practice is essential, and with it your proficiency will increase. In addition, you will find that magic performed in this state tends to be more effective.

Mirror working is very similar. There are two different types of mirrors frequently employed in the Art. Perhaps the oldest and until recently most common was the black mirror. This is generally a round piece of glass, ideally concave, that has been blackened on the back side. Silvered mirrors are also used but until the modern era these were very expensive and hard to obtain. In the Hermetic Order in which I trained we used a six foot tall silvered mirror mounted to a wall in the ritual room as a portal to other realms.

While there are many methods for mirror working, the basic technique involves the same preparation as had been used in the hearth working. That is, setting the Roth Fail with either a chair or mat facing the mirror, projecting the double and gently retracing the Roth Fail while in this form. Then, standing before the mirror the double picks up the Fe and traces the sigil of *Opening the Worlds*.

In doing so, as the tip of the Fe touches the mirror, the surface of the glass is envisioned as becoming liquid like in nature, or perhaps changing to a fine mist. Then as the sigil is traced, this is seen as electric blue and reverberating across the surface. The Fe is returned. The Witch then uses the gesture of parting the veil or pushing the doors of the portal gently open. She then steps through the surface of the mirror and is drawn into the realms beyond. In all other respects the process is essentially the same. On returning through the mirror the Witch closes the veil or doors of the portal, sealing the threshold. She then returns to her physical body as before.

As for which is more effective, hearth or mirror, that is a matter of personal preference. Hermetic Magicians almost invariably use the mirror. With this very elaborate preparations are frequently taken to 'tune' or 'load' the mirror to specific realms and worlds. We will be looking at some of these techniques in the third book in this series entitled *The Art*.

Chapter Nine

✤ DWELLERS IN THE FOREST ✤

There is something deeply profound and ancient in the forests of New England. There are places in these mountains where the worlds cross over, merge and intertwine; areas where the Annwn and Abred meet. It is in such places that the Witch is able to experience the many realms beyond the physical. It is also in these places that those of the Art can come into direct contact with entities that inhabit these other worlds.

Generations of Abenaki Native Americans have interacted with these beings. Calling them the Bokwjimen (pronounced 'book-wuh-dzee-mun'), these are known to be a race of beings, nature spirits, who inhabit the forests of New England. Generally they are considered to be benevolent yet, the Abenaki explain that these spirits can become dangerous if disrespected. Like so much in the Art, I find these beings and the faery folk described in European magical lore to be very similar. I have little doubt that these New England spirits are akin in type with those found across the sea.

In my experience, coming into contact with these beings is more common than one may expect. Even for the average person this can occur. At first they may be seen as fleeting shadows out of the corner of the eye, or as forms moving quickly through the trees. If one is in a state of 'becoming' one may see a form in the distance, or feel as if one is being watched when no one is physically there. Of course, these places exist throughout nature, the world over. They occur anywhere in nature that is remote, quiet and away from the overwhelming influence of society. Yet, I have to say that for me the mountains of New England seem to have a special resonance that bridges the gap between the material world and those realms that lay beyond. I don't know if it is because of the high quartz content in the Granite Mountains themselves, or if there isn't a much more occult reason. It is clear that H.P. Lovecraft had unwittingly become aware of the mysterious wonder of these mountains and the beings that haunt these forests, though he drew upon these forces for some of his darker interpretations and visions of the occult. Whatever the cause, we find this place to be very conducive to communicating, and ultimately forming partnerships with otherworld beings. No matter where one lives, this process is a vital part of Traditional Witchcraft. And, one of the first steps to forming these relationships is the ability to cross the hedge, traveling in spirit.

In looking to the records of the Witch Trials we find a remarkable number of accounts describing this. In these, whether the Witch had begun the process by simply lying in her bed or by having applied ointment and using the Besom or Stang to move through the hearth, the Witch frequently meets the Queen of Elphame or the Master (whom the Christians would identify with their 'devil'). These beings, in turn, take the Witch to worlds lush in the wonders of nature where frequently a gathering of others is occurring. Here rituals are performed followed by merry making and feasting. If not the Queen or Master themselves leading the Witch on these journeys, oftentimes the person is guided by a spirit that resides within the realm. These beings usually become familiars to the Witch, teaching them the Art and aiding with spells.

Today it is all too easy to chalk such accounts up to fanciful imaginings, or the forced confessions of the delusional taken under torture. Given our increasingly materialistic paradigm of the world most people find it hard to believe that such accounts could have any objective basis in fact at all. Yet, the reality is that these accounts are remarkably similar to those described in other Shamanic cultures the world over. For the Witch of today, the use of specific magical techniques does, in fact, bring about very similar results in quite stunning ways.

If you have been practicing the procedures outlined thus far, the next step in your development is to learn how to enter some of these other realms and interact with the beings that inhabit these places. The reasons for this are many. In our practice of the Art much of our knowledge and power comes through the direct relationship to the natural forces inherent in the place we live. This includes getting to know and form alliances with the otherworld beings who are part of the natural fabric of the land.

I am going to say from the outset that I don't know that these techniques would work well in a highly populated, urban setting. Living as we do, deep in the forest, I have seldom used these when in an urban setting. I suspect that, using these in a large city, one could easily open oneself to those humans who may have departed in the area and may be linger on, rather to 'nature' spirits.

Having said this, I do know from experience that certain Gods and Goddesses associated with celestial bodies can be evoked quite effectively in urban settings provided that the right ritual requirements have been followed. However, for the Witch who is working directly with forces inherent in the natural world, the further one can get from the bustle of human society the greater the connections that will be made. It is through these encounters with the spirits alive in nature that the Witch gains greater knowledge, experience and power.[55]

The following is one technique that has proven to be very effective. For this one should follow the same exact procedure as given in the previous chapter. This includes all of the preparations, timings, ointments and incense, as well as the mental imagery used to project energy and alter

---

55. A more detailed discussion on the practice of the Art in urban settings is presented further on in this book

consciousness. Once your Ka or double has moved through the hearth or mirror, rather than moving to a chosen physical location, I want you to envision a specific set of symbols and images that have meaning in the Art. Each of these images and symbols act as a catalyst that aligns one's Ka with specific dimensions. As one teacher explained this to me, each symbol can be understood almost as if it were a rung on a ladder, or doorway through which one steps, carrying the Witch to another level. With each successive symbol introduced the next realm is being entered. These are other realms laying just beyond this physical dimension.

So to return to our formula, once having moved through the hearth or mirror, envision finding yourself standing on a path in the middle of a forest at night. The air is calm and the starry heavens stretch across the sky. For a moment visualize a Tau cross, a "T". This is an ancient symbol reaching back to the earliest dynasties of Egypt and before that to such prehistoric sites as Göbekli Tepe which dates back nearly twelve thousand years. The use of this symbol clearly predates the Abrahamic Traditions.[56] After envisioning this let the symbol fade away.

Then proceed to walk along the path. Soon, directly in front of you, a Stang comes into view, standing upright in the middle of the trail. Its two horns frame the Full Moon that shines brightly. As you focus your attention on the Moon, allow yourself to move *through* the Stang and particularly through the horns. Then continue on the path that leads deeper into the forest. At this point it is common to find yourself confronted by specific beings or images. Or to find yourself approaching a new place or scene. Let yourself experience this realm and the impressions that come through during this phase of the process. If you find that a being has appeared, talk with it. Learn what you can from it. This is a very important part

---

56. It may be important to know that this symbol figured highly in the practices of Julie and her family.

of the experience and one in which spirits within the area will present themselves.

It is important to note here that at this point you are not imagining the experience. This isn't some type of 'guided meditation' or psychological venture. Such an assumption is only the underpinnings of materialistic conditioning and the result of a paradigm imposed upon us by our current culture. No, for all intents you are have entered an objective, albeit, alternative reality. A realm beyond that which most people are ever aware. This particular realm, brought through by the symbols presented thus far, is one which is tied directly to the experience that is the Willow Path.

Returning to the subject of the beings met here, as with any occasion when you first meet someone, use your intuition, common sense and good judgement as you assess the experience. Don't assume that this being has your best interest at heart. Like any relationship you need to get to know each other before any mutual work or connection can be made. If at any time you feel uncomfortable or threatened cut the experience off by telling the being to leave. If it persists envision yourself placing your hands to your forehead, forming a triangle with the thumbs and forefingers touching. Inside of this visualize the Witch's Foot (Pentagram) forming. Then, with all of your will 'throw' the Witch's Foot at the being by thrusting your hands forward, spreading your fingers wide as if forming the antlers of a stag. As you do this state firmly the word "Deoraidhin" (pronounced JER-rid-hin). This is a Gaelic word used to banish spirits.

In my experience it is extremely rare that you will find any negative beings intent on harming you during this exercise. However, much may depend on where you are physically when performing this rite. If you are performing this exercise in a physical location that has been inhabited by people over a long period of time it is very possible that contact with spirits of the departed may come through.

Assuming that all is going well, let yourself experience this realm. Get to know this place and any beings that may make themselves known to you. Don't try to force the experience, simply let the images and impressions come to you. When ready you can either return back the way you came, or you can continue on.

If you are continuing allow yourself to envision the path moving deeper into the forest. You may find that you are climbing the incline of a hill. Ahead a clearing appears. You can see fire light. As you approach envision the sigil of the *Transformative power of the Moon.*

See this as being made of a silvery, electric blue light as it hovers in the air directly in front of you. It hangs in the air for a few moments and then fades as you move through this and on toward the clearing. Overhead the Full Moon continues to shine brightly as you see a circle set in the clearing with a cauldron hanging over a fire at the center of this.

As before, let yourself experience this realm. Be aware of anyone or thing that may be present. Here you are much more likely to encounter beings of a more complex nature than before. Frequently elders of the tradition will meet with the Witch. Whether these are discarnate spirits of those humans who had gone before, or beings of a different order that are part of the fabric of the tradition, it doesn't matter. Once again, let yourself open a dialog with these beings. Learn what you can and form relationships with those who may be willing to do so and whom you feel comfortable in getting to know. Above all be respectful.

As a side note, this can be an excellent means of forming relationships with specific spirits as potential helpers in the Art. These, of course, would be familiar spirits in the classic sense of the word. In fact, many accounts exist in historical records of Witches obtaining familiar spirits through their encounters with them in nature, not unlike the conditions described here. As with any relationship both parties need to feel that they can trust each other and that the relationship will be mutually beneficial for both. My suggestion is to see if the same spirit or spirits appear frequently in your journeys into these realms. Each time be certain to open a dialog with them and listen to them. If they are to be your familiar they, in turn, will be respectful to you. In time they will almost certainly seek to return with you. If not, a pattern frequently occurs in which the spirit or spirits will visit you, or you will find it easier to move into their realm. In each case it is a welcoming experience for both parties. Again, be aware of the implications involved and be certain of the spirits' intentions.[57]

In most shamanic systems around the world much power can be obtained through these relationships, with some shamans claiming that *all* of their power derives from such entities.[58] For the Traditional Witch I don't believe this is solely the case. Much of a Witch's power comes from her own innate ability, determination, natural talent and training. Nevertheless, working with otherworld beings and forming lasting relationships with familiar spirits enhances ones effectiveness in the Art considerably.

Returning to our discussion regarding the ritual at hand, when ready to return, allow yourself to retrace your steps following the path back through the forest to the point at which you started. Then simply think of your physical body and allow yourself to return to it just as you had in the procedures outlined in the previous chapter.

As explained before, it is important not to over analyze the experience while it occurs. Rather, let the experience unfold naturally. At first you will have images emerge that clearly are products of your own mind's creation. Others will come that are completely alien to you. Remember that these images, all of them, are your mind's attempt to form patterns and meaning out of the forces

57. See the chapters on Familiar spirits in *The Willow Path* for much more information related to these alliances.

58. Harner, Michael. *The Way of the Shaman*, 1980.

encountered in these realms. Just as our physical brains attempt to form patterns and give meaning to the various wave lengths of light, color and shading that the eyes perceive. So too, when traveling in spirit, the mind (not the brain) is processing the information gathered about the influences it is encountering in these other worlds. To do so it uses the language of symbols to attempt to understand these. As discussed in *The Willow Path,* in the Art learning the esoteric symbols of any given magical or Shamanic tradition is essential for the beginner because these become the language through which otherworld beings relate to us and that we can use to communicate with them.

Whenever possible, it is important to keep a written record of your experiences. You are going to find that a tremendous amount of information is presented in a very short amount of time. All of it is important. In addition, you are going to find that as you continue to perform these procedures you will start to have information flow to you spontaneously, even after you have 'returned' to your body. This is normal. Pay close attention to your dreams. When physically walking in nature be conscious of any impressions and intuitions. Then, later, when you have time, go back and try to see how you can apply this in your personal workings in the Art. This is all as it should be and is very traditional in rural expressions of the Art.

The set of symbols described above are just a preliminary to the way in which different realms may be experienced. For now the reader should practice with these techniques becoming proficient, for they will form the foundation for future work in the Art.

Perhaps it may be helpful to relate one of my first experiences using this technique. At the time we had just purchased the property in the forest. It is a beautiful, heavily wooded plot resting a top a small mountain. We had begun clearing space for our cabin. The terrain is strewn with outcrops of granite and large white quartz crystals jutting out of the ground. There are long ravines with creeks that often run wild in the spring thaw.

As we began working the land there was the constant awareness that someone or something was watching. At times, the feeling seemed almost unwelcoming. Frequently we would have items go missing and, as noted earlier, voices could be heard coming from the edge of the forest. Yet there was a deep, rich sense of calm power and majesty that lay within the land itself. We were absolutely in love with the place despite some of the uneasiness that seemed to come from parts of the wilderness. I remember that on the occasion in which we had finished building our cabin and were placing a protective amulet over the outside door there was loud thud that emanated from the forest directly in front of us.

As members of the Art it was clear to us that there were spirits present who were not exactly happy about our presence. We decided to use a series of techniques to open a dialog with these forces and, hopefully, gain their approval and eventual friendship. These included leaving small food offerings in a natural clearing (this would later become the space in which we built our Coven's ritual stone circle). We also conducted rituals designed to call the *Sídh*, the natural spirits of the land, to introduce ourselves to them. However, in my opinion, one of the most important acts was to seek these spirits out through the technique laid out in this chapter.

Essentially I followed the same pattern. I conducted this on an afternoon just before the Full Moon. I decided to do this from my bed as I wanted to be completely relaxed. However, being during the day I was aware enough not to fall into sleep. I went through each of the procedures, eventually finding myself on the path that lead to the clearing where we had been placing offerings. Moving through the sigil of the Moon I became aware of a new path that appeared to circle around the hill on which the clearing was located. I recall having the strong impulse to follow that path instead of the one normally taken to the clearing.

As my Ka moved along this I became aware of a presence. It is hard to describe its form. It appeared to be composed of several different animals; from canine to bear, yet there appeared to be horns on its head and I had the distinct impression of claws. This being was clearly challenging me and my right to proceed on the path. As intimidating as it was I didn't show fear. Rather I explained that I had come to meet the spirits of the forest, to get to know them and if they desired, form an alliance. All of this was conveyed mentally. I don't recall any sounds of any kind coming from either of us. There was a pause and then the being let me pass.

As I continued to circle the hill, the path lead to a small opening in the woods where a table of flat granite stones had been set. As I walked toward this I became aware of the presence of a woman. She was covered from head to foot in a brilliant scarlet red cloak that had hints of gold on the cuffs of the sleeves and at the hem. A hood hid her face from view yet I had the very distinct impression of light emanating from under this. The only part of her body that I could see was her hands, and these appeared to be gloved in white. She beckoned me to sit at the table. On this was set a goblet filled with a liquid.

As we sat across from each other I proceeded to introduce myself and explain that we had moved to this beautiful forest and wanted to be friends with her and her people. I explained that we were very respectful of the land and forest. That we wanted to be stewards while we are here. In communicating this it was clear to me that she was not a human spirit. There was something ancient, even timeless about her. She was a being of immense age and power. Yet, this power seemed deeply majestic and calm. She was a being of a very different and more complex order than we humans. I have no doubt that if this forest had been located somewhere in Europe or Old England, she would have been seen as a local Goddess.

By contrast, I had the distinct impression that she saw me as somehow fleeting or transient. Yet she showed kindness and respect. And, while no verbal words were exchanged she called me "a walker on the land." There seemed to be an agreement of sorts. A sense of partnership. And I knew that given time a friendship could emerge from this. She nodded toward the goblet and the lifted this up, offering it to me. I have long been aware of the warnings never to partake of food or drink while in the realms of faery. However, this seemed different. Drinking from this seemed to be the way in which we were sealing the alliance. Placing the cup to my lips I could see that the liquid was a gold color with a wonderful sweet taste of mead. After taking a sip she, in turn, took one as well.

With that, the sense came over me that the meeting was over. It was time for me to return to my world. I don't recall if she left or if I simply began walking back. However, I did find myself on the path as I returned through the forest and eventually to my physical body that was lying prone on the bed.

Upon coming back to normal consciousness my critical mind instantly began assessing whether this had been an objectively 'real' experience, or had this been a clever act of imagination. I can't say that it was fantasy as in each moment that unfolded I wasn't creating the scenario, rather each seemed new and unexpected. This, of course, leads back to the teaching that imagination is the mind's way of making sense of the energies and forces encountered on an occult level.

As a follow up to this, at the next opportunity, I physically traced my steps along the normal path. When I reached the point at which I had 'found' the smaller trail that circled around the hill, I did in fact find a wildlife trail. It was a very narrow path apparently used by wild game. As I followed this, the path did circle around the hill. At precisely the point at which I had 'experienced' the setting of a stone table I found several huge flat granite stones, naturally formed and lying on the ground. Perhaps even more interesting was that, in the exact spot where I had first become aware of the Lady, there was a depression in the granite stone work, a hole or small well. At the top of this a granite stone stood straight up as if marking the spot.

To me the omens were quite obvious. This was an entrance to the hallow hill of this forest through which the worlds merge and open. It was here that this great Lady emerges and when she desires, communicates with those of us in other realms. Over time I have lined the 'well' with small white quartz crystals that I have found locally. In this I place offerings to the Lady and her kin. Also, in the years that followed this experience, I have taken the granite slabs and set these in place exactly as the table I had seen in the 'vision'. This particular spot in the forest has become an important part of my practice.

In the years that have followed this first experience I have had several other encounters with the Lady of the Forest. She always appears the same; cloaked and hooded in the rich scarlet red. As my proficiency with traveling in spirit has developed so too have my relationship with the Lady. Since those early workings the unwelcoming feeling from the forest has stopped. We no longer have items mysteriously vanishing. The sounds and voices do continue, however as already noted, with these has come new knowledge in the Art.

Your experiences may be different. In fact, they will be, simply because you will be doing these in a locale that is different from this place. Please know that you should feel free to change some of the imagery. For example, suppose you live in the grassy flat plains of Mongolia. Rather than project yourself into a forest, you would want to become familiar with the spirits of that location. So you would place yourself in those grassy fields. Yet, it is vital that wherever you do this work certain key symbols and images need to be used in order to be successful.

These, in order, are:

• The Hearth with fire. Ideally brick work with a checkered pattern should be visualized.
• Envisioning the sigil that opens the veil between the worlds.
• Address the Besom as before and then straddle this while in the body of the fetch – Ka.
• Allowing yourself to by pulled into and through the hearth, and preferably a sense of rising.
• In whatever locale you may be it is essential that you envision the scene as if at night under a starry sky.
• Take a moment to envision the Tau cross "T".
• As you walk along the path become aware of a Stang rising up to meet the Full Moon which is shining between the horns.
• Moving 'through the horns' and on into the scene.
• If desired, allow yourself to merge with the next realm by envisioning the sigil of the *Transformative power of the Moon.*
• As before, move 'through' this to a circle that has a fire in the center, with a cauldron placed over this. It is important that you are aware of the image of the Full Moon over head as well.

Those are the key elements of this procedure. Through it all allow let yourself to enjoy the experience. Take in its richness. Be aware of any beings or people who you encounter. When finished and you have returned to your physical body take notes on what happened. Above all, don't berate yourself for any apparent lack of success in this process. Like all crafts, this takes time, practice and persistence.

Chapter Ten

✤ CALLING THE SÍDH ✤

In the previous chapter I mentioned the use of a ritual intended to make contact with the spirits of the locale. We call this *Calling the Sídh*. The word *Sídh* or *Sidhe*, pronounced 'shay', is a Gaelic name meant to describe a particular class of nature spirits, the faery folk. This is a separate form of being that inhabits the wilderness just beyond the veil of the material world. Their similarity to the New England Bokwjimen is, in my opinion, unmistakable.

In the previous chapter I gave a description of my own encounter with the *Sídh*, particularly with one who could be classified as a *Sídh-bhean* or Faery Woman. Though, as I had stated, I have the sense that this being is far more powerful than a normal woodland spirit. If anything, she borders on being the equivalent of a 'mighty spirit' – a local Goddess.[59]

As part of our work in communing with these beings we not only use the methods of traveling in spirit, we also employ basic ritual techniques designed to call the nature spirits to our Roth Fail where we can then communicate

---

59. It may interest to the reader to learn that similar accounts of meeting a hooded woman in the New England forests have been published. In particular, Michael Finkel documents the life of a man who retreated to the forests of Maine, U.S.A. having no contact with humans for close to three decades. In Mr. Finkel's book, *The Stranger in the Woods*, 2018, he describes an incident in which the hermit was on the verge of freezing to death when a 'hooded woman' approached him, offering to take him with her. He declined, but in the years that followed he recounted some regret at not making the choice.

with them. Using traditional sigils and techniques of the Art, the ritual included here was written by us specifically to introduce ourselves to the spirits of the land. We did this in response to the unmistakable phenomena which presented itself to us once we moved to this place. I am offering it here in hopes that the reader may find this useful as well.

Keep in mind that when working in nature with the spirits, we, as humans, are almost always intruding in their space. Further, through the techniques of the Art, we are intruding into their *realm*. Respect and courtesy need to be observed in order to become familiar with these beings and ultimately gain their trust. In doing so, one can begin to form alliances and possibly even friendships with these beings. In time they can be very useful, helping to protect one's home, bring prosperity, as well as providing knowledge in the Art.

The timing and preparation for this rite depends largely on the locale itself and the types of *Sídh* one is calling. The following are a list of some of the different types of nature spirits. The sigils for each can be found in the Table of Sigils. Those used in this ritual are taken directly from seventeenth century manuscripts related to Witchcraft:[60]

Spirits of Air – generally called on in any high place, or where the winds tend blow strongly. Thus the tops of mountains, cliffs and bluffs as well as in open windswept fields and plains.

Spirits of Water – near lakes, rivers, oceans. The Abenaki of New England referred to Water spirits as the *Manogemasak* (*pronounced mah-nawn-guh-mah-sock*). They are considered to be a type of lake or river elf that are generally good-natured but can be mischievous.

---

60. Scot, Reginald. *Discoverie of Witchcraft*. From the supplementary material added by an anonymous author to the edition in 1665.

Spirits of Fire – in hot arid climates or where fire is a natural occurrence on a frequent basis. One could also call on these beings through the use of a ritual fire.

Woodland Spirits – when working in forested regions.

Mountain Spirits – when inviting spirits linked directly to the mountains that one may find themselves in.

On occasion one may combine these. For example, because we live in a mountain forest, it would be appropriate to use the sigils of both the woodland spirits as well as that related to mountain spirits.

The rite itself should be held during the Waxing Moon, the nearer the Full Moon the better. We prefer to do this on a Monday or Friday night. However, you may choose a different day based on the planetary resonance as you feel is best. For example, spirit evocation generally can be very effective on a Saturday.

Set the Roth Fail as normal outside in the locale of the spirits you are seeking to contact. In the north place the Stang, standing upright. Outside the circle's edge, just behind the Stang, place an offering of food and drink. European tradition strongly suggests that salt should not be part of the offering, nor as an ingredient in any of the food. Having said that certain folk traditions here in the U.S., particularly Appalachian magic, will often include salt in offerings for nature spirits. For our part, we keep this to a minimum. One of the best drinks to offer is mead. Also, milk or spring water are excellent. Do not have any iron or steel implements set with the offerings.[61] With either flour, or your Fe trace the sigil related to spirits you are seeking in front of the offering, outside the Roth Fail.

---

61. It is acceptable to have salt as well as the steel bladed black hilt knife present within the Roth Fail.

As an incense the first choice would be to gather ingredients that come from the locale itself. For us we may use pine resign, Vervain and Elecampane. While not indigenous to this area, we have also included Rosemary that we cultivate here. Rosemary is traditional for attracting nature spirits.

Once all is ready set the Roth Fail as you normally would. Be certain to take the time to ensure this is accurate and complete. The *Sidh* can be unpredictable. Nature spirits in general can be mischievous and their sense of what is right or wrong can be very different from that of most humans. As mentioned this rite is meant to be a 'get to know you' type of meeting. Thus, until the Witch and the nature spirits have become acquainted and have formed a mutual respect for each other it is best to ensure that the working space is secure.

After the Roth Fail has been ritually sealed the Witch stands in the center before the cauldron, facing north and the offerings. If working in a group, all clasp hands around the cauldron. Then slowly and steadily the following incantation is recited:

"Come *Sidh*,
Spirits of (the land, forest, etc. depending on the locale)
To this Roth Fail (circle, maze, etc.) set by our hand,
From tree and rock, hollow and pond,
We now call upon our bond.
Sidh
Ancient dwellers and friends,
The veil is thin, it parts and bends.
By these words of power we call to you,
Toghairm, Toghairm, Toghairm (pronounced "Tog-hrim")
Through sacred words we call you near,
Our voices strong, our intention clear,
Come *Sidh*,
Spirits of the land,
To this Roth Fail drawn by our hand!"

The line that refers to "tree and rock, hollow and pond" can be altered as needed for one's locale. As the ritual unfolds one may repeat the three Words of Power in a rhythmic chant, followed by "Come *Sídh*, spirits of the land." This may be chanted over and over, depending on your own inner sense.

As the chant fades away allow there to be a few moments of silence as you simply observe. Depending on your own talent at the sight, you may begin to perceive actual forms emerging from the natural features of the place. These will tend to coalesce at the point just outside the circle where the sigil and offering are placed. Even if you are not 'seeing' shapes it is very common to perceive a change in the atmosphere. The candle flames on the hearthstone may change in size or color. The temperature may suddenly change in the Roth Fail. Unusual sounds may emanate from the forest. If you had called air spirits the winds may rise. If you had been calling water *Sídh* you may notice unusual changes in nearby bodies of water.

Even if no perceptible change does occur don't assume that the *Sídh* haven't taken notice. If you did the rite correctly the *Sídh* will be aware of your actions. They may not make their presence known primarily because they are watching, waiting, trying to understand you and your motives. Be patient, courteous and respectful.

At this point it is best that you now make a simple statement that is sincere and honest, extending an invitation of friendship. This should include the desire work with them, acknowledging that you respect them and the natural realm which are part of. The key is to speak with integrity and sincerity. There should be no undertones of superiority, or of seeking to dominate them. These beings are very smart and in many cases have been part of this locale for a very long time.

It is in this that the Witch's approach is very different from that of most ritual Magicians. In ceremonial magic the Magician almost always seeks to assert control over such spirits, frequently by attempting to call on more powerful otherworld beings who may have a measure of authority in the realm being worked with. The Witch on the other had seeks to form partnerships and friendships with the spirits. She, too, may call on more powerful beings in the realm such as the Queen of Elphame, or the Woodland Master. But seldom is this done in order to subdue the other spirits. Rather it is done out of respect for these otherworld beings. I have found that once the Witch does make contact with those beings who are of a more complex or 'higher' nature (such as the Queen or Master), often times the other spirits then become much more open to working with the Witch. Still, the goal here is not to subdue or coerce. The purpose of this rite is to open lines of communication, friendship and partnership.

During this part of the rite it is common to have food inside the Roth Fail that you will now partake of. This shows a willingness of sharing and communion. Ideally this should be the same as the food as that left as the offering outside the circle. As part of this raise the goblet in a toast as you say:

"Banu earth,
Banu spirits of the land (or inject the appropriate 'type'),
Banu Great Queen!"[62]

After some time has passed thank the *Sídh* for their presence and let them know that you seek their friendship. Then recite:

---

62. This is similar to a Swedish chant used to greet the spirits of the land and help enlist their aid as spirits of the home once one builds this. The Swedish chant translated into English reads: "Hail earth,
Hail spirits of the land,
Hail family mother."
As quoted by Lecouteux, Claude. *The Tradition of Household Spirits*, p.15.

"*Sídh*, Spirits of (the land, forest, etc. depending on the locale)
I thank you for your presence and your companionship,
for this time spent here.
As you return to your realm,
Let there be peace and friendship between us.
I ask, may you come again when I call,
For between the horns lays the path we keep,
Through this bond our friendship we keep."

Finish the rite by closing the Roth Fail. Then you may either scatter the food and liquid offerings on the ground, or bury this in the spot where it had been set. Be certain the brush the sigil away with the Besom.

In the days and weeks that follow be very aware of your impressions, dreams and intuition. This is especially so if you live in the place where you had conducted the ritual. I have found that without a doubt the spirits will begin to make their presence known to you. Don't ignore these, no matter how minor or coincidental they may seem. I have found that this ritual frequently opens lines of communication with the *Sídh*. In time this has proven to be a solid first step to later works related to traveling in spirit and the means by which direct interaction grows.

Chapter Eleven

✤ THE DREAM OF NUADA ✤
TIME & THE ART

On a clear day during the early stages of the Waxing
Moon, particularly just before sunset, look into the
sky. Almost certainly you see the silver crescent of
the Moon following closely behind the Sun. If you did this
each day over the following week you would find that the
Moon steadily increases in size while moving further away
from the Sun. In the northern hemisphere the Sun appears
to move from left to right each day as one faces it. It is from
this apparent movement that the term deosil or 'sunwise'
comes from. During the waxing Moon, with her steady
progression each day positioned further to the left, the
Moon has the appearance of moving tuathal, 'widdershins'
or as we prefer to call it 'moonwise'.

I am not going to go into the tremendous amount of
negative 'press' that the tuathal direction has received in
contemporary occult circles. Like anything that involves
the use of power the intentions of the Witch determine the
ultimate end result of most procedures. For us the tuathal
direction is largely used in works meant to relate to the
Moon or to help us move into the Abred, the Annwn, as
well as when drawing on power in the land. Perhaps more
importantly though this apparent difference in the perceived
motion of the Sun and Moon sheds light on the currents of
time itself as this is experienced and used in the Art.

Throughout all of recorded history the cycles of the
Sun, Moon and stars have governed humanity's perception
of time. In fact, before our current era, our ancestors

experienced time very differently than we do today. For them time was regarded as limitless, complete and full, and yet evolving, as it circled back onto itself. The Sun rose each day, the planets cycled through the heavens and the seasons returned year after year. In essence, time itself appeared to return to its original spot. Yet the ancients (particularly the Ancient Egyptians) saw this as time somehow becoming more effective and maturing with each cycle.

In order to understand and experience some of the deeper aspects of the Art it is imperative that the student rethink their perception of time, moving away from linear models to the realization that it is much more holistic and complete. The Egyptians studied this in great detail outlining their observations in ancient texts. Yet, the view that I present here can also be found in most Shamanic cultures and esoteric teachings.

The current view of time in our culture, with is finite definitions as flowing in a linear path from an unknown future, to the present and then into the past would have been very hard for many ancient people to comprehend. Egyptologist, Dr. Jan Assmann, explains that our current perception of time is relatively 'modern' and that it arose almost exclusively from "Greek ontology and Christian dogmatics" resting on "systems in Western languages, which express the notions of past, present and future."[63]

To the contrary, in the Art time is largely understood as being composed of two parts. The first of these is 'change' or as the Egyptians called it 'neheh'. The concept of neheh is perhaps the closest to our modern perception of time. For essentially neheh is considered to be a view of time flowing in a steady fashion from morning to night, season to season, young to old, etc. However, the difference from this and the current 'Greco/Christian' concept is that neheh *returns back onto itself* to a renewed beginning. Egyptologist, Dr.

---

63. Assmann, Jan. *The Search for God in Ancient Egypt*, 2001.

Lanny Bell, explains that neheh time was understood to be rhythmic with a "regular or periodic return to the original starting point at the completion of each cycle or revolution." [64] So, for those of the Art, time is cyclic and self-renewing.

The second aspect of time that is taught in the Art is what the Egyptians called 'djet'. As Dr. George Hart explains, this encompasses "the idea of 'totality' in the sense of an ultimate and unalterable state of perfection."[65] It is that which 'remains,' 'lasts,' and 'endures.' This latter concept, djet, is almost certainly completely alien to most people today, yet we find references to this condition in virtually every mystical, Shamanic and esoteric system that exists. It is the state of being that comes over one when experiencing a sense of 'unity' or 'being one with the moment'. In this state one opens the gate to the Mystery of Becoming discussed earlier.

In Pagan traditions this dual understanding of time, change vs totality, was often exemplified in the two faces of male solar deities. In Egypt this was seen in the journey and transformation of Ra on the one hand, and in the eternal otherworld presence of Osiris on the other.

Each morning at dawn Ra was born, growing to adulthood at noon where he was at the prime of his life, only to grow old in the afternoon and then sink into the arms of the star Goddess as he died, entering the underworld. Yet his journey didn't end there. For, in the starry realm he underwent a serious of transformations which culminated at midnight. From there he journeyed again toward the eastern horizon renewed, where he was born of the sky Goddess to begin his quest again. As such Ra represents the very essence of neheh time – change and renewal.

64. Bell, Lanny. 'The New Kingdom 'Divine' Temple: The Example of Luxor.' *Temples of Ancient Egypt*, p.283 (note 10) p.127-184.
65. Hart, George. *A Dictionary of Egyptian Gods and Goddesses, p.*46.

This can also be seen in Pagan legends outside of Egypt. The legend of Tarvos the Bull is an excellent example. In this, Tarvos is born each spring, grows to maturity in the summer and then is sacrificed in the fall at the hands of Esus. This is essentially the same motif. For, after his death three cranes scoop up some of the bull's blood and carry this south. Then in the spring they return, pouring the blood on the ground, out of which Tarvos is born again renewing the cycle.

We can see this too in Traditional Witchcraft and folklore. It is shown in the Green Man, celebrating spring and summer. We find it in the tradition of John Barleycorn being sown, growing, then being cut down, only to return again and again. The great stag Cernunnos as lord of the forests represents both the God who goes through the cycles of change – neheh – growing to maturity only to sacrifice himself in the fall. Yet, he is also the hunter that slays the stag. In death he is also the Lord of the underworld. This latter point is important. For in the realm beyond our material world time becomes 'complete' or Djet.

In the realms of the Annwn time is described as being very different there. Folklore and legends both tell us that those who enter the Annwn experience time as slower or non-existent. There are countless stories of people entering the realm of faery and then returning years later, yet they thought that they had been gone only a matter of days.[66]

The Egyptians saw this aspect of time as literally embodied in their Lord of the Underworld, Osiris. Dr. Assmann explains that Osiris was seen as "the imperishable and immutable continuation of that which has been completed in time".[67] As such we see the Sun Gods as neheh time or that which changes, evolves and is renewed; while the Gods

---

66. Funk & Wagnalls *Standard Dictionary of Folklore, Mythology and Legend*, p.365.

67. Assmann, Jan. *The Search for God in Ancient Egypt*, p.77-78.

of the Underworld embodied time that is complete and whole. Dr. Assmann expresses this well when he discusses Ra and Osiris:

> "They were what they were only in relation to one another. Only the two together yielded reality, and it was only their combined effect that gave rise to the complex of neheh and djet that humankind experienced as 'time': a periodically consummated union of the two aspects, change and completion, from which reality proceeded as a sort of continuity of the life of the cosmos."[68]

In all Shamanic traditions the hour of midnight is of particular importance. For this is the time when the Sun God reaches the deepest levels of the underworld. Whether this is the Annwn of Celtic teachings or Rostau in Egyptian writings, in this hour a great mystery unfolds.

In the Egyptian books of the afterlife, particularly the Amduat, at midnight Ra finds his corpse as the perfected God Osiris, floating on the waters of the primordial sea. As a Ba, Ra and Osiris unite as one being. The two forms of time merge. In this way the Sun God becomes rejuvenated and begins His journey toward rebirth.

In ritual the Egyptians would depict this as an open coffin resting on a diadem in the middle of a man-made lake. This was always deep in an underground chamber. We find examples of this today both at the Osirian beneath Abydos and in the caverns below the Giza Plateau.

This same theme is clearly echoed in certain Celtic myths in which the solar hero journeys through the underworld of Annwn, facing trails and death, only to be renewed in the cauldron within the Castle of Glass. Frequently the Castle is located on an island in a lake. Avalon is one such example of this theme. It is only after

---

68. Assmann, Jan. *The Search for God in Ancient Egypt*, p78-79.

this merging on the isle that the hero can return to the material world renewed.

In djet there is no experience of past or future, rather there only 'is.' Djet is a mode of existence on a deeper level beyond the temporal world that we, while in the material realm, only occasionally experience. Nevertheless, this experience of oneness and of being in the moment with no boundaries, can and does occur.

Further, the state of djet-time illustrates how it is possible for the Gods and certain spirits to come to us from across the span of thousands of years in very real and vibrant forms. Rather than functioning solely through cyclic neheh-time, the Gods function in a dimension in which time and space are not linear. Because djet is a state of 'enduring-time' or 'oneness' the Gods can affect temporal time in which we normally function.

The state of djet also helps one to understand how otherworld beings may be called upon and communicate with people at any given location at any given time, even when being invoked through rituals that may be worked by several groups of people at the same time. Simply put, because there is no past or future in djet the Gods are able to communicate to those on the material level across seemingly vast distances, in multiple locations and across the spectrum of 'linear' time.

In djet, time "is", and the Gods are able to express themselves to us despite the seeming limitations we have imposed upon ourselves. This occurs simply because, for the Gods in djet time, a linear perception of time doesn't exist. Yet, it is vital to understand that the existence of the Gods, in fact all existence, is not one of "unchanging endlessness" but rather one of "constant renewal".[69]

While in physical form we can only occasionally experience djet-time. However, Egyptian teachings explain that those who have passed on to the 'afterlife' exist solely in djet. In

---

69. Hornung, Eric. *Conceptions of God in Ancient Egypt*, 1996

this way it was felt that the dead could see the past and know the future all because they live in the 'enduring' time of the djet. While coached in modern terms, perhaps the observations of Ceremonial Magician, Dion Fortune, sheds some light on this concept:

> "On the Inner Planes, time and space are modes of consciousness, as modern philosophy is beginning to realize. To consciousness unconditioned by matter, time present is that of which it is conscious; time past is that of which it is not thinking at the moment; and future time is that of which it is unaware. Space likewise is near or far according to its occupancy of the focus or fringe of consciousness."[70]

This description closely parallels the Egyptian understanding of djet time. For in djet it is only a matter of changing one's focus. Thus, time in the temporal sense merges as one in djet, only differentiating into boundaries and divisions by the focus of attention placed by the individual. As Ms. Fortune points out, on the 'Inner Planes' "what we are thinking of is present, and what we are not thinking of is absent."

In the Art the afterlife is also seen as a period of regeneration and renewal. The journey of the Sun God in the underworld exemplifies this state. It is here that the Sun God returns to the primordial waters of the mother's womb and is made new as He prepares for rebirth; whether cauldron, grail or lake the symbolism is the same. As with the Sun God, so too, do the deceased seek this renewal. Dr. Erik Hornung points out that in a Ramessid hymn the dead call out to the Sun God so that they too may be rejuvenated through the healing waters. In this way they "'slough off' their previous existence, and 'put on' another, as a snake does its skin".[71]

---

70. Fortune, Dion and Gareth Knight. *The Circuit of Force*, p155.
71. Hornung, Eric. *Conceptions of God in Ancient Egypt*, 1996

As we consider time and the role of masculine deities we have to ask what role do the Goddesses play? The reality is that while the male Gods embody these two modes of time, it is the Goddesses that are *beyond* time. They are both the cause *and* that which creates all. This is exemplified well in Egyptian esoteric teachings. In the Egyptian system the Sun is seen as flowing through three distinct daily phases: the infant born at dawn, the virile and radiant lover at noon and the elder Sun sinking in the west. These epitomize neheh time. Yet, in each of these stages, it is the Goddess Hathor as the embodiment of the divine feminine who is there compelling him, guiding him, encouraging him.

At dawn the sky fills with a reddish-pink glow. The Egyptians saw this as the birth of the Sun God from the womb of the sky Goddess Hathor. An ancient hymn describes this maternal connection between these two:

"Ra the beautiful;
The youthful;
Who is present as the sun-disc,
In the womb of your mother Hathor!"[72]

As the day progresses toward noon the relationship between Ra and Hathor changes. For while Ra has matured into a virile male in the prime of life, Hathor too transforms from the mother into the lover. At noon She is the Goddess of sensuality and pleasure. In this form these two dynamic and complementary forces merge in union so that life can continue.[73] High noon is exactly opposite the realm in which the dying Sun is renewed in the Lake and Cauldron of the Goddess' womb at midnight. Now at noon He merges with the womb of the Goddess in sexual ecstasy in order to bring forth new life.

---

72. Bleeker, C.J. *Hathor and Thoth: Two Key Figures of the Ancient Egyptian Religion*, p.48.

73. Pinch, Geraldine. *Votive Offerings to Hathor*, p.155-156.

Because of the tremendous attraction and affection between these two divinities, Hathor continues to call to Ra, leading ahead of Him as He grows older in His daily journey. As Dr. Alison Roberts explains:

> "Re's great love for Hathor inspires him to cross the sky each day, for it is her attraction which is the power motivating the circuit of the sun."[74]

As the day progresses Hathor changes yet again. She becomes the 'Eye of the Sun'; the protective daughter in the form of both a cobra on Ra's brow and as the lioness Goddess, Sekhmet, who is both respected and feared. As the daughter Hathor now greets Ra in the west where She guides him into the arms of the Star Goddess, the Mother and underworld.

A similar pattern can be found in Celtic myths, particularly those surrounding Morgana, whose name means Great Queen.[75] While She is primarily a warrior Goddess whom all fear, it was She who made love to the solar God Nuada, revitalizing Him while also giving Him the knowledge and insight, through a dream, to defeat the forces of chaos. It is interesting to note that while Morgana is largely known for Her warrior impulses, in fact She and Her two sisters were also held to be Goddesses of sexuality, plenty, nourishment and abundance.[76]

We see Goddesses across cultures and in many forms as the source and cause of all existence. She is ever present. Whether as the mother bringing forth life, the lover conceiving life or the warrior Goddess and daughter protecting life, the divine feminine remains fresh, exhilarating, and vivacious. While

---

74. Roberts, Alison. *Hathor Rising: The Power of the Goddess in Ancient Egypt*, p.60.
75. Paice MacLeod, Sharon. *Celtic Cosmology and the Otherworld*, p.112.
76. *Ibid.* p.113.

Above: Calling the Elders

Left: Calling the Sidh

Left: Fluid Condenser

Below: Condenser

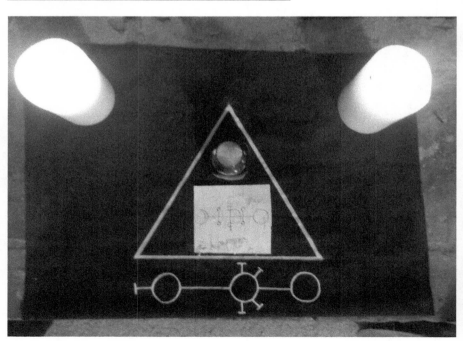

Top: Crystal Mountain

Left: Crystal Well

Entrance

Full Moon ritual

Hearth & mirror

Spell Casting

Horns of the Moon

Ladies of the Moon

Lady's Table

Lady's Table & Well

Above: Lady's Table

Left: Lady's Well

Mirror of Arianrhod

Outdoor Roth Fail

Sending the Fetch

Stang & Besom

Stang & Circle

Above: The Geassa

Left: Stang & Table

The Hollow Hills

The Sidh

Tracing the Willow Path

He grows old and dies, only to be rejuvenated and reborn through Her, She is not subject to these Herself.

In the underworld Her role continues. Here She is the Great Star Goddess through which transformation and rejuvenation occur. Perhaps most telling is the role of the feminine in the deepest portions of the underworld, at the sacred lake during midnight. In the annual mysteries of Osiris the twins Isis and Nephthys call Osiris with songs inviting him to "come to his house". In Ancient Egyptian symbolism the image of the house also represented the vagina and womb. Thus, this simple chant takes on a fuller meaning, for it is literally calling the God to sexually join with the Goddess, to return to his wife, so that creation . . . life . . . can be conceived. For it is through the arousal of the creative spark lying dormant in djet time that rejuvenation can occur.

As seen earlier, it is in this moment, the Sun at midnight, that Ra and Osiris are one being. Djet and neheh merge because of the intrinsic attraction and power of the Goddess. Without Her this simply does not happen. In this regard we see the divine feminine as not only the source, but also the motivating force behind and within all that is, arousing and awakening the potential for creation.

It is important to note that none of this conflicts with European Pagan traditions which frequently associate Goddesses with the lunar phases as maiden, mother and crone. In fact, these can be seen as complementary to this. The Egyptian motif of mother, lover and daughter represents the creative power and influence of the feminine as She relates to the masculine force in the daily cycle. However, in the lunar cycle the feminine manifests as the maiden or young woman and with it the new beginnings that are fulfilled through the burst of life, energy and sexuality. As the mother She is the Goddess in Her aspect of the Full Moon. She is the gate, the creator. In the crone phase the Lady is power! Here She is at once both the wise one and the death crone.

Yet, in neither of these two cycles, daily nor lunar, are the Goddesses seen at any time as infants or as eventually dying. On the contrary, the divine feminine is the ever present force behind all that is: the joy and ecstasy inherent in life, the gate through which all passes, and the eternal wisdom that guides all who are ready. That She neither dies nor is born, but rather transforms is exemplified in the many European legends of the young knights as solar heroes, who make love to the crone after which She transforms once again into the maiden. For us these two motifs, Egyptian and European, are equally important and shed immense wisdom on the nature of the Great Goddesses. Clearly these are powerful clues showing the dynamic nature of these incredible beings and, in turn, the Witch's understanding of reality.

Perhaps at this juncture I should mention that some Traditional Witches see the divine feminine as having only two aspects or sides: the Bright Queen and the Dark Queen. I explored this at length in *The Willow Path*. However, in relation to our current discussion it is important to mention again. In this view the Lady as the Bright Queen is seen as being a Goddess of light, beauty, passion, life and love. While the Dark Queen is seen as the death crone, the weaver of destiny, the destroyer who clears the way for rebirth and renewal. This dual nature is a very valid expression of the Lady.

My concern is that many within traditional circles feel that the image of a triple Goddess is a relatively 'new invention' with some feeling that this was a creation of Robert Graves in his book *The White Goddess*. In particular they take exception to the view of the Queen as maiden, mother and crone.

Without a doubt Graves had taken quite a bit of poetic license in his writing. However, there is tremendous historical evidence which shows that a number of Celtic Goddesses were very closely associated with the number three. In many cases a Goddess would be portrayed as having three different names and forms, or be part of a trio of 'sisters'. In truth, too, we find that there are Goddesses who were frequently portrayed in the three classic lunar 'phases'. The Goddess Ana or Danu gives us a clear example of this. She could be seen as a Wise Crone, an earth mother as well as a maiden depending on the mythological cycle being recounted.

In her work *Celtic Cosmology and the Otherworld*, Sharon Paice MacLeod explains that Danu appears to have been associated with two other Goddesses who appear to be forms of the same being. She goes on to explain that Danu could at once be seen as the "Mother of the Gods", associated with the land and its fertility, abundance and prosperity. She was also seen as a Goddess of Witchcraft and magic, wisdom and skill.[1]

To some extent we see this in the early representations of the Goddess Bridget as well. For she was seen as a trio of sisters. It may be important to note that in the earlier renditions of the Arthurian legends King Arthur is portrayed as being married not to one Queen, but three; all with the name of Gwenhwyfar.[2] Clearly this can only be a reference to the three forms of the same feminine force. It may be important to note that even Ceremonial Magician, Aleister Crowley, makes several references to the Moon Goddess as maiden, mother and crone in his book *Moonchild*. This was released a full twenty years before Robert Graves' writings on the subject.

For our part, we can understand and relate to both views of the divine feminine: Bright Queen/Dark Queen as well as the triple Goddess. Both views have their place in the practice of the Art. I can say that Grandma Julie clearly taught that the Great Queen had a triple nature.

---

1. MacLeoad, Sharon Paice. *Celtic Cosmology and the Other World, p.*110-111.
2. *Ibid.* p.122.

Chapter Twelve

✤ THE WHEEL WEAVES, THE THREAD SPINS ✤

Returning to our discussion of time, it is easy to see how, as we go through our daily life, we can get caught up in the idea that time travels from a distant future that gradually moves into the present, while the present quickly slips into the past. Time can appear to be like a road that is traveled, moving straight ahead on a flat surface as it slips behind us. Yet, to carry the analogy further, physical roads are situated on the round curve of the Earth. And the seemingly straight road moves in a bend over the surface of the globe. Follow a straight line around the Earth and one eventually ends up in the same place. As we saw previously, so too, time moves in a vast arc eventually spiraling back onto itself; this is the mystery of neheh time.

Thus, history tends to repeat itself. The seasons change in a constant pulsation, yet they return again year after year. All life begins with birth, followed by maturation, then death, only to be repeated in rebirth. The great stellar ages roll by, cycling through, only to repeat themselves.
Yet there is change. Each cycle evolves. Tomorrow will be different from today, the events in any season differ from year to year. Yet, the forces that guide the process remain the same. The patterns of each cycle follow in succession.

Those of the Art recognize that the cycles of time, the cycles of neheh, return to their beginning and yet this return occurs at a slightly different octave. We go through the cycle of the seasons only to arrive at each in turn. Yet with this passage comes *experience*, growth and wisdom. Time returns to its origin yet it has evolved and those

148

who travel the path of neheh change with this, in renewed forms and states of being.

As such, neheh can be thought of as a spiraling maze, ever returning to its source and yet, in doing so it moves to a different level. While traveling through neheh time we seldom realize the larger cycles that lead us on. Rather, we only see the path just ahead. Still, the cycle is ever present; life, death and rebirth, and with it growth and evolution in spirit and form. These are the overarching themes that characterize neheh. It is through this continuing cycle that we find ourselves in different sets of circumstances, yet these often times remain similar in nature because of the links forged by our actions in the past, resulting in the conditions to be faced.

In eastern mysticism this is often termed "karma". In Ancient Egyptian forms of the Art this was called "Shay" meaning fate, in Gaelic this was known as "Fáil". This latter term is tied to the ancient myths concerning the Lia Fáil, the Stone of Destiny, in Celtic traditions. It is interesting to note that Fáil, meaning 'destiny', is so similar in form to the Gaelic term 'Fail' meaning 'wheel' or 'circle'.

This is why the maze has always been such a vital part of Shamanic traditions throughout much of history. Neheh-time itself is a vast spiral returning over and over to its beginnings and yet moving steadily onward as all consciousness, the Geassa, experiences itself and grows.

The spiral of time is important, for as we travel through these cycles, time spins back onto itself, while reaching an ever richer octave; similar to climbing a spiral staircase. In our minds we feel as if we have traveled many steps, and in fact we have crossed a long distance. Yet, if we were looking at the staircase from the side it quickly becomes apparent that the point we are at on the stairway is closer in circumstance and relativity to those directly below, even though in a linear understanding more distance was traveled.

Take a moment to think about that analogy, for what it implies is that, if we can discern the cyclic pattern of a specific moment in our life and find a similar cycle in the past, no matter how distant, the events of that past are closer to us now and represent the root cause of the circumstances experienced today. From a magical perspective, those forces which we put into place now will likely manifest when a similar pattern of energy cycles through in the future. The wheel weaves, the thread spins, and the osiers of the Willow are bent and shaped to form reality.

To put this in other terms, in the Shamanic understanding of time, this model means that at any given moment in our experience we can access the circumstances of the past which to our 'normal' perception of time may seem distant, and yet on the spiral these are closer due to where in the cycle we are at. This offers insight into the Fáil or destiny of any particular moment. For we can look back to the cycle before to see the circumstances that helped to form us then, and more importantly, the actions we took which now are coming to fruition in this cycle.

This has a direct relationship on our ability to remember, or perhaps more accurately stated, to experience those forces set in motion in previous incarnations. Without a doubt I have found that memories, whether consciously or those 'felt' on an unconscious level, from past lives will return at key moments in the current life when those skills are needed. Importantly, too, these come through as joys to be experienced in new forms, as well as those experiences that are meant to act as opportunities and challenges to help resolve issues from the distant past. In either case, rather than these coming 'through' in a linear fashion from most recent to the distant past, they tend to coincide with specific patterns in life that resonate with these previous incarnations despite the seeming distance in linear years.

This also gives us an understanding of how future events unfold because the circumstance involved in the current moment will reach toward the same point in the cycle that is to come. Our actions now will directly affect the circumstances we will experience in the same point on the spiral in the future. Obviously this is a generalization that can only be spun out through intuition and meditation. Nevertheless, it gives a clue into the deeper meaning of the spiraling maze in the practice of the Art.

If neheh-time can be understood as moving in a spiral, djet-time, that which is completed and mature, can be understood as the circle. In djet, time is whole with no breaks, no beginning and no end. The circle simply is. It holds within it all potential; all that is or will be. Thus we see that in djet time is one, complete, and those beings within djet can experience all at once, depending on the focus of their attention on a given circumstance.

Yet, it is important to understand that in the Art one can slip back and forth between these two modes of time and awareness. Neheh and djet are in essence one in the same. For if we turn the model of neheh over, as if looking down on the spiral, the unending circle of djet comes into view, just as the architect looks down from the top of the spiral staircase and sees the circle of stairs. Within this lays the spiraling path of neheh, yet it is contained within the wholeness of djet.

This can easily be equated to our earlier discussion of the Worlds as presented in *The Willow Path*. In that discussion we saw that the Annwn in fact encircles and contains all the other Worlds, holding within it the potential for all that its. While, in the same understanding, the Worlds of Abred and Gywnfyd exist within this. All the while it is consciousness, changing forms, that moves across and through these in great cycles.

As the reader has undoubtedly deduced, the existence of reincarnation is a concept which our system of the Art embraces completely. This isn't a matter of faith. Rather it is a conclusion drawn from an assessment of the tremendous volume of evidence that has been independently amassed by researchers over the years. Further, this conclusion comes in part from personal recall.

In the first chapter I explained that knowledge of one's own past lives was one of the fundamental skill those of the Art should develop. This is perhaps one of the most challenging aspects of self-discovery in the Art. The reasons are many. I can only give you an overview of the techniques that I have found to be most successful for me. Some of these include spontaneous yet fleeting memories, self-induced reverie, as well as hypnosis. In addition, some vital clues have come from careful analysis of my Astrological chart.

Finding the right method or combination of methods that work for you requires time and patience. I would suggest that you begin by looking back through your life. Reach back to your earliest memories. Research shows that it is common for at least some children, up to about the age of seven and sometimes beyond, to relate experiences from previous lives. Generally these tend to be very vivid during those ages but fade with time and as one grows older. Barring that, think about your likes and dislikes as a child. What were your interests? Can you explain these as merely being due to events in this life, or do they seem to go deeper? As you contemplate different cultures around the world, or different times in history, are there any that stand out to you? What foods appeal to you? Music? Dance? Clothing? While being far from conclusive, each of these can become triggers, opening memories locked deep in the subconscious.

As noted earlier, you may not recall lives in a chronological order. Again, I refer you to the concept of the spiral. I find that memories come through as we face similar cycles in this life that were part of the patterns woven in previous existences. Thus, very distant memories may come through when those of a more recent existence have yet to surface.

I find that the best time for memory recall is in the twilight realm that occurs when I am just waking from sleep but haven't become fully aware in the normal mundane

152

sense of the word. In this state I can often gently nudge my memory, asking for information or simply allowing myself to wander back in time.

In doing this it is best to let yourself imagine a serene nature scene, perhaps a lush garden with a path that winds through this. Let yourself follow the path until you find a set of stairs that lead down gently to a lower level in the garden. In your mind allow yourself to slowly walk down one step at a time. With each stair let yourself relax as you suggest that you are moving steadily back through your past, leaving this current life behind for the moment. Generally I use a series of ten steps. With each stair I tell myself that I am relaxing further while I slip deeper into my past.

Once you reach the bottom of the stairway, maintain the image of the beautiful garden; however, just ahead envision three doors leading through a wall. As you approach tell yourself that at any time you may return to your normal waking self whenever you desire. Then let yourself chose one of the doors. Find yourself opening the door and stepping through.

Take a few moments to let your mind adjust to this setting. Generally I have found that this takes some time. And frequently I will get the impression of swirls of light, images that move across the field of vision, and a sense of moving. Nevertheless, if you persist, eventually a material scene frequently comes into focus. As you go through this just let it happen.

Once a material scene begins to form just let yourself become aware of the scene before you. Take a moment to look down at your feet and hands. This serves several purposes. It helps to solidify the moment, bringing your attention to focus readily on the memory itself. It also immediately establishes several factors. In seeing one's hands and feet it will almost certainly tell you the gender you are experiencing, possibly the race you were, a possible age, and even time period as you consider the types of footwear, or lack thereof. It can help to identify the possible location you are in as well. Then become aware of the type of clothing you are wearing. This will help to open the memory further.

Next, allow yourself to experience a particularly happy moment in this scene. Just let the first thought or event that enters your mind unfold. This is often very vivid and surprisingly rich in detail. Even if it isn't clear at first, just let yourself go with the experience as much as possible.

Imagine someone calls your name. What name comes to mind? Where are you? What do you see? In what context is your name being called? All of these will help to open the door to the past.

The images will probably come in a fleeting form at first. That is fine. Let them flow as you simply become the observer taking them all in. As with so much in the Art, don't try to over analyze these as they occur. There will be plenty of time to consider the details in the light of research and logic later. For now just be the observer taking in the details as much as you can.

When ready allow yourself to return to normal consciousness. You can do this by simply willing yourself back to the here and now. Or you may choose to envision turning and walking back through the door and walking up the garden steps, telling yourself that you are becoming more awake and feeling refreshed.

This simple act of reverie while one is in the transition state between sleep and being fully conscious can be very effective. Be certain to write down details of any recovered information from the exercise. It is important to not take these experiences at face value. Rather, take note of each detail. Then, over time, research these looking for any information that may lead to corroboration.

Beyond using reverie, take a look at those talents, skills and knowledge that seem to come easily to you. While we all learn new talents in our current life almost certainly there are those which we have gained in the past. In this life these will tend to come more quickly. Keep track of those skills, for they may also act as triggers for the deep mind as the doors of past life memory slowly open.

For me though, by far the best tool for past life recall has been hypnosis. But keep in mind that I am very comfortable with the subject. I have had extensive training and practice as a hypnotherapist for years. As such, I have no concerns about slipping into trance. I find that self-hypnosis is a little more challenging to use, as a part of the mind needs to retain a measure of cognitive awareness to direct suggestions.

Rather, under the guidance of a trained hypnotist, memory refreshment can be very effective. If you decide to seek out a hypnotist be certain to investigate their training, credentials and their methods. It is important that the hypnotist is trained in techniques that do not ask leading questions while their subjects are in altered states. This can cause some people to confuse the suggested statement given by the hypnotist with actual memory. Nevertheless, hypnosis under the hands of a skilled practitioner is an excellent way to open the doors of distant memories. In such cases be certain to ask the hypnotist to give you a suggestion that memories from previous lives will continue to come to you after the session is over. I have found this latter point to be particularly helpful.

Please note that it may take several sessions before anything meaningful comes through. This is quite normal especially if you are unfamiliar with hypnosis or if you are nervous about the procedure. Take the time to build rapport with the person conducting the sessions. Having trust in their skill as well as their ethical compass will go a long way toward gaining the success you seek.

Astrology can also be a tremendous tool for learning more about past lives. However, for this it takes someone who is very skilled. There are so many factors to be considered when looking into an Astrological chart. Nevertheless, the very premise of Astrology implies that we came into this life under certain planetary influences because of circumstances that had occurred in past incarnations. Thus, it is possible to look through a chart and see patterns that led to this life.

Sybil Leek's course *Astrology Dynamics* from the 1970's had a short but excellent lesson that discussed factors to consider in the chart when looking into reincarnation. Unfortunately this printed lesson is very rare. This was a supplemental monogram the school put out for those students interested. However, there are some other excellent resources available for students who are so inclined and have Astrological training. I can strongly recommend Stephen Arroyo's book *Astrology, Karma & Reincarnation* as well as Steven Forrest's *Yesterday's Sky: Astrology and Reincarnation*. These will give you a good starting point to understanding your past.

Each of these methods can be very helpful and over time work well in combination. Realize that any memories that come through need to be looked at as being subjective until you are able to find information that helps to verify these. This may be something as simple as learning that the name remembered was in fact only used in the region and time that the memory occurred. Or it may be a specific word that comes through, a type of food recalled, a simple article of clothing or an item seen.

What I find to be most interesting is how, at different points in one's current life, characteristics from previous personalities can manifest. Usually this is on a subliminal level and at times when one is required to react to a sudden situation, in times of crisis or in the ways we relate to other people. It is easier to slip back to old habits than to look at the situation fresh and try to approach it from a new perspective. Irrational fears too tend to have their origins in the distant past. All of these are the imprint left from past lives on the spirit of the individual. The key is to recognize these when they occur and begin to make conscious choices as to whether one wishes to continue in those older habits or look at situations from a fresh perspective.

Beyond this, the question arises, once the memories start to come through what do you do with this information?

Knowledge of our past helps one to see deeper into who we really are, gaining insight in the immortal self, the 'true self' or the Akh; beyond time, culture, race, gender and quite possibly even species. In reaching into past lives eventually the patterns found help us to see the real spirit of who we are and with this our connection to all else. It is through this connection that we are able to draw on energies and intelligences that are greater than our individual self.

Chapter Thirteen

✤ THROUGH THE MIST ✤

In considering the subject of time and its relation to the practice of the Art, the question arises as to the role of divination in this system. There are some who feel that divination really has no part in magical practice because the Witch shapes the future through her or his rituals today. This, of course, is an obvious over simplification and a somewhat simplistic attitude to take. Divination isn't solely involved in predicting the future. Rather it is the means by which those of the Art glean information about circumstances and situations. These can relate to events and people in past, present or future. Nevertheless, there are some who feel that because magic can and does alter events there is little need for divination. The reality is though that not everything is under the control of the Witch or Magician. And while we all have free will, some things happen simply because they are meant to. The reason for this is fairly obvious.

As we saw, time moves in cycles. What occurs at one point in the spiral will directly affect a similar point in the future. Many of the circumstances we face now are the direct result of actions we had taken in the past, including previous lives. Thus, these are the end result of choices we have already made.

This isn't 'karma' in the 'new-age' sense of the word. The Traditional Witch doesn't subscribe to the idea that 'bad things' happen because one was 'bad' in a previous life. Nor do we cling to the Wiccan idea that what one does returns three-fold. This, in my opinion, is a simplistic attitude meant to instill a sense of morals through the fear that anything

158

'bad' will come back to one three times. In my opinion, the origins of the Wiccan 'law of three' appear to be a distortion of certain concepts rooted in Celtic myth and thought.

In ancient Celtic magical practices it was common to call on a force three times, bringing its influence to bear on the goal at hand with triple the power and authority. As such we find such Gaelic terms as "tréan" used to describe "thrice richness" or "three times in strength". Conversely the word "tríbhás" refers to a "triple death" or death by three different yet simultaneous means.[3]

In Traditional Witchcraft it is a common to use such enchantments as "three times three" for this exact purpose, bringing forces to bear in combinations of three. This can be used for a variety of purposes. I have seen it used as a means of entering deeper states of becoming while working with different realms in ritual. It is also frequently used in defensive magic as a means of turning curses back onto the sender nine times stronger (three multiplied).

Nevertheless, I am not aware of any direct reference in lore or myth describing actions returning back on one in a threefold pattern *unless* this occurred through the agency of actively evoking forces three times through enchantments.

Rather, those of the Art recognize that at any given time, through our choices, we set into motion a series of events which ultimately have a direct impact on our future. This doesn't necessarily mean that if one harmed another in the past you must, in turn, be harmed in the future. To assume that the wheels of fate work in such a moralistic manner is spiritually naive. 'Good' or 'bad' are human values and vary from person to person.[4] Rather, everything we do has an effect on some future outcome in the spiral of time. To be sure, there is a price that has to be paid for everything. Yet the threads of destiny are complex. Perceiving these threads

3. Ó Tuathail, Seán. *Foclóir Draíochta*. Copyright, 1993

4. For a better understanding of the ethics followed by those of the Art, the student should read "The Counsels of the Wise" in *The Willow Path*.

and learning possible outcomes from actions taken is the real value of divination.

Further, there are currents and tides of power which flow through nature. Similarly these currents flow through the cycles of time itself. Part of the practice of the divination is being able to perceive these tides and understand the possible outcome these may bring.

When we look outside and see dark clouds moving in we know that there is a good chance that rain may follow. When the snows of winter begin to melt and the Sun is seen rising higher and higher each day we know that spring is coming and with it new life. How we react to these currents of power in the environment is our choice. If rain is coming we can chose to carry an umbrella to avoid getting wet. Or we can, ignore the dark clouds and then complain when we get caught in the rain. When we know spring is coming we can prepare the ground, plan the setting for our garden so that we can have food later in the year. Or we can ignore the warming weather and then find ourselves in need later in the season.

In a similar way divination allows us to prepare for circumstances allowing us to make choices to help enhance those things we want, while mitigating those which may prove challenging.

There are any number methods that the Witch can use for divination, far too many to go into detail of each here. However, I would like to mention some. Traditionally cunning folk and country Witches have used fairly simple methods. One of the most common was the pouring of melted wax or lead into water while asking a question, divining the shapes that formed from these. Until the modern era the 'sieve and shears' technique was very common. For this the points of a pair of shears are stuck in the side of sieve. This was then suspended, usually held by the fingers of two people. As questions are asked the entire device begins to spin. The direction of the spinning determined the answer to the question.

By far some of the most frequent means used by rural Witches involved scrying. This could be done in any number of ways. For example, the Witch may scry in a bowl or cup of water, a glass or crystal ball, a polished mirror, or semi-precious stone. Pools of ink were a common focal point in scrying, as were natural bodies of water. This was particularly so on the night when the Moon's reflection could be seen on the surface of the water.

Cartomancy has long been valued in the Art. Usually this was done using common 'playing cards' as these were easier to obtain then the Tarot. I have also seen examples of cards specially made by Witches and diviners for this purpose which appear to have almost no resemblance to either playing cards or the Tarot. In particular several examples can be found in eastern European and Russian forms of the Art.

More complex methods of divination including Astrology, Geomancy and Numerology were also used extensively. However, these were usually only available to those who had access to some of the occult texts that were available more to Magicians and those in urban centers. Nevertheless, clear records exist showing that many cunning folk did have some fundamental knowledge of basic Astrology.

Many Witches combined the act of 'becoming' or 'merging' with divination. For this they would seek out places of power deep in nature. This was usually done at night and more frequently then not during a tide of power, such as the Full Moon, Midsummer Eve or Samhain. Crossroads were frequently held to be excellent places for this exercise, as were hedges and natural trails. There the Witch would sit and relax, focusing on the issue she sought an answer to, while allowing herself to slip into the state of 'becoming'. Tradition states that during these excursions spirits would appear and provide the answers.

In my opinion the practicing Magician or Witch needs to have a minimum of two different techniques that they are fairly proficient at. This can take time to achieve. For in essence each form of divination usually involves using a set of symbols that hold some intrinsic occult power. As explained earlier sigils, tools and images become the outward manifestation of specific powers and frequently entities. In this understanding, each symbol used in divination, in theory, has a measure of power within it. Further, each potentially becomes a transcendent key allowing one to connect with the force the symbol represents. It is absolutely vital that the seer takes the time to not only learn the meanings of each token or glyph within the form of divination chosen, each of these need to become ingrained in her consciousness. For, in essence, one is learning a language through which to communicate with the force that governs the method chosen.

This applies even with the act of scrying, interpreting the shape of wax and lead, or in communicating with spirits. For inevitably the images that come through will almost certainly be in symbolic form. Learning how to interpret the symbols is vital. Just as one has to learn a written script before being able to read text in a book. This takes time. There is no substitute for this. Even the most gifted seer has to learn how to interpret the images she receives. And, of course, the more complex the system of divination the longer the training will take. Thus subjects such as Astrology and Numerology require any number of years, with constant reading, practice and in many cases personal tutelage. Nevertheless, the benefits can be tremendous.

Also, all symbols do not mean the same to each diviner, although some may usually be interpreted similarly across different systems. Thus, a white bird or dove may have different meanings depending on the scryer,

In approaching divination there are some important points that you need to consider. Almost always, the Witch will first appeal to her familiar seeking their aid in receiving an accurate answer to the question involved. Existing as it does in the 'spirit' world of djet-time the familiar has ready access to information that we in neheh-time can only glimpse once shifting into a state of 'becoming'.

If one does not at present have a familiar with whom they are working a different approach need to be taken. Magician Aleister Crowley felt that each form of divination has its own intelligence or spirit that speaks through the oracle. As such, one needs to appeal to this entity at the start of the operation asking it to give clear and accurate answers.[5] The method for doing this varies. For example, Magician, Stephen Skinner, explains that in consulting Geomancy one first determines which Geomantic spirit governs the question being asked. One then traces an invoking pentagram of Earth (as Geomancy is divination by earth). The sigil of the spirit is then drawn in the center of the pentagram.[6]

Crowley explains that most divination will fall under spirits associated with the element of Air, and that Tarot specifically is under the influence of the planet Mercury. Obviously one needs to research their chosen divination system to determine what spirit or spirits naturally govern this. From there it is only a matter of research and intuition to come up with a personal means for reaching out to the intelligence involved.

As noted above though, perhaps the easiest and most practical spirit contact is one's own familiar as she (or he) already has a relationship with you. She knows your situation. Further, being a spirit herself she can act as a liaison with the intelligence governing the system you are using.

In forming your question you need to be very explicit, avoiding any possible confusion or double meaning. You have to remember that in divination, like magic, you are working with both spirits and the deeper levels of the mind. And like these, oracles can be quite literal when approached. Any ambiguity in your question will almost always result in a vague or inaccurate answer.

---

5. Crowley, Aleister. *Magick in Theory and Practice*, p.156-161.
6. Skinner, Stephen. *The Oracle of Geomancy*, p.34-37.

For obvious reasons, when asking a question regarding one's own life there is a certain about of anxiety about the situation and bias in how one hopes the future will eventually manifest. If you have too strong of an emotional leaning toward a specific outcome almost always that bias will be reflected in the oracle itself. Rather, it is important to approach the oracle in as passive attitude as possible. The closer you can get to an approach of not caring about the outcome, other than being curious about the situation, the more accurate the reading will be. Clearly this is difficult to achieve. However, if you find that you are emotionally upset, or are strongly desiring a specific outcome it is best not to approach the oracle. Instead, either wait until you have let the intensity of the emotion pass, or else direct that energy into a spell that will help bring the desired result to you.

As we consider bias, more often than not the oracle will give you an accurate answer; however, one may simply not believe the answer given. Many seers can recount stories of having clients that insisted that the reading be done again in hopes of getting the answer they want. On other occasions the oracle will give a clear and accurate answer; however, the client only interprets it in the framework of their pre-disposed desires.

In approaching any method of divination that is dependent on the person performing a specific autonomous act (shuffling cards, pulling tokens or bones, tossing coins or stalks, etc.) it is important to simply let the hands work on their own. In handling the parts involved in the oracle one needs to simply let go. Don't try to control a thing. Just focus on the question and let the spirit and one's own intuition control the actions as you handle the oracle.

This can be very difficult to do. During this process one must stay relaxed and open, while focused solely on the question. Any intrusive thought will almost always interfere with the answer that will be given, confusing the oracle and resulting in a mixed reading.

Despite all of its challenges divination is a real art that is vitally important for the Witch or the Magician. In all regards I feel that the Witch has a real advantage in that all of her training centers around letting go and blending with the forces of the land and nature. The act of 'becoming' is one such example. This can be very conducive to successful divination.

As a final thought I strongly suggest that one not rely too much on divination. The energies and currents surrounding any given situation can be complex and often change quickly. At best divination shows the state of those energies at the moment the divination is being performed. In the vast majority of cases you have the ability to alter the outcome, even if only in a small way. Use divination to get a clearer perspective on the influences involved in any situation. But then use that information to bend your future into one which is in line with your goals.

Chapter Fourteen

❖ THE LADIES OF THE MOON ❖

Having examined the cyclic nature of time I'd now like to give our technique for refining the use of tides of power. In *The Willow Path* I discussed the cycles of the Sun, Moon, as well as the use of planetary days and hours. A solid understanding of these is important, for the timing of rituals can be critical to the success of the enchantment. As we have seen, the Moon plays an enormous role in this. Beyond an understanding of the basic uses of the phases we have found that each day has its own lunar influence as well. We call these *The Ladies of the Moon*.

A lunar month can vary in length, running anywhere between twenty-eight to twenty-nine and a half days. In this system we count twenty-eight days, with each being ruled a different Lady of the Moon. The lunar month begins with the first sliver of the Moon's crescent appearing just after dark Moon. We then count each day through the lunar month. If the lunar month does run into a twenty-ninth day we look to the overall appearance of the Moon as she moves through the sky. This gives us a sense of the energy that this additional day is emphasizing. In practice the divisions between the lunar days are subtle in nature. As you will see, frequently the influence of each day tends to blend into the next, transitioning in meaning over the course of several cycles. As such, when it occurs, the impact of an additional day will fall within the orb of one of the twenty-eight Ladies. In working practical magic we have found this system to be quite effective.

It is important that the reader not confuse this technique with the *Mansions of the Moon*. The Mansions have their roots in Arabic teachings. Yet, they were frequently employed in medieval European ritual magic. Henry Cornelius Agrippa discusses this system at some length in his sixteenth century work *Three Books of Occult Philosophy*.[7] A number of contemporary magical orders today continue this practice, using the *Mansions of the Moon* on a consistent basis. This is particularly so in Hermetic Orders that follow the Ogdoadic stream of wisdom.

Essentially, the *Mansions of the Moon* is a system which observes the position of the Moon as it travels through the signs of the zodiac. In addition, it takes into account the Moon's interaction with certain celestial objects; namely, specific stars. There is some controversy as to whether the tropical zodiac or the sidereal zodiac should be used when considering the Mansions.[8] For our discussion here this is a moot point as the *Ladies of the Moon* are *not* determined by the zodiac position and are not related to the system of the *Mansion of the Moon* in anyway.

Rather, the *Ladies* look to the interplay of energies between the Sun and Moon, tracking their movement each day. In this way we gain an understanding of the realm that the Moon is moving through as shown on the glyph of the Stang Rising through the Worlds as found in *The Willow Path*. In fact that drawing delineates in pictorial form the essence of each lunar day. As such, I recommend that the reader refer to the drawing while studying this chapter.

---

7. Donald Tyson's edited and annotated version of this work is an excellent reference for the serious student of the Art. Tyson, Donald, *Three Books of Occult Philosophy* written by Henry Cornelius Agrippa of Nettesheim, 2006.

8. For those interested in learning more about this subject the best book that I have found is: Warnock, Christopher. *The Mansions of the Moon – A Lunar Zodiac for Astrology & Magic*, 2006.

The Worlds, as the reader will recall, correspond to specific realms, energies and states of being that are best understood through the ancient teachings of Celtic myth and legend. These are the Annwn, Abred, Gwynfyd and Caer Wydyr. The Moon travels through these realms monthly. As such each day of the month brings with it a different energy, related to the realm it is in that can be used. Beyond this the *Ladies of the Moon* strongly consider the angular aspects formed between the Sun and Moon. These are very powerful and will directly influence the types of forces, spells and rituals that can be most successful on any given day.

I want to make sure that the reader understands that this system is one which we had researched, developed and put into practice over years. We were careful to base this on actual occult teachings related to Astrological and Numerological teachings, coupled with specific traditional instructions regarding lunar phases. This was coupled with our knowledge of the realms noted above. While I am aware of other esoteric systems that also involve specific qualities and deities associated with the daily movement of the Moon, primarily in ancient India, we did not look to these in our research. Rather this system came about gradually after much observation and magical working. To my knowledge, this method is unique to our practices. I offer it here for the first time in a public format so that others may work with this, building on the success we have seen.

As you read through these descriptions you will see that I have included basic talismanic images meant to embody the essence of the energies for each day. These are drawn from traditional sources, yet they are purposely kept simple. The reason for this is so that one can hold the image in the mind easily while pulling the energy of the day into the work at hand, whether this is a spell, potion, or a more complex rite.[9]

---

9. Each of these are portrayed on the painting of "The Stang Rising through the Worlds" in *The Willow Path*.

As already noted the lunar month begins with the first appearance of the waxing crescent Moon and follows through the twenty-eight day cycle.

Day One: Lady of the Horns

Appearing in the western sky as the Sun sets, the slim crescent of the Moon can be seen just as she begins to wax. Her horns are sharp as they point upward. On this first day we see this orb as being in the Annwn resting at the base of the Stang as the World Tree. It is from here that she begins her ascent through the worlds.

Today marks the point of transition of the Witch Goddess from the Wise Crone during the Dark Moon, into the Maiden at the New Moon. In Celtic myth this occurs when the Sun God as consort – often depicted as a knight – makes love to the Crone. It is during this that She transforms into the beautiful Maiden. An example of this is portrayed in the Irish legend of Niall discussed at some length in *The Willow Path*. In making love to the Lady she reveals that she is none other than the Goddess of the land itself. And it is through their union that Niall becomes the high king, serving the Great Goddess.

This first day of the lunar month brings with it the energies surrounding new beginnings, initiation and transformation. As such this is an excellent day for any workings involving fresh starts and bringing in new opportunities. This crescent phase gives energy to any project, expressing this in fresh and vital ways. Rituals performed today will be given power and the innate potential for future growth; not unlike the promise of life that lies at the heart of every seed.

The Lady of the Horns is an excellent period for rituals which require a sudden burst of energy. New projects, spells designed to attract or maintain love, as well as all rites of prosperity which are meant to come to harvest at a later date can be done now. This is also an excellent day to set magical protection around oneself and one's property.

In our system we use the image of the new crescent Moon with her horns sharply pointing upward to represent the forces of this day.

Day Two: Lady of the Star

On day two of the lunar month the Moon is waxing just past new. She is still in the Annwn as she continues her journey as the Maiden. As with the previous day, today may also be used for providing bursts of energy toward the achievement of long term goals, as well as, to bring energy to new projects just begun. It also brings with it a certain continuity and sense of endurance that the Witch can tap into.

In practical terms the energies experienced on this second day can be applied effectively to attraction, fascination, love, as well as those of lust. People in authority can be approached easily and spells used to influence them can be cast with confidence. Successful proposals can be made on this day. This energy can be used for prosperity spells as well.

The Lady of the Star also brings with it the opportunity to work well with meditative and contemplative exercises. This may seem counter intuitive given the emphasis on energy and new beginnings. Yet, this day also opens the gates to wisdom. Being near the time of the New Moon any type of work involving looking within can be very effective. Hypnosis and exercises related to past life recall will be beneficial today.

As a talismanic image we portray this day with the ancient Egyptian five pointed 'seba' or star, often in a lapis blue and gold pattern.

Day Three: Lady of the Besom – The Llawforwyn

The Moon continues to wax in Annwn as the Maiden, the Llawforwyn. Today is excellent for any spells in which the goal is prosperity, fertility and abundance. The Besom has a long tradition of symbolism surrounding sexuality and pleasure. This is an excellent day for all rites of love, rituals meant to arouse and excite; sexuality, sensuality, as well as any enchantment meant to bring joy and pleasure.

The association with the Besom indicates that this is a good day to practice forms of astral travel; sending forth the fetch, the formula of the Swt, and trance work generally. This is especially so if this is the first day in a series of exercises to be conducted over the period of the waxing Moon. As the Moon nears full you will find each attempt becomes stronger.

This is also a good time to successfully call on or become aware of spirits. Having said this though, their messages may not be clear. Be aware of this as you continue work with otherworld beings. As the Moon continues her journey during the waxing phase these messages should become clearer.

This is also an excellent day for rites intended to bring strength, passion and power to oneself or arousing this in others. This day is alternatively known as "The Lady who fights for Her Lord." This evokes the images of ancient warrior Goddesses, from the Celtic Great Queen Morgana, to the Egyptian lioness who protects the Sun as Sekhmet. As such, rituals of counter-magic and protection will be beneficial today. Setting protections around the home or one's property will prove to be very effective.

This can be a powerful day for rites related specifically to Goddesses and women's magic. This is especially so for those corresponding to the Queen as the bright Goddess of spring, growth and beauty.

In practical magic we use the image of the Besom itself to represent this day's energies.

Day Four: Lady of the Fe – The Adorer, the Trulliad

Named after the Celtic word for 'wand', as well as Faery, the Moon as Lady of the Fe is waxing in the Maiden phase. Today though she crosses the threshold between the Annwn and Abred (see *The Willow Path* for additional information of this). This is the threshold on which our world, our dimension exists. This is the Middle Earth of old Pagan legend, also known as Midgard in Germanic and Norse culture. As such the Moon's influence on material affairs is very strong now. Rituals designed to create objective physical changes in one's material circumstances will have a greater chance of success.

On this fourth day of the lunar month the worlds of the Annwn and Abred blend and overlap. Thus these worlds tend to be much more accessible for those of us on the material plane. In turn, our realm is much more available to the influence and visitations of otherworld beings. Messages from these can come through strongly. Listen to your instincts and intuition. This is an excellent day to seek out contact with spirits and beings in the secret places of nature. Divination conducted today is likely to reveal very accurate results. So too, communication with spirits of the deceased can be very successful.

The Moon here also gives energy to new enterprises and projects. As with the previous day, this is an excellent time to reset one's magical protections and boundaries. Too, this is a good time to use the Fe (Wand) to project one's goals into the astral; building these forms so that they can eventually manifest in this realm.

The Moon's energy this day can be used for works related to abundance, success and prosperity. As the "Adorer" the Moon's energy can also be used for works related to friendship, love, seduction and the ancient occult art of fascination.

This can be a powerful day for any rites involving the evocation of woodland spirits. This is also an excellent time for rituals involving the God of the forest, and experiencing him as the young lord of nature, abundance and virility. As such, the talismanic image we use to tap into the day's forces is the Fe itself pointing straight up.

Day Five: Lady of Desire
The Moon continues to wax as it moves through the Maiden phase and with it the themes of new life and

growth continue. This day brings with it energies which can be used for all matters of attraction, desire, strong sexual feelings, as well as new friendships, associations, and social gatherings. Creativity, the drive to try the new and the unique all tend to manifest today. Innovativeness and inventiveness also come through now. As such workings meant to bring any of these influences into one's life can be performed today with success.

The Lady of Desire is also an excellent day for healing spells and rituals, as well as any that are life affirming, positive, and renew strength. It is the perfect time to prepare herbal recipes and potions related to health and wellbeing. The time is also right to banish negative forces and spirits, setting protective barriers and creating protective amulets.

The Moon is now in the Abred, as such astral workings, 'traveling in spirit' and magic generally can be effective under this influence. Any of the procedures described earlier as part of traveling in spirit are likely to be successful today.

In our system the outline of a red oval meeting sharply at the top and bottom (sometimes known as a "vesica piscis") exemplify the energies of this day.

Day Six: Lady of the Mysteries

On the sixth day of the lunar month the Moon is continuing in the Maiden phase as she rises further into the Abred. Astral influences are very strong now. For the Witch or Magician this is an excellent time to work with, and create on the astral for magical effect. This can include creating forms and images with the goal of these eventually becoming manifest in the material realm. It can also involve working with otherworld beings, familiar spirits, as well as 'thought forms' purposely created by the Witch.

Experiences with otherworld entities or forces are very possible today. Thus mediumship, trance work, spirit scrying, necromancy, evocation; all of these can be very effective. Listen to your intuition and impressions. If desired seek out spirits in remote places. Related to this, today is a good time for the making and consecration of amulets related to spirit summoning and those meant to protect one from malicious entities.

This is the first of the 'Moon Days' that relate directly to one of the five elements. This day corresponds to the element of Air, as such evocation of air elementals can be very effective. This is also a good time to blend incenses, as they will be particularly powerful.

Divination is favored at this time. It is also an excellent day to work rites designed to gain skill and knowledge, or to seek out a teacher. Finally, as with many of the other days noted, the energies today can be used to perform rituals of protection and drive away negative influences.

As this day relates to the element of air we use a medieval sigil, often employed in Traditional Witchcraft, corresponding to this. Which is the outline of an upright triangle with a flat line resting across the upper point. From this three vertical line rise; one on each end of the line while a third rises from the center.

Day Seven: Lady of Beauty

This marks the first quarter phase of the Moon. She is still in her form as the Maiden. Here she continues to raise in the Abred. Also, when we look to the placement of the Moon on glyph of the Stang rising through the Worlds, this lunar day has a resonance with the Celtic Fire festival of Beltane. As such, the energies today can best be used in spells related to love, as well as sensuality and sexuality. This can also be an excellent day of gatherings, friendship, social events.

Beyond this though, we have found that the Moon's energy today can be applied aggressively toward achieving desired goals of most any kind, provided these are of a constructive nature. Thus works aimed at building, attracting, strengthening, providing, bringing abundance – all of these can be worked toward now. The energy of this day lends itself to regeneration and renewal. Healing rites can be very powerful.

This can also be an excellent day for seeking a deeper understanding of oneself. The Mystery of Becoming, or merging in nature, can be very effective. The day can even be used to help induce a measure of spiritual transformation and renewal through nature. This spiritual transition may come through ritual, personal mediation or spontaneous gnosis.

Pay attention to intuition at this time. Communication with spirits and otherworld beings can occur now. If desired seek these out at this time. So too, communication with the Gods is possible under the Moon's influence today. As such, it is an excellent time for evocation and rites of invocation. Work with familiar spirits will be productive. This is a good day for spirit scrying, summoning and mediumship generally. Divination performed under this influence will likely yield important results.

As a talismanic symbol used to tap into this day's energies we depict this as a green circle resting atop a single stroke or 'handle' below.

Day Eight: Lady of Abundance

The Moon continues her journey through the Abred, waxing in the Maiden phase. This day brings with it energy and life. All is moving toward fruition; however, it isn't ready for harvest yet. Steady progress can be made today and with it success and prosperity are within sight. Rituals and spells meant to continue this effort, reaching toward one's goal, will be powerful. I have seen rites performed to bring opportunities for future financial success be exceptionally powerful when done on this lunar day.

This is the second of the 'Moon Days' that relate directly to one of the five elements. This day corresponds to the element of Earth; as such, the seeking out of material magical objects can be very successful now. Fashioning the actual physical tools used in the Art will prove productive. The making of talismans for material prosperity will yield powerful results.

This is also an excellent day to seek out the truth of a matter. As such, divination will be advantageous.

As the Moon is in the Abred and the number eight relates strongly to the Hermetic path, complex ritual techniques will be powerful when working directly with astral forces and influences.

The talismanic image we use for this day comes from medieval sources, and Traditional Witchcraft. This is a green circle with horns atop this. A green line is drawn down the middle of the circle, as if splitting this.

Day Nine: Lady of Illumination

The ninth lunar day corresponds to the final stages of the Maiden. Today the Moon is in the upper regions of the Abred. This is the third of the 'Moon Days' that relate directly to one of the five elements. This day corresponds to the element of Water. Potions, philters and condensers brewed today will have be very powerful capturing the fluid essence of the Moon's power. This is also an excellent day for evoking water elementals, or to seek out nature spirits near bodies of water. Thus rituals done near lakes, rivers, streams or the ocean will be powerful.

This day is very good for any rituals involving recognition and communication with any of the lunar Goddesses. Cerridwen, Arianrhod, Diana and so many others come to mind. Works involving the use of the cauldron will be powerful today. This is a time to seek higher knowledge or spiritual insight.

This is also an excellent day for anything having to do with communication in general whether this be writing, music or speaking. All forms of verbal expression are strong today. As such, ritual invocation, enchantments, chants and the use of Words of Power or 'charms' will be more powerful. If you are preparing a document meant to influence another person, this could be the center of a spell in which it is infused with your intentions and desires. Rites related to birthing are important today. As is the ability to seek clarification on any matter. Divination will prove effective today.

The magical representation we use for this day is a traditional symbol found in Witchcraft and medieval grimoires. This is a blue circle topped with a trident.

Day Ten: Lady Whom the Gods Adore

As the Moon passes from Abred into the realm of Gwynfyd she changes from the Maiden to the Lady, the Mistress or Mother. Rituals related to harmony, love, growth and continued prosperity can be very effective, as are works that are meant to bring birth, gain, devotion, praise, abundance, as well as material and emotional fulfillment. There is an underlying current of sensuality present in the energy as well.

One tends to be more psychically aware, possessing innate perception. As such, communication with, and evocation of, spirits can be very effective under the Moon's position today.

With the Moon crossing the threshold of Gwynfyd, this is an excellent time for 'traveling in spirit'. If you had begun a working with these techniques earlier in the month as part of a progressive process, you will probably find that you have marked success today. In fact, this is an excellent period to work with the techniques meant to move one's awareness into the utopian worlds ascribed to the Gwynfyd. As a result the presence of the Gods can be sought more easily today. Magical invocation of these powerful beings will be very effective.

Our talismanic image used to draw on the energies of this day is the Ancient Egyptian 'tyet' depicted in a brilliant red.

Day Eleven: Lady of Fire

The Moon is in the Lady phase as she continues to move into Gwynfyd. With this element of fire is highlighted. The Witch may use the energies of this day to remove obstacles which may be holding one back from success. This, too, is an excellent day to evoke fire elemental forces and beings.

The illumination of fire – the flame of the Lady – exposes one's enemies and those who would mislead. As such, divination used to reveal the truth surrounding a difficult matter can be very accurate.

Fire, too, brings with it a strength of will and the passion that can be highly effective in ritual. Being so near the time of the Full Moon, those of the Art often use this to ritually direct immense passion toward the manifestation of a goal. In doing so it is important to remember that this is the 'Moon Day' related to the element of fire. So the Witch should think in terms of those goals that she would like to apply drive and passions to, those goals she would like to 'heat up'. Today is also an excellent day for the blending of ritual oils as these, generally, are ruled by the element of fire.

As a talismanic image for drawing on the power of this day we use a traditional sigil from Witchcraft and medieval sources. This is a red triangle, pointed upward with a stylized flame rising from the midpoint on the base and shooting off to either side.

Day Twelve: The Lady and the Master

The Moon is in the Lady phase as she continues to rise higher in the Gwynfyd. As the title implies, this aspect of the Moon corresponds to the union of the Mistress and the Master. Works of magic designed to draw joy, abundance, success and prosperity will be powerful, as will rituals intent on increasing courage, determination and fortitude.

In the glyph of the Stang rising through the Worlds, the Moon is crossing over the left horn of the Stang. The Master, as the God of the woodlands and the spirit in the wind, is powerful today. So, too, is the Lady of the forest in her bright aspect. This is an excellent day to seek them through ritual, as well as in the secret places of nature.

Rites designed to bring vitality and good health will be strong now. This phase of the Moon is strongly related the ancient deities associated with the Green Man and the

Horned Gods of nature such as Cernunnos, Cernowain, Herne, Faunus, Pan and Khnum.

As a magical image, we portray this day's energies as a green circle topped with horns.

Day Thirteen: Lady of the Portal
This is the first of the three days of the Full Moon. The Moon is in the Lady phase just one day from her apex. She is near the upper regions of the Gwynfyd just before passing into Caer Wydyr. As Lady of the Portal today is a time of passage or transition from one place to another as well as a transition from one state of being to another. This transition can be a movement in location, a change in one's situation, or a transition to another state of being. Astral work and positive magic of most any nature will be very powerful now. This is an excellent time for practices of 'traveling in spirit', working with the fetch or Swt, trance work and all that these techniques entail.

This 'Moon Day' also relates directly to the fifth element of spirit. Being one of the days of the Full Moon itself, this is an excellent time for initiations, as well as the consecration of ritual tools. Communication with spirits and otherworld beings will be very effective under this influence. This can be a wonderful time to perform rituals to Goddesses generally, as well as to the greater deities of nature overall.

This is an excellent time to cast spells meant to influence other people; however, this should be of a positive and constructive nature. As this can go both ways it may be advisable to use this time to cleanse your home and set your Watchers/Guardians.

Under this influence the use of the Besom and Stang as ritual tools facilitating transition and movement between the worlds will prove highly effective, as will mirror working, scrying and hearth for the same purpose. Preparation of oils, incenses and potions designed to aid 'traveling in spirit' as well as communication with spirits in general can be effectively done today.

As with most phases of the waxing Moon this is a perfect time for rituals meant to bring prosperity, abundance, love and happiness. This is also a perfect time to help bring goals to a head, the final transition before complete fulfillment.

Deliverance of an important message, whether through mundane means or more esoteric methods, will be very positive helping to bring goals into fruition. Divination will be much more accurate on this day than on most.

We use two different images to represent the forces of this day. Usually we will portray this as a solid purple oval. However, on occasion, we will use the traditional Witchcraft image of a trident, with the right hand tine curved inward.

Day Fourteen: Lady of the Silver Cauldron – The Mistress
The Moon is in the Lady phase and at her height in the month. She has crossed the threshold of Gwynfyd and now rests as the Silver Cauldron at the heart of Caer Wydyr – the Castle of Glass, the Crystal Mountain. This is the Mistress, she who is the Great Goddess, the Full Moon shining through the trees in the clearing.

Without a doubt this is one of the most powerful nights in the month for magic. The energies that flow through 'the astral' are more fluid and abundant now than at other times. But there is more to this than astral influence. Here the Moon sits in the heart of Caer Wydyr beyond the astral realm of Abred. Her light flows through the worlds transferring this into the astral and finally emerging in the material. Thus this is spirit, as the essence of life, embodied and clothed within nature! It is because of this that magic is so powerful now. For the energies now come through shining in all worlds in this one brilliant moment.

Rituals intended to bring happiness, abundance, fulfillment, as well as sex, love and celebration will all be powerful now. Gatherings of associates and close friends, as well as romantic encounters all can be successful, as will rituals performed now for these purposes. Rites for acquiring prosperity and good fortune will be effective. And like the previous day, this is an excellent time for rites of a spiritual nature calling on the Gods, communing with spirits, evoking the Great Goddess. Astral projection, 'traveling in spirit', 'rising on the planes', mirror working, scrying, all will be powerful today.

This also resonates with the same type of energies found at the Summer Solstice. Magic, communion with nature spirits and otherworld beings are all possible. As is summoning the spirits of the dead. Fertility of the land, the body, the mind as well as one's fortunes can all be worked toward on a magical level. The talismanic image we use for this Full Moon day is a silver cauldron.

Day Fifteen: Lady of Jubilation
The Moon remains in the Lady phase while moving out of Caer Wydyr and is now returning to the Gwynfyd. This is the third day of the Full Moon though She is just beginning to wane.

As the title implies this is a time of celebration and contentment. Works meant to stir strong emotions and passions will be effective today. As such, rituals designed to incite love, joy, eroticism, sensuality and sexual seduction all are possible under this influence, as are rites for prosperity and abundance.

Communication with spirits and Gods can be very strong at this time. Works related to understanding or awakening an awareness of one's true self can be very effective. Anything having to do with conception as well as birth can be powerful under this phase of the Moon. This is a very positive influence. In our group we represent the forces of this day in the talismanic image of an upraised goblet, as if toasting the Gods.

Day Sixteen: The Lady and the Stag
On this day the Moon is in the Lady phase, waning in Gwynfyd. When placed on the glyph of the Stang rising through the Worlds, the Moon has crossed the right horn

or path. The title "the Lady and the Stag" is a reference to Diana the Huntress, as well as to Herne the Hunter.

The energies of this day can be used for all situations in which adjustment or change is needed in order to bring about a goal or to bring a harvest. This Moon can used for all rites of 'gathering' in order to prepare for challenges to come.

The energies of this time often involve giving back to the land, to the spirits and Gods. As such, rites of offering and sacrifice will be effective with the spirits accepting the gifts more readily today. As with its counterpart, the "Lady and the Master", this day can be very powerful for rituals involving the evocation of the Horned Gods of nature. In this respect though they are called upon in their role of the harvest, the hunted and the hunter, the stag who is both begetter and slain.

This is a powerful day to use magic to influence others, though because the Moon is Waning care must be taken. Rather than being used to enhance or encourage existing desires and traits in others, the energies of this day are better used to change the other person's mind. It is a good time to present alternate views from those the other person may have had.

As a talismanic image we represent this day in the form of a stylized stag's head. This is a brown circle topped with the antlers of a deer.

Day Seventeen: Lady of the Cloak
The Moon is waning, in the last phases of the Lady. While still in the Gwynfyd this day is characterized by the strain that comes with transition, for the Moon moves toward the Abred and into the Crone phase.

As the Lady of the Cloak this day can be used for rituals of a guarded nature or for those intended to keep matters hidden or secret. This is also a good time to perform rites intended to move one away from difficulties. Rites designed to create barriers or prevent others from achieving their goals can be done successfully. Rituals meant to sow confusion will be effective. Also be aware that with this day the influence of unseen forces and negative spirits may be strong as well.

The talismanic image we use to characterize the forces of this day is that of a figure cloaked in grey and black.

Day Eighteen: Lady Who Lights the Dark

The Moon continues to wane as she passes into the Crone phase and out of the Gwynfyd, lowering into the astral realm of Abred. The wisdom of the spiritual realms of Caer Wydyr and Gwynfyd illuminate the Crone as She travels through the Abred.

While the previous lunar day had been one of hidden and deceptive forces, this day brings wisdom and guidance. Divination can be very effective now. Seeking the counsel of the Crone will prove useful.

On this day magic is strong, astral workings will be powerful under this influence. However, this is best used to clear away any negative influences or evil entities, removing that which is out worn in order to make room for eventual new and healthy growth.

While divination can be very effective today, understand that it is easy to mislead oneself under this influence. It is important to keep your inner vision and goals clear. For us, this day is represented by the symbolic image of a lit torch.

Day Nineteen: The Lady Who Binds

The Moon continues its journey through the Abred as she manifests further as the Crone. Under this day's influence spirit hauntings are likely to be much more active than normal.

Be careful of deception or illusion on the part of others. Take your time to appraise the situation at hand. Inner wisdom and a good understanding of your true self will aid you now.

This period can also be used today to influence others; however, be very careful as these are likely to manifest in negative patterns. This is an excellent day for setting oaths, commitments and obligations. Ritual bindings of all kinds can be done now with success. This is also a good day to explore the bonds one has formed over time with others. As such, past life recall techniques may be more successful under this lunar force.

The image we use to manifest these energies is an "X" with one arm being black and the other grey.

Day Twenty: Lady of the Fading Light
The Moon is in the Crone stage lowering further into the Abred. In many respects this lunar day resonates in meaning with the Celtic fire festival of Lugnasadh. As such, rituals of harvest in all its aspects can be done. This includes rites designed to gather resources whether on a material or spiritual level as one prepares for the challenges to come.

Along with harvest, this day can be used for rituals in which giving back to the land, the spirits and Gods is very appropriate. This is also a powerful day in which determination, and steadfastness can be evoked within oneself or to motivate others.

In a more negative view the influence of this day can be used in removing or cutting away those forces, obstacles or people that challenge one. Be prepared though, as a price for this type of work will be needed to be paid for this is also a day of sacrifice and offerings.

As a talismanic image we see the golden sickle that cuts the wheat as being emblematic of this day.

Day Twenty One: The Lady Who Rends
The Moon is waning in the Crone phase as she continues her descent through the Abred. This is a day when rites designed to bring about transformation and transition can be very effective. The Lady who Rends tears away old and

outworn forms, transforming that which was previously not used into that which is valued.

Under this Moon's influence rending in all its forms is effective. Skill and patience during this process will produce positive results. As such, rituals used to tear down barriers, stop the efforts of one's foes, and remove obstacles can be performed with success.

It is important to understand that dark works will be very powerful as well. Thus, curses or 'blasting' can be undertaken today. Setting one's protections may be very prudent.

As a symbol for the energies of this day we see this as a red circle that has been split in half spreading open at the bottom.

Day Twenty Two: The Lady of Wisdom – The Baisleac
The waning Moon continues to move through the Abred as the Crone. Here she is the Wise One, the Baisleac – the female 'folk' wizard, the wise healer and Witch.

This is a powerful day for any acts involving artistry, skill, knowledge and wisdom. This is also an excellent time to seek counsel through divination, spirit communication and trance. One can get highly accurate information today as well as real wisdom. It is best to follow any advice received today through these sources. This is also an excellent day to put closure to matters, render judgement, or make a final and lasting decision.

All of the processes involved in 'traveling in spirit' can be undertaken today, provided these are done in the Roth Fail, or the chamber one is working in has been sealed well.

This is also an excellent day for rites dedicated to the Great Queen in Her form of the Wise Crone.

The talismanic image we use for the essence of this lunar day is simply that of an eye.

Day Twenty Three: Lady of the Harvest
The Moon is in the Crone phase lowering in the Abred – the lower regions of the astral just before crossing the threshold

of this, our material realm. As with its counterpart during the waxing period, the Moon's placement here increases the ability to affect change on this 'material' level more easily. However, whereas the waxing period would be used more for applying energy toward the beginning of projects and goals, the waning Moon position is used for gathering in and harvesting the 'rewards' of what one has accomplished. Thus this is a period for pulling together resources, consolidating these, and for solidifying the efforts of work done to date in preparation for challenges to come.

Yet, as this is a waning Moon the energies of this day could easily be used for darker, negative magic that is meant to directly affect events on the material level.

Because the Moon is crossing over the threshold between Worlds, this is also an excellent day for communication with spirits and entities. However, caution will need to be exercised as some of these may be of a negative nature.

The image of a harvested sheaf of wheat tied together, sometimes known as 'the neck' in many folk traditions, is used as a talismanic symbol capturing the essence of this day.

Day Twenty Four: Lady of the Hearth

The Moon crosses the threshold of Abred and slides into the Annwn. For this one moment she rests in this world, the material world, as the astral tides turn. The gates between worlds are open now.

As noted elsewhere in these writings, the hearth is the center of the home, the 'altar' of the mysteries. It is here that the forces meet. So too, this lunar day brings the influence of the Moon to rest on the hearthstone in this plane of existence. Magic can be very powerful today, especially those works which are meant to specifically make real change on a material level. It can be very useful for communication with spirits and entities. Again, care must be taken as negative influences may try to come through at this time. As the hearth is the altar of the mysteries on which the fires of wisdom are kept burning, this is an excellent day to seek counsel through divination. As the astral tides turn on this day, this may be a time to reset one's boundaries and protections.

The talismanic image we use on this day is a simple representation of the hearth with a fire set within.

Day Twenty Five: Lady of Blood

The Moon is in the Crone stage, lowering further into the Annwn. Great care is needed at this time. From a magical point of view this is a period when very negative workings can be done. Keep in mind, too, that one's enemies may be able to use this period for these purposes against you. It is also likely that hidden influences behind the scenes can be at work. Set your protections, for with defense malicious forces and entities can be repelled, sending them back to the source from which they were sent. The fire cauldron, protective mirror workings, the White Eye, certain herbal charms, as well as techniques for setting wards at the quadrants all will be powerful allies for this.[10]

For the adept the energy of the day can be used to bring energy to a goal or project. Blood is the essence of life. It carries a force that is vital. Magically the energy contained in blood can be almost tangible when used properly. Thus, rituals performed today can be given real power through this placement of the Moon. Still, because the Moon is waning and very near to being dark, great care has to be taken. It is very easy for the energy of this day to back fire against one when trying to apply this to constructive goals. As such, we focus more on the day's ability to repel evil and to remove unwanted influences.

The image that we have found that best captures the power of this lunar day is a red tear drop representing blood.

---

10. These techniques will be discussed at length in the third volume of this series *The Art*.

Day Twenty Six: The Lady of the Claw

The Moon is in the Crone phase, continuing its descent into the Annwn. The Lady of the Claw is a period when magical workings designed to tear down or remove that which is unwanted may be performed with success.

Those rites meant to 'test' one, or to be an ordeal in order to facilitate personal transformation can be powerful now. This should only be done with the goal that such a test would be to carry the individual to new levels of being and awareness.

As with the previous day this can be a very negative period in which some of the darkest forms of magic can be performed. Protections should be used to avoid any negative influences at this time.

It should be noted that this lunar day holds a certain resonance with the Celtic fire festival of Samhain. Communication with otherworld beings, whether spirits of the deceased, the inhabitants of the Annwn as well as the Gods themselves, all are possible. Supernatural experiences including hauntings are likely now.

The symbol of a single white claw or talon is used to exemplify the essence of this lunar day.

Day Twenty Seven: The Lady of the Tooth

The Moon is nearly dark as it sinks low in the Annwn. This can be a day of change and transition. Wisdom and desire, age and power bring a measure of plenty and satisfaction. The tooth crushes the husk so that the true essence of the matter at hand remains. This influence can be used magically to get to the truth of a situation. Divination can be very good today. This lunar day can also be used to cause change in a situation. However, keep in mind that as the Moon is waning, very near dark, this change will almost certainly involve the tearing down of the old and outworn.

As with the other days in the final waning period, this can be a very powerful time for negative magic. Again, use this day to set your protections. As a talismanic image we use the basic form of a tooth.

Day Twenty Eight: Lady of the Black Cauldron

The Moon is in the final stage of the Crone, resting at the bottom of the Stang in the Annwn. Where the Full Moon is the silver cauldron, the Dark Moon is symbolized by the black cauldron. On this day the twin sisters unite to bring transformation to the God. Here the Crone and Maiden meet; wisdom transforms into youth.

This can be a time when the most negative, destructive forms of magic are at their most powerful. However, this period can also be used to bring about positive transformation. This is the Sun at midnight, the Phoenix and Benu that dies only to rise again even more splendid than before. It is only through the Goddess as both the dark death Crone merged with the bright life-giving Maiden that the Sun can be renewed.

Keep your defenses strong. If you have enemies who are familiar with esoteric techniques, it is likely that the more dedicated of them will use this period to strike.

This day though is also an excellent time for quiet contemplation. The Wise Crone at Her cauldron can advise. The Lady weaves the thread of fate at the distaff. Divination, mediation, communion with the forces in nature can be very effective today.

In practice I have found that using these daily lunar tides, the Ladies of the Moon, helps to clarify the energies of the phase. With careful planning their influence can be significant.

Chapter Fifteen

✧ ALIVE WITH POTION AND FLAME ✧

On a warm summer night during the Full Moon, take a walk outside. As you look up at the starry sky let yourself experience the beauty of the moment as the moonlight washes over you while illuminating the land. Take your time as you drink in the natural wonder that this creates. It is such a simple experience, so common as to be all but ignored by the average person. Yet there, in that one moment in time, the rich vastness, awe and beauty that is the universe enfolds you in the essence that is all. These are the experiences that the Witch relishes. For it is in these moments that so much becomes possible. In these moments worlds and dimensions merge, pathways open and the mystery of who we are begins to coalesce in ways that simply defy definition.

In this state of mind take some time to find a natural source of water. It can be a brook or stream, a creek or river, a pond, lake or well. Wherever you find yourself let the moment unfold naturally, unhurriedly. Once found, look at the surface of the water and the reflection of the Moon shining on this as a mirror. You could have chosen the site earlier in the day. However, now, under the light of the Moon just let yourself relax and simply experience the energies that have gathered there.

We have already seen that power collects in various places in nature and during different tides. The Full Moon's energy is particularly drawn to water resonating with it, and, under the right conditions, gathering in this. Basque Witches have a tradition of collecting water from springs, wells and brooks on the night of the Full Moon because of this concentration of lunar energy.

190

On this night, as you gaze intently into the reflection of the Moon, gather some of the water up in a clean container. Then return to your place of Art. If privacy permits, an outdoor ritual site would be perfect for this rite. If not, an indoor Roth Fail will work well.

There you will have prepared the Hearthstone (altar) in advance, placing two white taper candles at the back corners. On the center of the Hearthstone place a white ceramic bowl that is new or has only been used in the Art. In front of the bowl a piece of parchment or high-quality paper should be set. On this you will have drawn the sigil of the *Transformative Power of the Moon*.

To the side place a piece of sterling silver and a set of metal tongs. Traditionally a fire with red glowing coals either in the hearth itself or, if outdoors, burning in the center of the Roth Fail should be present. I have seen some references to using a candle for the following; however, this really can't generate the heat needed for this operation.

Pour the water you gathered into the ceramic bowl. Normally a cup of water will be more than enough for our purposes. Now, carefully proceed to heat the silver on the coals of the fire. This needs to become as hot as possible.[11] Then, with the metal tongs dunk the silver into the water.

As this happens silver 'slag' from the piece will dissolve into the water. Once it is cool repeat the process again, doing this a total of nine times. After this is complete remove the piece of silver, setting this aside. Once all is safely taken care of return your attention to the water itself.

If working outside, sit in a manor so that you can see the reflection of the Moon on the surface of the water. If indoors allow yourself some time to envision the Moon while gazing intently at the water. In either case, become aware of the Full Moon's energy filling the space. Let this

---

11. If a fire is not practical in your situation a somewhat 'untraditional' but convenient means for generating the heat needed maybe to use a hand held torch created specifically to heat metal.

build as you begin the rhythmic breathing you had used in your work with the fetch. In doing so allow energy to steadily grow in intensity, drawing this in while you breathe in through the nose, extending the abdomen to a count of four. Hold this to a count of two, then breathe out through the mouth to a count of four. Hold your breath again to the count of two, and then begin again. Continue this technique until you feel that your entire body is filled with the energy evoked through the Moon. Then, with one final deep breath, gently release the air through the mouth, allowing this to flow gently and smoothly onto the surface of the water. Let the energy permeate the water, filling it with the power. In your mind's eye see the energy filling the water.

Immediately following this, return your focus back to your breathing. In doing so, once again, build the lunar energy up within yourself. This time however, once you feel that your entire body is filled with this essence, allow this to well up from your torso, move through your arms and out through the palms of your hands. Remember 'force follows will'. See this as a silver-white energy flowing gently from your palms. Begin by passing the left hand over the water three times while the energy flows into this. Then do the same with right hand. As with the breath, feel the energy flow from your hands into the water. Envision this as glowing with the power you have passed to it.

Now, pick up your Fe and with this trace the sigil of the *Transformative Power of the Moon* above the water. See the sigil glowing in the air, as a brilliant electric blue and silver in color. Even after you replace the Fe the sigil remains, suspended above the water, radiate with the power you traced, as it becomes a portal through which the otherworld essence of the Moon flows.

Assuming the conditions are such that you can, either leave the bowl under the Moon's light, or if indoors, leave this on the Hearthstone. Before sunrise retrieve the water, bottling this and placing it in a dark safe place.

To help preserve the water so that bacteria doesn't grow in

this I will often divide this into smaller portions. In each of these I will mix a quality vodka at a ratio of two thirds vodka for one third *Moon water.* These are sealed and then labeled.

Traditionally this was called Moon Water.[12] This is a classic example of a condenser used in Witchcraft. The process just described comes directly from Basque and Italian sources. Fundamentally it is meant to draw in and contain the magical influence of the Full Moon, storing this in the water for use later. Thus it 'condenses' this in a concentrated form. Moon Water is made specifically to capture the power of Full Moon itself, storing this for use later. In practice this can be used in any rites related to the Moon; from divination, spirit summoning, traveling in spirit, to rites related to invocation of the Great Queen.

The use of condensers in the Art reaches back through both Traditional Witchcraft and Hermetic magic. In all probability it has roots reaching into Alchemical systems as these frequently involve heating metals and applying these in combination with other ingredients. As will be seen, herbs too, frequently figure highly in these formulae and in some cases replace certain metals altogether.

Condensers can be immensely important to the practice of the Art. Because of the condensation of power that these hold, they are used primarily by applying a few drops to objects imbuing them with their essence. This can be very useful when creating magical tools, talismans and amulets, as well in ritual when working with mirrors or show stones.

In the Art there is also the use of what has been called a 'universal condenser' which falls under the grouping of 'fluid condensers'. Where Moon Water was very specific in its alignment and function, the universal condenser is intended to function almost as an all-purpose 'battery' in

---

12. It is important to note that the formula I have given here is drawn directly from traditional sources including those given to me privately during my training. The method given is very different and unrelated to the many commercial sources found on the internet for 'Moon Water'.

which magical power is condensed and, thus, available for use later in virtually any ritual.

In recent years much has been written about these. As such, I was reluctant to present this here. However, I find that it is too valuable a tool not to discuss. The method for creating this that I am about to give is one that we use. This comes after much experimentation with formulas researched from older magical works and private documents made available to me during my training.[13]

We call this "a Witch's Condenser" because it is made specifically by the Witch herself, for her use only. As will become apparent, the process of creating this ultimately links the Witch with the condenser in very personal ways. Thus, once made, it needs to be guarded carefully. Yet, it is because of this link that the power involved can be directed by the Witch alone.

Essentially, the Witch's Condenser is her will and personal magical power focused in this single potion. Should the condenser fall into the hands of one whom the Witch may not be predisposed toward, the results could be a major concern. In such a case, if the person had training in the Art, the condenser could be used against the one who created it. So, think carefully before making your own condenser. Having said this, without a doubt the condenser can be a vital substance that will enhance one's overall magical effectiveness.

The Formula of the Witch's Condenser

The process of creating this is somewhat lengthy involving several steps. According to some early recipes the first step involves the creation of a 'gold tincture'. This should be done during the waxing Moon, on a Sunday, preferably under

---

13. These include Sybil Leek's formula found in her 1969 book *Cast your own spell*, Franz Bardon's books on Hermetic Philosophy and Magic, references found in several older herbal sources, as well as teachings given to me in private.

direct sunlight. Similar to the process used in the creation of Moon Water, this involves taking a piece of gold (rather than silver) and heating this, then dropping it into water that had been collected under the Sun. This should be done a total of six times, in each case heating the gold to a nearly red-hot temperature before each submersion. In doing so the 'slag' from the gold dissolves in the water. If desired, like the Moon Water, this may be divided up and then mixed with a quality vodka to help preserve this.

For those who do not wish to go through this process, both Sybil Leek and Franz Bardon had recommended using gold chloride. Chemically this contains pure gold within it and is a good substitute rather than potentially ruining a beloved piece of jewelry. I found this to be easily obtainable through credible internet sources. However, as would be expected, it can be quite costly.

I need to point out that, while Hermetic Magicians and Alchemists of the middle ages may have had access gold, it is very doubtful that the average country Witch would have this luxury. As such, there are other substances which are available. These will be presented as the process unfolds. In my experience, while the gold tincture is highly desirable and does add a measure of power to the overall condenser, it is optional providing the other ingredients are used.

The second step in this process involves selecting herbs that will form the foundation of the condenser. Multiple sources suggest the use of Chamomile flowers because of their strong resonance with the Sun. In practice I have used Chamomile for this. However, through experimentation I have found others herbs that have proven to be more effective overall for attracting and containing power which I could access in ritual later. In particular Vervain has shown itself to be very adaptable for this.

Some in the Art will use a combination of seven herbs, corresponding with the seven planets traditional planets. I advise against this as almost certainly the condenser will be used at different times, and in rites related to specific

195

planets. Rather, I find that Vervain with its wealth of overall lore and ability to be used across a broad spectrum of magical purposes is the perfect herb for an all-purpose condenser. Perhaps an overall understanding of the uses of Vervain is in order.

Known as the sorcerer's herb Vervain is by far one of the most powerful and versatile magical herbs in the Witch's garden, being highly prized by the Druids. It may be used to enhance the power and success of almost any spell or ritual. In rites of protection it both dispels evil and creates a barrier of safety. I have often combined Vervain with salt and scattered this on thresholds and throughout areas. Carried as an amulet this herb brings luck, popularity and drives away evil. Hung about the house this herb will keep the place free from negativity as well as help draw wealth and prosperity. Hung over the bed it helps to prevent nightmares. For cleansing an area some will tie Vervain and Hyssop together and use this as a broom, dipping this into a mixture of salt water and white vinegar. This is then used to sweep the area clean of negativity. A spell found in Charles Leland's book *Aradia* notes that collecting and carrying Vervain and Rue together will protect one. He cites the following incantation:

"O Vervain! Ever be a benefit,
And may thy blessing be upon the Witch
Or on the fairy who did give thee to me!
It was Diana who did come to me,
All in the night in a dream, and said to me:
If thou would'st keep all evil folk afar,
Then ever keep the Vervain and the Rue
Safely beside thee!"[14]

Keeping a sprig of Vervain in one's bag or wallet ensures that there will always be money there. Growing Vervain

---

14. Leland, Charles G. *Aradia, the Gospel of the Witches*, 1899. From the Invocation of the Holy-Stone.

around one's home causes a constant flow of money. Vervain and Elecampane can be used together to bring success in business. In this case it can be carried in a bag, burned as incense, or scattered at one's place work or business.

Vervain added to the bath will dispel evil and help to bring luck, love, personal power and protection. The bath also helps one to exude happiness to others. If facing a court case or some other judgement bathing in an infusion of Vervain will aid in achieving victory.

Vervain is a frequent ingredient in love and sex potions, philters, sachets, powders and incenses. It is considered to have aphrodisiac qualities. Rubbing one's hands with the herb and then touching others helps stimulate their friendship and love. Placing Vervain in your mouth before kissing the one you desire helps to cause the other person to love you. Scattering the herb on a bed or in one's home disperses negativity, and brings love and harmony. Vervain reignites the flames of love.

One recipe for increasing love is to coat dried apricots in honey, then sprinkle dried and powdered Vervain over these. Place these in brandy to soak for two weeks. Then serve the brandy to your lover during the waxing Moon. Vervain combined with Elecampane and infused in wine makes a powerful love potion.

Ancient sources state that burning Vervain and Frankincense as an incense during love and lust spells will cause the object of one's desire to become aroused and passionate for the person. To help turn adversaries into friends make an infusion of Vervain and Orris Root. This is added to one's bath taken prior to meeting with the people.

In her herbal books Sybil Leek explained that Vervain oil is used to bring prosperity and success in all matters, especially in business. She used this to avert hexes as well as remove curses that may already be in place by anointing the person with this.

As you can see Vervain is a very powerful, seemingly all-purpose herb. For us, in our locale, both the European

Vervain and American Blue Vervain can be grown here, with the Blue Vervain being particularly abundant. As such, fresh Vervain is relatively plentiful. When considering herbs for your condenser, fresh herbs grown in your location are much better than any you may obtain from a distributor.

Once you've chosen the herb or herbs you will be using place a generous handful in a pan. Sybil Leek suggests using a ceramic pot for this. Cover this with water gathered in nature. Spring water or water from a well is very good for this. With the lid on the pot bring the water to a boil for twenty minutes.

Remove the pot from the heat and let it cool, keeping the lid on this. When cold, strain the decoction through cheese cloth or linen. Then boil the filtered liquid down until about 4 tablespoons remain. Let this cool, again with the lid on this. Now mix this with a quality vodka at a ratio of two parts vodka to one part herbal condenser.

At this point it is necessary to form the link between yourself and the condenser. While the boiling of the herbs was probably done in one's kitchen this next step is very personal. As such this should be done in private, preferably in one's own Roth Fail, or if outside you will want to ensure that no one observes you.

For this you will need to add a few drops of your own blood. The life force inherent in blood has many of the qualities that gold tincture possesses. Yet, it has the added benefit of being uniquely yours. Ideally this is drawn with the ritual black handled knife. However, the use of a sterile needle or pin will do just as well.

Traditional sources also suggest that the Witch include a few drops of their own sexual fluids.[15] Because the occult

15. Traditional Witchcraft, especially those forms originating from central and southern Europe, frequently use sexual fluids as ingredients in a number of practices. This is because of the inherent life force that these fluids contain, both physically and on an occult level.

essence inherent in blood and sexual fluids dissipates relatively quickly these need to be freshly added to the Condenser. They can't be collected earlier and added to the mixture at a later time.

As you can understand the personal nature of the operation is such that it lends itself best to solitary work. It is vital that *nothing* from any other person enter the Condenser, especially during its creation. I can't over state this. A stray hair, saliva, blood or sexual fluids, in fact any taglock from anyone else that may accidently get mixed into the Condenser will render the operation ineffective.

Essentially, in such a case, the Condenser would be linked to both people, yet diluted in power. It would no longer be the concentrated will of the Witch, rather it would manifest as unfocused confusion and an inability to direct the natural forces flowing through it.

Once the blood and personal fluids are added, shake the mixture well. Then filter this again through clean cheese cloth or linen. At this point, if you have made the gold tincture, or you are using gold chloride, place ten drops into the decoction. This is then corked and shaken well. Store this in a dark, cool place.

A condenser prepared in this manner will last for years. As such, the choosing of the timing for making this is important. Especially so for the final step in the process. The ingredients themselves prepared in this manner form a natural battery of sorts for the attraction and retention of power. Yet no fluid condenser is complete without ritually aligning this with the energies sought. This was evident in the preparation of the Moon Water described earlier.

To ritually energize the Witch's Condenser this, of course, should done during the waxing Moon. The best lunar days for this would be day nine "Lady of Illumination", day thirteen "Lady of the Portal" and day fourteen – the Full Moon – "Lady of the Silver Cauldron". While not essential, ideally this should coincide with an additional power tide in the year. This could be one of the four Celtic Fire Festivals, as well as one of the solstices or equinoxes. Which one will depend on the type of energy one wishes to have their condenser resonate with. Please refer to *The Willow Path* for a good understanding of these tides. One could also choose an eclipse of the Sun or Moon. If this is done care should be taken to determine what sign and house it occurs in, as well as any aspects this makes to other planets.

In energizing this, follow essentially the same formula that was used in last half creating the Moon Water without the use of the sigil of the Moon. Begin with a slow rhythmic breath as you allow energy to steadily grow in intensity, drawing this in while you breathe in through the nose, extending the abdomen, to a count of four. Hold this to a count of two, then breathe out through the mouth to a count of four. Continue this, allowing your body to gently fill with energy. Then, when ready, exhale air out through the mouth, allowing this to flow slowly onto the surface of the condenser through the opening in the bottle, filling the condenser with power.

After this return your focus to continuing to build energy up within yourself. In doing so allow this to well up from your chest and then move down through your arms and out through the palms of your hands. First pass the left hand over the condenser three times. Then do the same with the right. With each pass envision the condenser glowing with power. At this point cork the bottle and place this is a safe dark dry place ready for future use.

As mentioned earlier, the condenser is one of the most powerful potions a Witch can create. As we proceed in the third volume of this series there are a number of ritual techniques that will recommend the use of this. Nevertheless, because of the link to the Witch's will, the condenser needs to be kept secret and safe.

Chapter Sixteen

❖ THE HOLLOW HILLS ❖

In the Art as we practice it, much revolves around forming a relationship with the natural world, particularly one's own locale. Certainly the processes and techniques of magic remain relatively the same and can be easily adapted across cultures, regions and even the expanse of time. After all, the Art is also a science and technology involving interaction with forces and beings in multiple realms. Nevertheless, the essence of our form of the Art requires that at some point the Witch or Magician must form a link with the spirits inherent in the natural space that she finds herself.

Not all forms of the Art require this. Hermetic magic with its emphasis on precise procedures, the application of fundamental concepts and correspondences, lends itself well to a more 'standardized' methodology. Perhaps it is for this reason, along with its emphasis on intellectual analysis throughout portions of its repertoire, that many Hermetic ritual lodges have been centered in larger cities. The ability to set a specific building, temple or room aside, designed on symbolic patterns lends itself well to urban living. In these cases the goal is to draw on specific energies through the use of symbology and sacred geometry. If the structure can be set properly, this is a valuable and effective form of magic. Yet, in my experience, there are severe limitations that come with this. For while it is highly effective for 'attuning' to specific celestial intelligences, it seldom makes any connection with the forces inherent in the location. In fact, many Hermetic Orders strive to separate themselves from the physical locale as they reach for these other realms. I think that this is a grave mistake.

Keep in mind this isn't the case in all ritual magical groups. Some are very specific about the locations which they practice. In ancient societies the features of the land were always taken into account when building ritual centers. We see this in the sophisticated temples of Egypt and the Greek Mysteries, the features surrounding the ritual centers of the Mayans, Aztecs and Incas, the stone circles of Europe and the British Isles, and so many other places. The Giza plateau on which the Great Pyramid rests has a number of natural underground tunnels and water ways, many of which were used in ritual. The Greek Oracle of Delphi was centered over a natural fissure in the earth, while the temples of Mesoamerica almost always incorporated the labyrinth of limestone caves and underground cenotes that crisscross the region.

In more recent centuries the Knights Templar were exceptionally adept at incorporating the energies of the land into their understanding of the Mysteries. A particularly striking example of this can be seen in the beautiful structures found in Quinta da Regaleria near Sintra, Portugal. This is a complex of buildings that were built specifically around the features in the locale. From the inverted tower that spirals down into a complex of natural caves, the use of underground lakes and rivers, to the eventual emergence into daylight where they built a 'chapel'. Into all of these features the Templars blended a rich mixture of ancient Celtic pagan symbolism, Hermeticism, as well as traditions brought from Arabic and Egyptian sources. Then, in an act of genius, they merged all of these into their own brand of mystical Christianity. For the initiate the symbolism and power of the site is unmistakable. Like the Alchemical Splendor Solis paintings and texts from the same general time period, this site is a fantastic and successful attempt at pulling these systems together.

Such examples though are rare. Especially so today. Seldom do we find city planners attempting to draw on the natural features of the land, let alone taking into account the spiritual forces present as well. Rather, society today is bent on simply plowing over the land, pretending that nature itself has no effect on those who will live there.

It is vital that one seek a connection with nature itself, no matter where one may be. The Old Ways aren't limited to any one location. Rather the Geassa can be found inherent anywhere in nature. However, for city dwellers who wish to follow the Willow Path this can pose a real problem.

Please don't misunderstand me here. The methods taught in these books most certain do work in any setting, whether country or urban, providing the instructions are followed carefully. Julie herself lived in a major metropolitan community at the time I was training with her. However, those who live in remote, rural areas have a distinct advantage over their city dwelling sisters of the Art.

My own experience in city settings is that one has to work very hard at making connections with nature. Like the ritual Hermeticist, this may mean carefully selecting a series for symbols and images when setting up a place of working. For me this meant converting an attic into a ritual chamber in which I could carefully control all aspects of the room itself. As noted above this worked well for complex rites designed to bring through certain celestial intelligences. In my case, these were primarily the Egyptian Neteru: the Gods. However, this room was not well suited for the techniques of Traditional Witchcraft. In time I found that, for Willow Path practices, I had to spend a tremendous amount of time in the garden, working with the earth itself as well as the plants we were cultivating there, all in an effort to renew the connection with nature.

In the city I would make a point of going outside under the Moon whenever possible. There I would perform a regular routine of meditative exercises as I blocked the noise of the traffic and attempted to slip into a state of Becoming. Even so, there was always a part of me that remained innately aware in case an intruder happened along.

We were lucky in that we did have an enclosed courtyard that opened to the sky. As such, when working in this space, I didn't have to worry too much about intruders. This made merging easier. Still, the noise from the city, along with the simple fact that my sole connection with nature was a small patch of land only a few square yards made this less than ideal. Too, the light pollution from the street lamps blocked out much of the star filled sky. Obviously, the conditions were less than ideal for a nature based system of the Art.

Further, even in this walled courtyard privacy was not assured. I recall one sunny day when I decided to step out into the courtyard to enjoy the Sun. The fencing was over six feet high so I felt comfortable going out with no clothes on. Within minutes of being out, enjoying my small spot of nature I suddenly heard a man yelling. Looking up there was a construction worker in a 'bucket truck' who had been hoisted up in order to work on the powerlines directly over the courtyard. Apparently he was not pleased at seeing a naked man enjoying his garden. I simply waved and stepped back inside. I can only imagine his reaction if I had been performing a full ritual with cauldron, staff and the other regalia one uses in the Art. The experience taught me that the city really is not conducive to the workings of a Traditional Witch, clothed or not.

The first few times we camped on the mountain, the effect was almost overwhelming. I recall that I felt as if I had been a deprived of water without knowing it, only to be given unlimited access to the rich well of the Annwn itself. It was exhilarating. For days following each visit the richness of images and information that came flooding through was incredible. In the city it would take weeks of ritual work to open the gates enough to have these types of experiences. However, a few days in the mountains, performing simple Craft workings opened my senses to realms I had only glimpsed in the past. In my opinion, the country Witch, nestled far off in the hidden recesses of nature has access to energies and beings that the urban Witch and Hermetic Magician seldom does.

So, as one reading these books, seeking to advance on the Willow Path, you need to find a way to make those connections with nature in your location. Whether this be the forests of New Hampshire, the moors of England, the windswept meadows of Mongolia, the rain forests of Central America, desert canyons or the ocean shores that lap so many coasts; wherever you find yourself, go into the wild places of nature. Take time to drink in the energies there. Open yourself to the spirits. If you do this, access to worlds will open to you beyond anything that can be experienced solely behind secret lodge doors.

The lodge has its place. I have had incredibly powerful spiritual experiences behind those walls. But the temple only fulfills a portion of what the Mysteries have to offer. The rest lays right in front of us if we will only step into nature itself. Having said this I do need to explain that the work of a Hermetic Order that has formed otherworld contacts is exceptionally valuable for many people. I would not be nearly as far along in the Arts without having gone through the training and initiatory practices within such a lodge. Both forms of the Art have their place and complement each other in many ways. Both can learn much from the other.

As noted earlier in my writing, the system which we practice represents a synthesis between these powerful forms of magic. As such, if one is to follow the methods outlined in this series of books, it is absolutely vital that a link with the natural world be formed and maintained. I don't know of any substitute for this.

While I'd like to advocate that every apprentice of the Willow Path move deep into the forests as we have done, I understand that for most this simply isn't possible. We all have bills to pay, children to raise, careers we are following. Further, most don't have the time or desire to begin to

205

learn the skills needed to live in more rural settings. The clear alternative is to begin to seek nature out. Take the time to travel outside of the city. Visit those places where you feel most in awe of nature. I mentioned that here in New England such places as the White Mountains with the forests that stretch across these are perfect for making these connections. The sea coast is also a wonderful place to feel the shear elemental force. If you have sympathetic friends who have access to private property deep in nature perhaps they may allow you to occasionally practice there.

Wherever you find yourself remember that you are part of nature. You are another animal, moving in your environment. The city may cause us to feel separate from nature, but ultimately we are part of all that is.

Having said this, at some point you will want to become aware of the specific energies and spirits that inhabit a particular location. This should be the place you go to renew yourself, making that connection and drawing energy for your Art. In doing so you will find that each location has very specific beings who manifest there. Our ancestors knew this, recognizing different Goddesses, Gods, nymphs and otherworld folk tied to locations. Immediately such places as the Isle of Man, named after the Celtic God Manannan, as well as the Danube River with its association with the Goddess Danu come to mind. Europe and the British Isles have long traditions recognizing specific places with otherworld beings.

Here in the Americas it can be more difficult to discover these connections. A considerable help to the American Witch is to look to Native American lore surrounding the area. This can yield important information. Too, local folklore often gives clues to the types of otherworld energies or spirits that may be present. However, for me, the greatest method to learn is to spend time in the locale itself. In fact, there is no substitute for this. Wherever you live in the world, you need to take time exploring the locale; 'feeling' the energies, experiencing these. This can't be forced. This is a natural process of gentle unfoldment. Just let it happen. Above all you have to perform ritual in the place.

Sometimes the simplest rituals are the best. This can be as basic as spending time merging with the energies, drawing a basic compass or Roth Fail and appealing to these forces. Offerings of food, wine or physical gifts are an excellent way to open the doors of communication. These should be left at places of power in the locale.

As Gemma Gary points out in her writing, places that represent a transition from one state to another tend to be points of power. So we find that river banks, small ponds, clefts in a large rocks, cliffs and bluffs, the hedge between forest and field, hollow trees, caves, waterfalls, all are excellent places of power where the worlds tend to meet and merge. Here, on this small mountain I have found several such places. When we first were exploring this area we found a clearing at the top of the mountain in which the soil gave way to flat granite bedrock. The feeling there is unmistakable. It was here that we decided to set our permanent outdoor ritual site.

Further down the side of the hill we found a natural game path. Some would call it a faery path. In following this a series of flat granite stones protruded out of the side of the hill forming a natural stairway. This leads to a circular impression in the forest. To one side two large granite stones set upright pointing toward the sky. In front of these a natural bowl can be found in the earth as if ready to collect water. Over time I lined the walls of the bowl with small pieces of white quartz that I founded throughout the property. To the other side a series of large granite slabs lay on the ground. With these I set a small stone offering table. This was the very site that I first encountered the Lady of the Forest at, described earlier in the book.

Further into the forest, at the base of the hill, a simple glen can be found. From this a small water way circles around the hill. Glens have always been seen as gateways between worlds. These can be found in myths and occult lore around the world. This place is no different. The sense of otherworld presence, along with the simple flow of fresh natural energy is palpable.

Yet another source of power that we have found is a very large old Oak tree, standing very tall near the place we built our cabins. This is perhaps the largest tree in this section of the forest. Clearly it had been struck by lightning at some point, as there is a huge gap in the side of the tree, and a portion to the side is dead. Yet the tree stands tall and beautiful, while the gash in its side forms an opening leading deep within. We call her 'Grandmother', with wide legs stretching to either side of the hole; the trunk coming together rising majestically up. Remarkably to either side, the trunk then splits into two massive branches rising high into the sky forming a natural Stang.

There are other places of power as well that I could describe. My point in discussing these here is that similar contacts are present throughout nature. As one following the Willow Path you need to seek these out. For it is through such places that contact with other realms can come through very easily. It is in such places, spending time, doing ritual, leaving simple offerings, and just merging with these forces that you will come to know the primary spirit, Goddess, God or other entities inherent in the locale. It is through such contacts that familiar spirits as discussed in the first book usually make their presence known. And it is through such contacts that the Traditional Witch receives much of her training and power.

In time the connections with these beings grow stronger. Once you have gained their trust and a mutual bond develops between you, natural 'gifts' or items of power will be 'found' in these same locations. Invariably you will find these out in the open, in places you have traversed countless times. Yet somehow, at this moment these items now appear. These can be anything from specific rocks, to bones, a specific plant, the limb of tree lying in the path that is exactly the staff you needed, to herbs, roots, tufts of animal hair, feathers and more. Not long ago a perfectly formed unbroken circlet of birch bark, complete with a beautiful pattern of lichen around this was found in the middle of a much traveled path in the forest. It is the exact size of a woman's bracelet. The Mistress who found this felt it was a gift from the Lady of the Forest. Given the significance of the silver bracelet in some forms of the Art, this seemed to be a very important token between us and the Lady who governs these woods.

To those not involved in the Art these will seem to be coincidental occurrences. However, for the Witch such objects are both gifts and a sign that the bond has been made. Further, these indicate that the spirits of the locale not only accept you, but also want to continue the relationship. Such objects should never be discarded. Rather accept these rare and wonderful items, for their use in ritual can be considerably powerful.

Finally, I want to say that if you are in a situation in which forming this natural link to the land just isn't possible persevere with the practices and exercise as best you can. Ultimately the way will open for you bringing these links into your Art.

Chapter Seventeen

✤ MY VOICE RINGS THROUGH ALL WORLDS ✤

The title of this chapter is taken from a line in an invocation of the Ancient Egyptian Goddess Hwt-Hrw, whom the Greeks later named 'Hathor'. It exemplifies the power and majesty of one the most complex otherworld beings that has made Her presence known. In these books I have talked at length about various forces, beings and intelligences that help to form the fabric of the Art. At this point it is important to continue with a discussion on the basic nature of these beings, how they relate to each other and to the Witch.

In reading through this please realize that this is my understanding of these forces, based on in-depth research into various texts, teachings I have received through initiation, as well as my own personal experience. Having said this, I have little doubt that it is limited in scope. Like all arts and sciences, this view may change as new information and work with these beings continues to unfold. Nevertheless, my intention is to provide a summation and starting point from which the serious student can gain an understanding.

As noted in the first book, most people have a very limited view of reality. Yet for those of the Art we realize that, in essence, all is consciousness. All of nature – everything – is an expression and manifestation of consciousness. Within this consciousness there are 'pools' of identity. The universe, or more accurately, the *universes*,[16] experiences itself in multiple

---

16. Quantum Physics is just beginning to come to conclusions that occultist have held for centuries; that is that there are almost certainly multiple universes.

forms and states of being. Some of these 'pools of identity' are highly complex, being primordial forces in and of themselves. Each of these is unique, sentient beings of an order that is exceptionally difficult for us to understand. So we create myths and symbols that form an analogic language through which these highly complex forces begin to relate to us. Yet, there are other means of communicating with these beings. By changing awareness and altering consciousness, we can move into realms that are closer to the essence of these intelligences. Nevertheless, beings of a primordial level manifest across the span of worlds in a variety of forms.

Some call these beings the 'Mighty Ones' – the Gods of nature. These are deities who, while able to traverse many realms and states of being, manifest in our world as various phenomena in nature itself. We hear them in the wild winds that rush through the trees on a stormy night. We see them in the mysterious glow of the Full Moon, and find them in forests and fields, or the power of the sea. In nature they are all around us, and each is capable of communicating with those of the Art, provided these beings are moved to do so.

As I have mentioned, these are real living beings. While it is certain that humans have dressed these forces up in the images and symbols of their own cultures, it is vitally important that the student understand that these beings are not 'archetypal' constructs or 'personifications' of the human mind. To think of them in such a way is to do them a grave disservice and is, in my opinion, insulting. The student who approaches the Gods under such an assumption will never gain the deeper essence and wisdom that lays at the core of the Art. So it is that the Witch learns how to discern the presence of these beings. As noted, each manifests through different aspects found in nature; this may be as forces found in the seasons, energies inherent in specific places, or as the weather itself. They are also found in plants, minerals, animals and more. All of these express varying aspects and qualities of these Mighty Ones.

Humans, too, can be 'called' to certain beings. Often times this comes through as a natural affinity for some aspect of the Goddess or God involved. It is in this respect that we find different temples in the ancient world dedicated to specific deities. In these cases, people who have a natural resonance with a particular otherworld being come together forming a system of the Art dedicated to that deity.

A similar pattern often forms in Traditional Witchcraft. It is very common for Clans or Covens to have contacts and affinities with specific otherworld beings different from each other. While the overall methods and structure of the Art will remain remarkably consistent, different rituals will take precedence over others, depending on the otherworld beings whom each group has formed contacts with. This doesn't mean that there is necessarily any conflict in the methods, practices or even in the overall structure of traditions. In their most essential form the *techniques* used in magic represent a form of technology, or scientific methodology. If you follow the steps correctly results will follow. This is an Art that is universal and applicable across the spectrum of magical practice.

When these contacts with specific otherworld beings is firmly established there comes a measure of 'hyper-awareness' or otherworld consciousness initiates within the group have access to that is uniquely tied to that being. I have no doubt that many groups do share some of the same otherworld contacts, working with many of the same beings. But this isn't true of all of them. Not every magical Order or Coven is guided by the same intelligences.

This then leads to a common question. Many people new to the Art will ask an elder in the group 'who' they, the apprentice, 'belong to?' Which deity do they have a natural affinity for? No one but the person themself can readily answer such a question. Nor am I convinced that everyone has a single otherworld being whom they are permanently tied to. However, we all have certain qualities and characteristics which tend to fall under the general guidance of certain beings.

In my experience, if one is meant to work with or has a natural affinity for a specific being, that otherworld intelligence will make its presence known in unmistakable ways. This can begin very subtly by finding that one has an interest in a number of mundane activities related to the being. Often times, the being will begin to appear in dreams, in mediation or even in rituals – even rituals which were not originally meant to call this deity. All of these can occur over time. One may find that they are drawn to specific tools associated with the being before knowing that the tool had anything to do with the entity.

One's astrological chart can be an excellent tool for helping to determine what types of beings one may be drawn to as well. Look to planets placed in prominent positions in the horoscope. In particular look to those associated with the ninth, first or fifth houses. Also, twelfth house associations can show links to unfinished ties from previous lives. The date of birth itself can be of interest too. I have often found that a person's birthdate will fall on or very near to dates important to the deity whom one may have an affinity for.

Again, I am not convinced that everyone does have a natural affinity for any one particular otherworld being. Rather, I feel that this is fairly rare. Further, I have seen that overtime, contacts with several different otherworld beings can form.

Always keep in mind that we all have free will. Ultimately, no matter the apparent connection with beings in other realms, each person can chose whether to cultivate the connection or not. The best advice I can give is to let this unfold naturally, overtime. If it is meant to be a lasting relationship, the means will become obvious, allowing this to happen.

I can say that forming such links with otherworld beings, particularly those whom we call the Gods, can be immensely rewarding. Again, quite often different Orders, Covens and Clans will have specific contacts whom they work with. This is normal, natural and healthy, providing that each party to the relationship is treated with respect with no attempt at domination. This includes no attempt by the humans involved to subjugate the entity. Nor should there be an attempt by the otherworld being at controlling the actions of the human members. No matter how much more evolved or powerful said being is, guidance, the recognition of wisdom, love and respect between the being and the Coven should be present. There should never be a sense of blind allegiance or dogma. If one finds that the being involved begins demanding actions that are against one's moral code, cut the ties with this entity quickly and without hesitation.

This is done by removing all symbols, sigils, and rituals associated with the entity from the group's practices. Even then, it is common for some entities to continue to 'haunt' the site where meetings are held, as well as attempt to influence the more psychic members of the Coven. In such cases, a more direct ritualistic approach may be needed to sever the ties. Having said this, generally, if the Coven's intentions are earnest and spiritually motivated, contacts with positive and powerful beings will occur and should be welcomed.

In our attempt to understand the Mighty Ones, the occult principle of resonance needs to be considered. For it is in this context that we recognize certain celestial and planetary spirits. This is an integral part of almost all forms of the Art. The spirits and various intelligences associated celestial bodies are well attested to. To understand this though, keep in mind that these beings are not limited to this one place in the vast universe. Rather, we realize that these beings also express themselves beyond the scope of the physical planets. As such, these same forces find expression in other natural forms. The planets in this one small solar system are simply one of many ways these spirits choose to 'come through' at this time, in this realm.

For example, a deity may manifest through the energy of the Sun and yet also be seen in the hidden spirit of the woodlands. I don't think that it is out of the question to assume that, eventually, we may very well find that this same being is able to manifest as other phenomena in totally different and distant environments beyond our known star system. On the other hand, I am certain that some beings are tied specifically to certain locations. Much depends on the level of complexity and development of the being itself.

There are also specific entities that resonate with the traditional four elements. We looked at some of these in *The Willow Path*. These included a discussion on "the Watchers" or "Guardians". These are a class of being that embrace the qualities and essence of the element with which they resonate best. As such, these Guardians can be called on to bring through those elemental forces in a measured yet powerful manner.

Sybil Leek referred to these as "the Watchers of the Night".[17] This is extremely similar to a title used in Strega, Italian Witchcraft. In this the guardians are often referred to as "the Night Watchmen".[18] Perhaps this is no coincidence given that Ms. Leek received her initiation in the south of France, near Italy. As for the term itself, one can speculate that this may be a reminder of ancient times when sentries for communities kept watch during the night. On an esoteric note, it may also represent those who watch the celestial vault of the night sky.

In all forms of the Art that I am aware of, the four directions correspond to the corners of the Universe and with it the four elements. The assignment of each particular element to specific directions often varies from culture to culture, or between magical systems. Nevertheless, this pattern itself is virtually identical in the vast majority of esoteric disciplines.

---

17. Leek, Sybil. *Driving Out the Devils*, p.236.
18. Howard, Michael. Liber Nox: *A Traditional Witch's Gramarye*, p.51.

Within the elements themselves there also exist primal energies that possess very focused yet, somewhat limited levels of consciousness. Different from the Watchers, these are the traditional *elementals* of medieval magical grimoires. Folklore states that these tend to manifest in the forms of specific creatures: fire as salamanders, water as nymphs, air as sylphs and earth as gnomes.

In practice, I personally have not had these beings appear in these forms. Rather, in going through the ritual evocations, I have always had these beings come as intense sparks, or flecks of energy rushing through the portal between worlds. The colors vary depending on the element, yet the impression I receive has always been of a rush of flickering energy that coalesces at the quarter and triangle that they are called to.

I have to say that the first time I attempted an elemental evocation, while I was impressed by the intensity of the energy and light that formed, I was disappointed. I had fully expected to see a manifestation of the traditional elemental beings form in front of me. Obviously, though, the ritual was a success. Further, the fact that a different phenomenon from that which I had expected occurred is evidence that I hadn't imaged the experience or 'made it up' from preconceived expectations.[19]

The elementals have a rudimentary intelligence. When evoked they need to be given very specific goals and tasks. Their time on our plane must also be clearly defined by the Magician who should set specific details for when the elemental is to return to the place of working. Upon its return it is thanked for its help and is sent back to the element from which it came.

---

19. At the time I was training in an Ogdoadic Hermetic Order. I related my disappointment to the Grand Master of the group. He congratulated me on my success, stating that this was exactly how the elementals usually do manifest. To say the least I was stunned, yet pleasantly elated that the phenomena I experienced was that which should have occurred.

As noted, elementals are not the same as the Watchers. While elementals are extensions of the actual element from which they are summoned, the Watchers are sentient beings of a complex order which resonate with the element associated with them. As such, the Watchers govern over elemental forces. It is for this reason that in a formal evocation the Watcher's name, or 'word of power', is used to control the corresponding elemental.

Some groups will work only with the elementals themselves, calling these to the quarters at each setting of the circle, rather than going through the Watchers. I have practiced with this technique. The effect is completely different in feel and intent. When using this technique there is a rush of energy that floods the space, yet control of this can be challenging. Further, in my experience, these energies don't serve to protect the space, nor do they regulate the flow of energy in the way the Watchers do. Rather, there is an overwhelming sense of energy flowing into the Roth Fail at each point. And with this, each form of energy is very different, opening the space to multiple realms at once.

The effect can be very exhilarating. Yet, unless the Witch is very talented, these energies either tend to cancel each other out or flood the space in such a way as to not be usable toward any one specific goal. It is for this reason that we are very careful to call on the Watchers themselves, with the appropriate calls and Words of Power.

A word of advice when working with either the Watchers or the elementals. Always have the Roth Fail set properly before beginning the evocations. Without this the effects can be quite alarming. I recall a time early in my training when I had arrived home late from a long day at work. I had planned to perform a solitary ritual.

The circle was marked clearly on the floor. I had placed lit taper candles at each of the quadrants. I began the invocations of the Watchers. Facing south I called upon the elemental forces of fire. As the words were said the south candle flared up, then fell out of the holder. The flame from the candle began burning on its side threatening to catch the carpet itself on fire. Quickly I snuffed out the flames. It was then that I realized, in my tired state of mind, I had failed to trace the circle with the proper tools. By not doing so I had left the working space open to the elemental forces. Essentially I had created an imbalance in this space between worlds. I was lucky that I hadn't burned the place down. I stopped the ritual and cleaned up the mess. I took a moment to recompose myself, and then started over, carefully following all of the steps the ritual called for.

Within different paths of the Art, inevitably one will also find that there are also those beings whom we have come to term "the elders" – spirits who act specifically as teachers and guides in the particular tradition involved. Essentially they are older spirits who are in many ways the repository of knowledge and wisdom for the tradition itself. Some Magicians believe that these are actual ancestors who have reached a level where incarnation is no longer needed. Rather, they now work toward keeping the ancient practices alive and available for those who seek them. Other Magicians feel that these beings aren't discarnate humans at all. Rather they are entities of a more complex level who have taken an active interest in presenting certain techniques and teachings to those who are sincerely drawn to the path that the being represents.

I personally think that both are correct; some are elder human ancestors or adepts, while others comprise a richer order of being beyond that of human level. In either case, these beings are frequently called on to aid the Witch in her knowledge as well as in casting of spells. For example, in our Samhain ritual we specifically open a portal through which such spirits of the tradition are encouraged to come.

In addition to these contacts, it needs to be recognized that there are great spirits – intelligences of varying powers and abilities. These are not necessarily Gods in the sense of being primordial forces. Rather, they exist as inhabitants of specific otherworlds and realms. Some of these spirits can move through the different worlds and are able to influence matters in each. However, generally, they seldom venture far from their own dimension.

Some in the Art refer to these types of beings as demons or angels. I personally do not like either of these labels. The beings I am referring to represent a class of entities that function primarily in dimensions very different from ours, each with a set of values that we as humans may find very difficult to relate to. Still, these beings can be an important part of the Magical Arts. This is especially so in Goetic practices where they are called on to perform specific tasks for the Magician or Witch.

It is in this regard that the ritual act of evocation helps to create a space that allows the spirit to temporarily manifest in our realm. This is done through the proper use of color, timing, symbols, and incense, all of which resonate with the spirit creating an environment that they can function in more easily while on our 'plane'.

As for who these various spirits are, there are literally thousands that can be called. Grimoires from across history give long registers of spirits, including their names, sigils and characteristics. It is in this tradition that Goetic magic has its strength. Undoubtedly there are many other powerful spirits that have never been documented in any Magician's works.

An interesting aspect of Goetic magic is that many of the spirits listed answer to other beings who are said to govern them. In order to gain the favor of these lesser spirits it is often necessary to use the name of the governing spirit in order to control them. Similar concepts are found in Ancient Egyptian teachings. For example, texts show that the Goddess Sekhmet has a number of spirits who are in Her following and who answer to Her. The God Heru, whom the Greeks later called 'Horus', also has a similar following of otherworld beings. This doesn't necessarily mean that *all* spirits fall under the domain of another. There are many examples in magical lore and in ancient texts which suggest that at least some spirits act entirely independently.

Ancient teachings also speak of spirits that function as guardians at the thresholds between different realms. This is seen most dramatically in the underworld texts of the Sun God Ra as He transitions through the different hours of the night. In ritual I have encountered similar beings. The spirit guarding the path during my experience with the Lady in the forest is one such being.

As I have already discussed, there are also the many different types of spirits that exist in the hidden recesses of nature. Legends of brownies, dwarves, elves, water nymphs, fauns, trolls, djinn and many more all have their origin in this class of being. For many in the Art much of their practice involves working with these types of beings. As already shown, our system is no exception. Living in the mountains and forests of New England, it was inevitable that some aspects of our otherworld contacts would be with these wonderful entities.

Folk magic across Europe discusses the ways that many of the spirits found in nature become attached to families and homes. It is very common among those of the Art to have 'house' spirits. These generally help to protect the home from outside forces, particularly occult influences that may be directed against the family or Witch. They also help to protect the home from theft, fire and poverty. In many legends these beings are described as helping to bring prosperity and happiness to the home.

When they are attracted to a home, generally they are most strongly drawn to the hearth. As such, Witches will set food out near the fireplace for them. Some in the Art set up actual small dolls meant to give the spirit a form in which to reside. No matter how one choses to acknowledge them, be aware that nature spirits will be attracted to your practice. Speak to them and show them respect. A simple offering near the hearth is an excellent way of creating a link and opening a friendship that can be very rewarding. Traditionally this may be a small dish of milk as well as sweet breads. Having said that, you will soon learn what the spirit likes and dislikes.

There is also the very real class of spirits who are people who have passed on yet maintain a level of contact with the living during their time between incarnations. Frequently these spirits can be called on to help the living. In many Shamanic traditions these are referred to as the ancestors. Ancient Egypt had a rich culture and system of magic surrounding maintaining the links between the living and those who had passed on. These are different from the elders described earlier in that they are not, necessarily tied to the magical tradition of the Witch. Rather, these are simply spirits of the dead coming through to make their presence known.

I want to stress that extreme care needs to be taken when working with the departed. For just as one needs to use discretion when confiding in or working with living people, the same applies when approaching the dead. Just because a person has passed on doesn't necessarily change their motives. Having said that, there are times when specific spirits of deceased humans can be very helpful. As always, good judgement and common sense will be your best aid.

As can be seen, in Shamanic practices, Witchcraft or otherwise, partnership with otherworld entities is a vital part of these practices. Some of these beings are more accessible and more easily communicated with than others. Sybil Leek makes this quite clear in stating that within Witchcraft there are specific rituals, "invocations and incantations" used to communicate with these beings.[20]

For us, in our practice, we use a variety of techniques. The use of the bullroar or windroar in rituals the world over is meant to call the spirits to the working area. I also recommend that students create a simple incantation to be recited at the beginning of any working to invite positive entities to join in with the rite. In using this, I often suggest

---

20. Leek, Sybil. *The Complete Art of Witchcraft*, p.155.

that the area be secured with protections in place before
hand so that only those beings whom you wish to aid can do
so. As such, the bullroarer is used to get entities attention,
then the Roth Fail is set. After this the personal spirit
incantation is recited. The following is one adapted from
that which I use:

> "Three worlds encircle the one,
> Annwn, Abred and fair Gwynfyd.
> The Lady calls from Caer Wydr,
> Her cauldron deep, pool clear.
> I call to the sky, to fire bright,
> I call to the land and waters deep.
> Comes ancient ones.
> Come and be here!
> Come good spirits with your powers near!
> Between the horns lays the path we keep.
> I call to you, come ancient ones,
> Join with us this night!
> Bandia (pronounced BAHN-JEE-uh)!"

This simple invocation carries within it images and words
meant to draw entities of a positive nature to the place of
working. In particular, it is meant to attract those beings
who are specifically aligned with the form of the Art which
we practice. In this way it will help form the other world
'contacts' with the elders of this system. Key phrases include
the intoning of the names of the four major realms of the
Art. The four elements are a central part of this chant.

In particular though, the phrase "Between the horns lays
the path we keep" is important. This exact phrase is meant to
be a formula specifically aligning the Witch with the forces
we use. If you use this, this term is not be altered in any way.
For it acts as a 'bridge' or 'portal' both opening the inner
abilities of the Witch to this system, and in bringing the
otherworld beings linked to this system through. It would
be better not to use the term at all than to alter it in any way.

The last word in the incantation is a Gaelic term meaning *Goddess*. It is used here as a Word of Power and is meant to align this invitation of the spirits with the Mistress of the Path we follow.

Again, this is only an example. Feel free to use this, or create your own. However, if you do create your own, take your time to think of the meaning of each word. In ritual words are vehicles through which currents of power can be directed. Each phrase can have far reaching effects, some of which may be unintentional. Nevertheless, a personal invocation created by the Witch herself can have tremendous power if for no other reason than the fact that it comes from deep with her.

Chapter Eighteen

❖ SILVER CIRCLE ❖

Much of this book has been focused on practical application, as well as understanding, of the different types of beings that those of the Art work with. This is as it should be, for the Art is and always has been used to assist people through the challenges of life. As far back as Ancient Egypt, magic was seen as the means by which one could help avert, or at least soften, the blows that life throws at us. Yet there is another side to the Art that few traditional crafters discuss: enhancing the spiritual awareness and development of the individual.

I can almost see a number of people rolling their eyes as they prepare to close this book, feeling that 'spirituality' has no place in Witchcraft or practical Magical Arts. However, before you do, keep in mind that Traditional Witches define spirituality in very different terms than most people in our society do. As we've seen, the Witch's paradigm of reality is unique, having little or no resemblance to that which has been propagated by the Abrahamic systems. Yet, because western culture is so imbued with the views driven by Abrahamic religious dogmas, we need to draw a clear distinction between these *assumed* meanings and those that the Witch actually embraces.

Remember, Traditional Witchcraft has its roots in ancient shamanic and animistic teachings. For us all of nature is alive and vibrant, filled with spirit. Spirit isn't something separate from the material world. As such, we don't ignore or despise the material realm as somehow less than spiritual or, as some Abrahamic sects believe, that the material realm is evil.

For the Witch there is no sin, no sense that we need to abandon natural desires or pleasures. For us life is a wonderful adventure to be enjoyed and experienced. Further, to the Witch there is no belief that some worlds and realms are somehow *more* divine than others. Certainly, there are realms in which beings of a more complex nature can function and manifest in more easily. However, this doesn't mean that these are necessarily better, just different. Thus, the many legends surrounding utopian realms throughout Pagan lore exemplify these other worlds but don't, to my knowledge, imply that they are more divine. As one Traditional Witch had written "utopia is now".[21] No matter what realm we may be functioning in we create our own opportunities and challenges through the effects of our thoughts and actions.

This lack of belief in 'sin' doesn't mean that those of the Art lack morals or ethics. On the contrary, both Julie and Sybil Leek stressed a strong understanding of certain modes of conduct that are directly related to natural principles. I outlined these in the chapter entitled *Counsels of the Wise* in *The Willow Path*. As such, I won't spend any more time on these here, as what I wish to present has little to do with ethics at all.

For the Witch spirituality is one's ability to enter into a state of awareness in which the deeper essence of nature is present, vivid and accessible. Beyond what we experience with our five senses, there is a richer reality alive in everything that is. For the Witch spirituality is the experiencing of the deeper essence inherent in all, transcending the limitations placed on us by our normal physical senses.

This comes in those moments when the connection to all that is becomes so tangible that this awareness expresses itself as reality. It isn't a 'belief' or a conclusion drawn through deduction. Rather, in those moments when this connection is made, the certainty of this transcendent essence is inescapable. There are no words that I can write that can clearly describe this state of being. Because

---

21. Leek, Sybil. *The Complete Art of Witchcraft*, 1970

of this, those of the Art have long used myths, symbols, song, incantation and ritual to try to capture this essence in terms that others can begin to glimpse. In all cases, this awareness begins in the simple technique of *Becoming* or *Merging*, described earlier. Whether the awareness comes spontaneously or through ritual it always starts the same. One of the most profound experiences of my life was quite spontaneous, yet the memory of the event has remained with me through these many years.

It was a still summer evening, the air mild and comforting to the skin, as I sat alone cross-legged on the front lawn of our home. Facing east, I was gazing up at the night sky as the Full Moon rose above the horizon. There I sat in quiet contemplation, relaxed and peaceful. The sky was clear and full of stars while the soft silver-white light of the Moon shone down on me, its iridescent glow surrounding me, mingling with the shadows of the trees and shrubs that lined the edges of the lawn. I was just a child, only thirteen years old, a boy entering adolescence, living in the Midwest of the United States. That evening though, sitting quietly, alone, my life would change: a change that would propel me into a journey that would affect all that would happen from that time on.

As I sat there, I slowly became aware of a presence. The very real sense of a woman grew more and more. At first this seemed to be coming from the Moon itself, yet it also seemed to be coming from the Earth. It wasn't that I could see her. There wasn't any form or apparition that appeared. Rather, there was the very real sense of this female presence. It was almost like those occasions when you know someone has entered a room before you turn to greet them. Yet it was much more powerful. This feeling was there, all around me.

All of nature, including myself, was engulfed in the essence of this beautiful feminine presence. With this came the recognition that I knew this being, I knew this intelligence! At the time I didn't know how I knew Her. Yet I did. It seemed as if She had always been present, somewhere in the background.

Time itself appeared to stop. For there, in that moment, I became aware of an otherworld being who was in Herself timeless and beyond comprehension, yet She was there, fully aware, accessible, and real, reaching out to me! I use the word 'otherworld' to describe Her, and yet there was no doubt that She was both of this world and yet transcends this realm in so many ways.

Further, this was no 'archetypal' subconscious imagining of an adolescent boy. She was real, as real as you or I. There was the distinct recognition that She had Her own identity and sense of self. Yet, without a doubt She was also the essence of nature. At least nature as it was present in that moment, under the Moon, sitting on the green Earth, with the star filled sky overhead. Looking back now, I can't think of a more invocative scene in which the Great Queen would appear.

Words really can't express the intense spiritual nature of this experience; suffice it to say that nothing up to that point in my life prepared me for this. The experience under the Full Moon was completely new and quite surprising to me. In this moment there were no sudden revelations or inspirational messages that came from Her. Rather, it was simply a sense of awareness, of knowing and experiencing Her as nature itself. And with this there was an exchange, a type of conversation on a very deep, non-vocal level. I really am not sure how to express the deep, peaceful and yet ecstatic feeling that filled me throughout the experience.

How long the episode lasted I really can't say. However, as I returned to my bedroom, I realized that something had changed in me. For now I knew that there was much more to life than we normally accept. I had come into contact with an otherworld intelligence, a spiritual being beyond anything I could have imagined. I no longer depended on 'faith' that such a reality 'may' exist. I now knew. A spiritual force, a being who was distinctly feminine and quite familiar to me made Herself known in a very real way and I would never be the same.

For many years I kept this secret, only rarely discussing the incident with a few trusted associates. Years later Grandma Julie had been one of these. That experience, the first of many such encounters, stayed with me. This memory has remained as a marker, a coming of age of sorts, which punctuated my journey into esoteric and spiritual matters. More importantly though, it remains as a reminder of the richer reality that exists in nature, guiding me as I continue to learn and grow.

When I told Julie about the experience she took it as a matter of fact. She explained that in essence, when this occurred, the time was ripe for such an experience. She felt that clearly there I had a connection in past lives to the Art. She explained that also, as I was just entering puberty at the time, my psychic senses were likely to have been more acute. Sitting under the Full Moon, these senses budding into life, I was ready to perceive energies and beings easily. The circumstances were well set for the Lady, the 'Witch Queen' as some traditionalists call Her, to make Her presence known.

I wanted to give this account in order to show how spontaneous and natural these events can be. I think that experiences such as these are far more common than most people will admit.[22] While the feelings that occur

---

22. In fact these experiences are fairly common. In his book *Greening the Paranormal: Exploring the Ecology of Extraordinary Experience* editor Dr. Jack Hunter documents a number of incidents in which normal people describe encounters in which they experience very similar events as that which I am discussing. One interesting case noted is that of a solider during World War I who recounted an evening in the forest in which "the moon, when I looked up at it, seemed to have become personalized and observant, as if it were aware of my presence". The account goes on in considerable length discussing the consciousness he felt in all of nature during that moment. This is just one such case noted in the book which speaks to the inherent spiritual current that flows through nature.

during such events are very real, they are so subtle and so different from anything our materialistic society has prepared us for that we have nothing to compare them to. Afterward, when recounting the event, most other people simply won't believe you. They may think you are looking for attention, or worse yet, suggest that it was a 'hallucination'. In my situation I was simply a pre-pubescent boy who happened to be in the right place, at the right time. In that moment the Queen found a way to let me know that She was there. Other than this, there was nothing 'special' about me per se.

In the Art the Witch learns to open herself to such experiences. She trains to become aware. When it happens, for her, there is no doubt of their reality. This is the spirituality of the Witch. There isn't any sense of being unique. Rather, the Witch has simply become aware. And with that awareness these wonderful beings, whom we can only refer to as Gods, make their presence known.

Almost all aspects of the training that occurs in the Art, whether it be spell casting or the ability to open oneself to these powerful beings, are essentially the same. That is, the training involves the cultivation of certain mental functions, while learning to relax and open one's awareness. Yet the *techniques and rituals* involved in the training vary greatly.

Perhaps the most common method for opening awareness is simply to go out into nature and quietly allow oneself to merge with the forces within the land. As mentioned, the simple act of *becoming* is the first step in the process. In those times, deep in nature, listen with your intuition and, over time, if so inclined the forces will come. These may be quite subtle at first, yet you will feel them.

When this begins to happen, the first few moments are critical in the process. For many people, in their sudden realization that something more is taking place, they become excited. Unfortunately, in many cases this excitement tends to close the connection, jolting one's state of mind back to mundane awareness quickly.

Rather, it is best to just relax and let the event unfold, keeping the quiet openness needed for the experience. If you can, maintain this calm state of mind as long as possible. In doing so your perception of the presence of otherworld beings will grow, becoming unmistakable.

In my experience, on those occasions when the presence of the Lady comes, this is frequently accompanied by a powerful sense of inner calm, connection and quiet ecstasy. Yet for me, when occasions occur in which other beings have come forward (other than the Lady), there is still as sense of calm and a distinct awareness of their presence. However, the deep seated spontaneous sense of 'spiritual' connection and 'ecstasy' seldom accompanies their appearance. I am not sure why there is such a difference. It may be because of my own connection with Her reaching across several lives.

Please don't misunderstand this last statement. I am not implying that contact with other beings is any less meaningful. I have had many experiences involving complex beings who have long been described as Gods, all of which have been exceptionally moving. Rather, my own experience with the Lady appears to be on a different level evoking emotions that reach very deep within. Your experiences may be different.

I can say that once an awareness of the being's presence (no matter which being this may be) has been established, it then becomes easier to communicate directly. This can be quite in-depth. Again, the critical point occurs when you first begin to feel the presence emerge. When this happens don't force it. Don't get too excited. Just let it unfold.

It is important to know that this same awareness can also be achieved through ritual. In the Art as we practice it, we use a ritual technique that is strongly tied to the symbolism surrounding Caer Wydyr, or the Castle of Glass. As the reader may recall from *The Willow Path*, Caer Wydyr is a Gaelic name for the realm which, legend explains, contains the Cauldron of Inspiration and Rejuvenation. Undoubtedly this was the forerunner for the legends surrounding the Arthurian quest for the Grail. In Europe similar legends exist surrounding the Crystal Mountain or Mountain of Glass, except in these the solar hero seeks to climb the mountain to find the beautiful Goddess as his lover.

In each of these, the person seeking to reach the center of the Castle, or the top of the mountain, must first undergo a series of challenges, and with these, transformations. Often these include facing different otherworld beings. These could be anything from ogres and sorcerers, to swan maidens and spirits of the dead. In the course of the hero's journey he was often depicted as using bones and animal claws, thrusting these into the glass using these as a ladder to climb the mountain.[23]

The similarity of symbolism between these legends is clear, with the overall meaning being essentially the same. In these the divine feminine is represented either by the Cauldron, Grail or by an actual woman. Crystal and glass have long had occult meaning. As discussed elsewhere in the Geassa books, natural crystal is known to be a conductor of power, storing, transferring and amplifying the energy used in magic. Its association with the Moon, and ability to act as a medium opening pathways between worlds is well documented in esoteric literature.

Glass, too, has long been held to have some of these properties. In particular it has been regarded as having the ability to hold psychic images and impressions. The making of glass was considered an arcane art, with its roots reaching back to Ancient Egypt and possibly before. Glass often adorned the coffins of Egyptian kings.

I find it interesting that some authorities feel that Amber was the original substance inspiring the esoteric understanding of the Mountain of Glass. They cite that the myths surrounding this mountain appear to have been most prevalent along the routes through Europe in

---

23. Funk & Wagnall's *Standard Dictionary of Folklore, Mythology and Legend*, p.456.

which Amber was traded. Thus, Amber itself may have been seen as physical pieces of the Glass Mountain. The word 'glass' originally had meant 'resin' or 'Amber'.[24] In traditional Witchcraft Amber is used in amulets to hold energy that is used in ritual later. As we saw in *The Willow Path* frequently the Mistress will wear an Amber necklace representing her connection to otherworld forces and reinforce her connection with the divine feminine residing in the Crystal Mountain.

The hero's use of bones and animal claws to climb the mountain indicates the otherworld nature of the mountain itself. These substances, too, harken to the rich tradition of animistic totems and use of animal spirit familiars in the quest for spiritual understanding. Both figure highly in traditional rural practices of the Art.

The themes found in these myths are extremely reminiscent of the challenges that the Egyptian Sun God Ra undergoes in his nightly journey through the underworld. Following Sunset, with each hour, he faces different guardians of the various realms. Meeting these trials he eventually reaches the heart of the underworld, the isle in the lake where he is transformed through the power of the divine feminine. I won't go into the details here as we have discussed this in other areas of these books. Nevertheless, the similarity is very obvious.

Traditional Witches in Wales have long used the legends surrounding the Goddess Arianrhod as well as the sorceress turned Goddess, Cerridwen, in their techniques for ritually reaching the awareness I have been discussing. As such, I feel it is important to present some of the key elements of these here.

While both stories are filled with drama and express very human characteristics, many esoteric images and procedures are clearly represented in highly symbolic form.

---

24. Funk & Wagnall's *Standard Dictionary of Folklore, Mythology and Legend*, p.42.

Perhaps more importantly though, the pattern in which these elements are presented gives an overview of the way each of the elements of the Art are usually introduced to the new initiate.

In *The Willow Path* I discussed some the more important aspects of the legend surrounding Cerridwen. Of particular interest is the account of shape-shifting as the Goddess chases the attendant. In the legend the attendant transforms into a hare, to which Cerridwen changes into a hound in order to pursue him. The attendant then changes into a trout, so the Goddess becomes an Otter. Finally the attendant becomes into a kernel of grain. Cerridwen changes into a hen who then eats the grain, only to give birth to him later. This symbolism is complex and important, yet, the esoteric meaning hidden within this is unmistakable.

While there isn't room here to present all of the details surrounding the legends of the Goddess Arianrhod, I would like to mention certain aspects that are very important. Arianrhod is a celestial Goddess often linked to the weaving of fate. Legend explains that She has a physical castle often believed to exist under the sea off the cost of Wales. She also has a celestial home. This castle is equated with the star constellation of the Corona Borealis also known as the 'northern crown'. In legend this is frequently called Caer Arianrhod. Located near the Big Dipper, it is visible in the northern hemisphere.

Perhaps it may be important to recount as well that the Greeks saw this same constellation as being linked to their Goddess Ariadne, a deity tied to weaving and to mazes. As we saw in *The Willow Path*, Her name turns up in the prophecies of Merlin in twelfth century Europe and may have distinct ties to Arianrhod. In similar fashion, it can be argued that Ariadne may have been the root deity called upon later by Italian Witches as Aradia, daughter of the Moon Goddess Diana. As a unique 'coincidence' not only is Arianrhod associated with the star constellation of the northern crown, her name means "Silver Circle" and may be a reference to the Moon itself. While far from conclusive, it is interesting that the overall character of these three otherworld beings are linked in these ways.

One of the key legends of Arianrhod, as described in the Mabinogion, gives clear reference to sexuality in several places. Of particular importance is the scene in which the Goddess is asked to 'step over a wand' to show that she was is maiden. It is important to note that a maiden wasn't necessarily considered to be a virgin in Celtic culture. Rather, a maiden was one who had not given birth. What is interesting is that the act of stepping over the wand is often seen as a reference to ritual intercourse.[25] The connection between the Besom, Wand and Staff in this context was discussed at length in *The Willow Path*.

Other parts of the legend give further reference to sexuality in a possible ritual setting as well. These can be found in the opening of the legend in which the God Math insists that He must have His feet placed in the lap of maiden when He is resting and not in battle. Later in the myth, Arianrhod is fitted for shoes. Feet and shoes have long been seen as analogous to the sexual act itself. This belief was so prevalent that for centuries shoes have been placed inside walls, foundations and left on ledges especially built into chimneys of homes to bring luck, prosperity, good fortune and fertility. These have been found in older homes throughout Europe, the British Isles, Colonial American buildings and even in older homes in Australia.

From the original act of stepping over the wand, Arianrhod produced two sons. Both are clearly otherworldly beings. The first, named Dylan, is a creature of the sea returning to that element almost immediately. The second has no name. Arianrhod's brother, who is also a Druid, takes the boy away and raises Him. Later in the story He returns with the child seeking audience with the Goddess. Her brother is welcomed, but She does not recognize the child.

---

25. Illes, Judika. *Encyclopedia of Witchcraft*, p.686.

Without a doubt the legend is a clear reference to the motifs contained in initiation. Her brother is an equal to the Goddess, an initiate and thus welcomed into the circle of Caer Arianrhod. In the legend He is clearly acting in the role of sponsor, raising and training the seeker, Her son. Before the seeker can be admitted He must pass three tests, or Geassas, that the Goddess places on Him. The first Geassa is that only She can give Him a name. The second is that only She can give Him weapons; the tools of the Art. Lastly, She places a Geassa that He shall have no human wife.

Each step within the legend represents specific ritual acts in the course of initiation. Because of oaths taken I can't go into detail on the specifics of the actual ritual, however, each of these Geassas figure into the rite itself. It is through the meeting of certain challenges that these three gifts are bestowed in the initiation rite. And as a result the seeker is admitted into the group. When looked at this through the lens of this legend, the Castle of Arianrhod is the equivalent of the Coven, and having met the challenges and received the gifts the candidate is admitted as an initiate into the Mysteries of the Queen – the marriage to the non-human woman.

It should be noted that the Mabinogion goes on to describe the eventual death of the Arianrhod's son. The means by which this occurs is interesting. Again, filled with all too human emotion, frailty and drama (perhaps to keep the story entertaining for the non-initiate), this part of the legend harkens to the many accounts of the divine victim, the death of the king to rejuvenate the land. This same motif can be found in the development and transformation of the initiate in the Art today. Particularly so for male members of the Art. Normally this will occur sometime between seven to nine years after their entrance into group. While these are *not* an actual physical death of the person, the event nonetheless is highly transformative and life altering. It represents a key moment in the initiate's development. When this occurs it opens him to new realms and possibilities. In my opinion it is significant that in the legend, upon His death, Arianrhod's son transforms into an eagle, the very symbol of spiritual transformation in so many cultures. Much more could be written on this subject, particularly the role of female initiates in this process. Having said this, I really can't go into more detail here because of the nature of the subject. However, I feel enough has been presented to show the rich, though highly symbolic wisdom hidden in this and other legends.

The reason I have presented this information here is because these myths are an important part of a traditional formula used for entering states of awareness in which communion with more complex intelligences and otherworld beings becomes possible. Certain traditional Witches refer to this as "Entering the Castle of Arianrhod".[26]

This can be done in a number of ways. Each involves both the use of ritual acts and active visualization on the part of the individuals involved. The following is a method which we call *The Castle and the Cauldron*. While this is very simplistic in form, it can be used as a foundation on which the student or a group can begin to develop this state of awareness.

The Castle and the Cauldron

Ideally this should take place on a clear night, when the Moon is full, and if possible outdoors. In such case, you may want to have a fire set in the center of the Roth Fail. Over the fire a cauldron can be suspended.

For this it is advantageous to brew an herbal potion that is meant to represent that which Cerridwen Herself had made. The actual recipe for Cerridwen's potion is the stuff of legend, and while different ingredients are named in different versions of the myth, I don't have the expertise

---

26. See William Gray's *Western Inner Workings* for his experience with Traditional Witches and a discussion on "Entering the Castle of Arianrhod". Beyond this book, letters that were made public show that Mr. Grey was very familiar with the Cochrane system of Traditional Witchcraft.

to attempt to replicate it here. As an alternative one could easily brew a simple infusion of spring water and Vervain. This tea is often used by traditional Witches to help with the sight.[27] This could be done beforehand and then placed in the cauldron to be kept warm. Or, one could easily let this brew in the cauldron during the ritual itself.

The Roth Fail should be prepared and ritually hallowed by the Mistress and Master before the other members arrive. For this the Sang is placed in the north with a lit candle placed between its horns. On the shaft beneath the horns a wreath of greenery and fresh red and white flowers should be hung. These are meant to represent the Red and White Dragons, the complementary opposites found in all of nature.

After the circle is prepared, the Mistress and Master will welcome the spirits of the land and those tied to the tradition. If specific deities are normally called as part of the Coven's working, this is done with great care now as well. Upon finishing, both the Mistress and Master will want to take a moment and envision the star filled sky, the Moon, as well as the northern crown of the constellation of Arianrhod. It is helpful to then allow this to merge with that of a crystal mountain rising into the stars atop of which rests a castle or tower shining like glass, almost as if glowing from the hearth fires within that heat the silver cauldron of the Great Queen. The crown of the tower reaches deep into the stars themselves which appear to swirl slowly in a steady labyrinth against the dark azure night sky.

This shouldn't be forced. Rather, the two will gently relax and let the images form. If desired, it is common in some occult groups to actually verbalize the description of the image so that both the Mistress and Master bring the visualization into actuality through incantation. Perhaps the following may be helpful:

27, Pearson, Nigel. *Treading the Mill: Workings in Traditional Witchcraft*, 2016.

"In Moon and Stars the Lady's Crown is found
Deep in azure keep.
For the tower of glass reaches into the night,
Atop lucent crystal's rugged peak.
It is from this realm that the Lady calls,
Her voice ringing through all worlds.
While nine ladies breathe life into the flames,
And the Cauldron simmers, the potion swirls.
Apple isle and limpid mountain, rising from the lake,
The castle walls of glass aglow,
Amber fires burning bright.
We tread the mill and climb the heights,
Through hollow and cliff, past each spirit plight.
For the wheel weaves and the thread spins.
Between the Horns, Lays the path we keep.
The Lady calls from Caer Wydyr
Her song of beauty we now hear.
For Crown and Cauldron are what we seek,
Through the maze to the Lady's keep!"

Enough has been said about imagination that the reader should now understand that the simple act of employing the creative imagination in a disciplined manner forms the matrix through which forces in different realms can come through and begin to manifest. Further, these images represent the symbolic language we in this realm use to relate to, or reach out to, these otherworld energies.

At this point it is often helpful to intone the note of 'high C', corresponding to the realm of Caer Wydyr. In doing this the note needs to come from to deep inside, felt as a vibration that moves through the entire being of each of them. It takes practice to develop the technique, however, it has proven to be very effective. When finished, the Master 'cuts' an opening in the northeast quarter of the Roth Fail and signals the Coven to come forward.

The rest of the Coven should have been waiting at a considerable distance. Either the Trulliad, in the role of the Summoner, or the Llawforwyn as Maiden will then lead the group to the ritual site. As the Mistress and Master had done, now each participant needs to envision themselves following a path through a maze as they climb the crystal mountain of legend. The greater each person can envision this, the stronger the effect will be for all. Thus, it is important that, as one walks to the Roth Fail, one sees in their mind's eye the labyrinth path through the forests that leads upward along the cliffs and ravines of the mountain. See the star filled sky overhead, as the Moon shines down lighting the path. Imagine the rocks of the mountain as being of solid quartz. This walk should be an active meditation in which one immerses oneself in the invocative experience of these images. As before the incantation noted above may be recited by the group as they approach the circle.

At the Roth Fail each member enters into the circle through the door left open in the northeast quarter. Once inside the Master will seal the circle. The Mistress then addresses the gathering:

"Merry meet under Moon and Stars,
For tonight we seek entrance to Caer Wydyr
To drink from the Sliver Cauldron."

Beginning in the north, the Mistress begins to walk slowly in a tuathal direction. Each member in turn follows, with the Master at the rear. In doing so, each should envision the ancient triple Celtic maze:[28]

---

28. While this symbol has been used both in Celtic Christian beliefs, as well as by neo-pagan groups, in fact it is very ancient, dating well before the current era. Clear examples of this can be found inside the prehistoric site of Newgrange, Ireland. I find that in practice it is a very potent talismanic image related directly to some of the richest understandings of Celtic Witchcraft.

This should be 'seen' as a brilliant electric blue hovering over the cauldron. As the group starts to circle the Mistress begins the following incantation as the rest of the group joins in:

"By hare and hound
By fish and otter,
By grain that falls for the hen to devour.
With dragons red and white,
We climb the mountain in the night!
Three times three the mountain we climb,
Three times time three the maze unwinds,
For the Lady calls from the Northern Crown,
In Caer Wydyr Silver Circle is found!"

In doing this, each person has their body facing forward, and yet they should have their heads turned toward the cauldron, as they continue to envision the triple maze. There is no need to move quickly. You aren't trying to create a sense of dizziness. While part of the intent is to direct energy through the talismanic image of the spiral into the potion, at the same time this process is meant to alter one's awareness, moving into the state of mind in which the Castle of Arianrhod can be experienced. As such, this circling can continue for some time, and with it the chant can be repeated for as long as necessary. Once the full chant has been repeated, it may be easier to continue with the last two lines:

"The Lady calls from the Northern Crown,
In Caer Wydyr Silver Circle is found!"

In practice it is best to simply 'let go' and move with the chant while seeing the triple maze form over the cauldron. There may be a tendency for some to becoming louder and chant faster as these last two lines are repeated. Remember though that the object isn't to raise energy. Rather one is seeking to alter consciousness. As such keep the chant steady, flowing and rhythmic.

In time, a change in atmosphere, the 'feel' of the ritual site itself, will occur. Frequently members will become aware of a broader reality. Otherworld beings will become apparent to some members. There may be a noticeable change in the temperature. If outside, the wind may change, or specific sounds from the forest become apparent. This is as it should be. Let it happen.

Eventually the circling will stop. This will come at the direction of the Mistress. Given her training and experience, she will be able to determine the most appropriate moment for this.

Once this has stopped all will turn to face the cauldron. The Mistress stands near the cauldron placing her palms over the potion. As she does so the rest of the group link hands and begin to intone the note of high 'C'. As the note begins to flow from the group the Mistress envisions the triple spiral. In doing so she forms a link with it and the otherworld energy flowing from Caer Wydyr, completing a circuit of power through the worlds. And it is through this process that the energy reverberates in her and out through the palms merging with the potion. As this is happening the Mistress will intone the following Word of Power:

"Bandia (pronounced BAHN-JEE-uh)"

In doing so, the word itself becomes a vehicle for the power to flow, resonating with the essence of the Great Queen Herself. How many times the word is intoned is entirely up to the Mistress. However, throughout the process, the Coven should be intoning the note of high 'C'. This will continue until the Mistress signals that she is done.

At this point the Trulliad (Coven Cup Bearer) will then step forward and hand the Mistress a goblet or bowl which she will dip into the potion. Then, holding this out in front of her, she recites:

"From the circle of stars
The Lady's voice is heard
Ringing through all Worlds.
Drink of the potion,
From the Cauldron of Caer Wydyr
That you may be as the Gods."

The Mistress takes a sip and then hands this to the Master who sips as well. He then passes this to the Llawforwyn (Coven Maiden). She will sip this and then she carries this to each member who, in turn, takes a sip and hands it back to her.

As simple as this rite is, its purpose is to produce a natural state of awareness in which the connection with otherworld beings and realms become much more accessible. Beyond this though, the drinking of the potion is meant to have a longer effect on the individual. By ingesting this the power drawn from the realm of Caer Wydyr is becoming part of the Witch herself. In this way these forces will stay with the person for a much longer period than just the limits of the immediate ritual.

What happens at this point in the ritual is entirely up to the Coven. Frequently this can be used as an opportune time to allow one or more members to "travel in spirit". In doing so, experienced members are very likely to have direct access to the realm of Caer Wydyr, bypassing the other realms normally experienced.

Magic can be very effective following this procedure as well, largely because the energies brought through from the Castle of Arianrhod are of a level that can bring lasting results on the material.

Given the nature of this exercise, it may be desirable to set in motion the means by which this connection with otherworld beings inherent in the tradition itself can come through in stronger, vital ways. In doing this, information from these ancient and primal sources are invited to manifest in the consciousness and practices of the Coven itself. As such, the following rite may be in order. I refer to this as, *Calling the Elders*. This is to help bring through the presence of otherworld beings tied to the tradition itself, whether these be actual spirits of former Witches of the past, or those beings who seek to teach us through the Art.

Calling the Elders
For such a procedure, have set on the Hearthstone/altar an equal sided triangle traced in powdered Wormwood and Vervain. In the center place either a natural quartz ball, a black mirror, or a scrying bowl filled with spring water. Some Covens will place either an actual human skull or a representation of the same (ceramic or other material) in the triangle in place of a scrying tool. We normally uses a natural quartz crystal ball, otherwise known as a show stone. Nearby we will place a combination of Vervain and Wormwood as incense on hot coals, allowing the smoke to permeate the area.

Once the potion from the cauldron has been sipped by all present, the Mistress turns her attention to the triangle. Using the Fe she will trace the *Lunar sigil of Spirit Summoning* above the show stone.[29]

---

29. A lunar sigil for evoking spirits is used because the Moon figures very highly in this rite. It is important to provide a channel through which the forces can move into this realm. The Moon acts as that gate. As a further note, some may recognize this sigil as being part of the 'Fifth Pentacle of the Moon' found in *The Greater Key of Solomon*. This sigil was given to me early in my training as part of the techniques for calling on spirits. At the time I had no idea that it also appears in the Solomonic grimoire. All I can say is that in the Art there is much that is transferred across different facets of these practices. This is yet another example of Hermetics influencing cunning Witchcraft. As Julie once said to me, "A Witch uses what works for her". I find many of the sigils from certain grimoires to be very effective if used in the proper context and method.

She then recites:

> "I conjure you, I conjure you,
> Elders of the Willow Path.
> By these words I conjure you,
> By will and breath I conjure you.
> By smoke and fire I conjure you,
> By stone and bone I conjure you,
> By the waters of life I conjure you.
> Come good spirits of the Art!
> Neamhshaolta, Neamhshaolta, Neamhshaolta[30]
> (pronounced NAV-HEALTA),
> By the Lady of the Silver Circle,
> By He who rides in the night,
> The gate is open!
> Between the horns,
> Lays the path we keep.
> Come good spirits,
> Your wisdom we now seek!"

As with the Moon Water, the Mistress passes her left hand over the triangle three times, and then does the same with the right hand. Then she, or one in the Coven gifted with the sight, gaze into the scrying tool. She will take as long as needed as she reaches into the well which is the Willow Path.

No matter the results, the scrying tool is left for the remainder of the ritual. This is meant to be a portal, opening a gate through which the otherworld beings who are directly tied to the tradition can come through and communicate with the members of the Coven. This may come as intuition, dreams, omens, or even as direct manifestation. Ideally, if the rite is being conducted indoors, it may be desirable keep this scrying devise in place overnight.

---

30. A Gaelic term used here as a Word of Power for evocation of Otherworld beings.

The rite should be concluded with the normal offerings of food and wine to the Gods, including the spirits of the tradition who were called through. Then the group should retire, to have a meal and socialize.

It may be important to note that while this latter operation specifically calls on spirits, no traditional 'license to depart' is used, nor are the traditional protective lamens or talismans worn. The reason is that those beings evoked are spirits and Gods who are part of the tradition. They are essentially the unseen contacts of the Coven itself. As such, this was an invitation to them to continue to manifest, influence and otherwise take part in the practices of the group.

These ritual techniques can be easily adapted for indoor locations. In such cases, one wouldn't have a fire in the center of the Roth Fail. Rather, the Cauldron would be placed directly on the floor. The Vervain potion would have been prepared in advance and placed within the Cauldron prior to the rite. The group, other than the Mistress and Master, would assemble in a separate room, preferably as far from the ritual chamber as possible. Then, at the appointed time they would begin the procession, making their way to the Roth Fail while using the appropriate imagery.

All of this, too, can be adapted for solitary workings. In such case, the Witch will perform all of the ritual functions and visualizations described herself. The only aspect of the ritual that would not be done would be the procession from a more remote location to the circle. Rather, this could be done as a lead up to the point at which the Roth Fail is set.

Like so much in the Art all of the techniques described here take time and practice. Further, you may not perceive any noticeable difference in your first attempts with these. Rest assured though that if you approach these with care and sincerity the forces and beings involved will take notice. Invariably I have found that for days, sometimes even weeks after such methods are used, very distinct impressions will come. Further, I have found that specific events in this realm often occur. While some might chalk these up to coincidence, these events invariably represent key elements that the Witch needs as she continues her journey on the path.

Again, I want to emphasize that the spirituality of traditional aspects of the Art is not some blinding white light experience endowing one with messianic insight. Nor do such experiences instantly bestow one with some special status as if it were a form of 'self' initiation or adepthood. I suspect that such claims are the result of over inflated egos rather than having gone through the experiences I am describing here.

Rather, the spirituality of the Witch is the natural unfoldment and awareness of the richness that is her true self, her Akh. With this comes the ability to experience the divine in nature itself. For ultimately, they are both the same. It is in this state that the Witch perceives forces and beings alive in many realms. She isn't special or 'chosen'. Rather, she is alive! She is filled with the wonder and beauty of all that is! That is the spirituality of the Witch.

Chapter Nineteen

✤ MARE TO THE GODS INVOCATION ✤

Throughout Europe, the British Isles and parts of Colonial America there are older homes and buildings which have odd markings carved or burned into them. In Massachusetts, U.S.A. a colonial inn dating to the early 1700's actually has such a mark forged into the metal of the front door handle.[31] Known as 'witch marks' or 'apotropaic marks', these serve largely as talismanic images meant to protect the building and to draw good fortune. One of the most common of these is a design that appears almost as two inverted letter "V", or as an upright capital "M", usually with the two middle legs crossing over each other.

Contemporary anthropologists are conflicted as to the actual meaning of the symbol, with the general consensus being that it may represent the first letter of the name "Mary". They see this as a possible reference to the Christian religion and its mythology surrounding the birth of its founder. This may very well have been in the minds of 'some' of the people who had carved these symbols. Yet occult tradition tells us that the symbol stems from a different source.

Rather, in occult practices, the image of the two inverted V's with the middle legs crossing has long been seen as representing the Horse or, more specifically the Mare. With this comes strong associations with a number of ancient Goddesses. These may include Epona, Macha, Mongfind,

---

31. The Salem Cross Inn, Brookfield, Massachusetts. www. salemcrossinn.com

Rhiannon and others. In practical magical application this symbol is often used to bring in the passion and power of the Great Queen, the Witch Goddess Herself.

Beyond this, in the Art the symbolism of the Mare or Horse is frequently meant to convey the idea of the vehicle through which power flows. More specifically the Mare is the means by which an entity can travel, manifest and ultimately experience the realm of its choice. Thus you will see references in Traditional Witchcraft to 'Riding the Mare' or 'Riding the Hag'. I discussed this briefly in *The Willow Path* in relation to the use of the Besom as a means for altering consciousness. However, these same terms are also frequently used when referring to the possession of a person by an otherworld being.[32]

Historical records are filled with accounts of unwanted spirit possession from virtually every culture around the world. However, in the Art there are those occasions when possession is not only welcomed but, in fact, it is the primary goal of specific magical rites. We find it in the ceremonies of Ancient Egypt with local Magicians and sorceresses often wearing masks of specific Gods and Goddesses while casting spells.[33] The objective in doing so was to assume the personality and thus, call into themselves a measure of the power of the deity being invoked.

This exact same technique was used in temple rituals as well. Numerous carvings have survived showing different members of temples donning headdresses and full masks of different Gods as they then enacted legends designed to draw the power of the Gods into them.

In the annual Mysteries of Isis and Osiris, twin sisters were often chosen to represent the Goddesses Isis and

---

32. Morgan, Lee. *A Deed Without a Name: Unearthing the Legacy of Traditional Witchcraft.* p.27.

33. Pinch, Dr. Geraldine. *Magic in Ancient Egypt*, 1995.

Nephthys as they performed the ritual to awaken Osiris. During this a priest assumed the role of the dead God. At some ritual centers this was conducted in subterranean chambers. The Osirian located at Abydos is one such chamber used for this invocation. Another has been discovered beneath the causeway leading from the sphinx to the Great Pyramid at Giza.

In these rites the priest would lay in a coffin on a platform surrounded by a channel of water. Standing beside the coffin, the two sisters would sing the enchantment calling Osiris back to life. Then, in an act intended to bring new life and prosperity to the land, the sister representing Isis would make love to the priest. In doing so the goal was to enact the conception of the Sun God Horus.[34] The following is one of the text reciting during this ritual:

"I, Shentayet [Isis] residing in Busiris,
Mistress of the golden-seed,
Mistress of beautiful Iunet, come to you, rejoicing in love.
I sit on your phallus, so that your semen enters me,
I become pregnant with the Ba of my beloved, Ausir [Osiris].
I, beautiful of appearance,
Mistress in the temple of Gold,
For whom the two lands become excited when I give birth to the Neter."[35]

In reading the above text, it is clear that the priestess is assuming the role of the Goddess Shentayet – Isis, speaking in the first person as if she were this otherworld being Herself.

---

34. It is important to note that beside the obvious example of an actual couple having intercourse, often times the ritual involved a 'symbolic act' in which the priestess representing Isis would plant barley seeds in a mold shaped as Osiris and then tend these as they grew. Nevertheless, in the ritual actual participants assumed the roles of the Gods involved.

35. These and other ritual texts describing this rite can be found in: Cauville, Sylvie. *Dendera: Les Chapelles Osiriennes.* Volumes I & II, 1997.

During the festival of "The Beautiful Embrace", the Goddess Hathor is reunited with Her lover Horus. In this a priestess representing Hathor would travel from her temple with a statue of the Goddess, in a barge on the Nile. Arriving at Horus' temple of Edfu she would be greeted by a priest representing Horus. There, among days of celebration, the couple would ritually mate. Then she would return to her temple at Dendera.[36]

Interestingly inscriptions describing the conception of King Hatshepsut appear to mirror the same magical formula. Hatshepsut was one of the few female kings of Egypt. Ancient texts explain that the God Amun came to Hatshepsut's mother, making love to her in order to conceive the next ruler.[37] Most contemporary Egyptologists feel that these texts were pure fiction, meant to help legitimize the female ruler's claim to the throne. However, I find this doubtful. The mere fact that the account would be accepted by the populace lends itself to a wide spread belief in possession for the goal of begetting a divine, but mortal, child.

It seems obvious that this is another example ritual possession. Here a priest, or quite possibly the King, would have invoked Amun through ritual during which the sexual act was performed. In fact, hints of similar rituals in the temples of Amun can be found in the role of some of the female members of the high priesthood. In this capacity they were seen as the wife or concubine of Amun, with all that this entails.[38]

---

36. Schumann Antelme, Ruth and Stephane Rossini. *Sacred Sexuality in Ancient Egypt: The Erotic Secrets of the Forbidden Papyrus, A Look at the Unique Role of Hathor, the Goddess of Love*, 1999, 2001.

37. Manniche, Lise. *Sexual Life in Ancient Egypt*, 1987.

38. Even the Abrahamic tradition hints at a similar theme in which the lead deity impregnates a virgin to bring a divine mortal into this realm. In light of the Egyptian rituals discussed here one has to wonder if the culture in the Levant wasn't also using a similar ritual for this purpose.

Of course, the conception of a divine child wasn't the only reason invocation was used in Egypt. There are many examples of invocations being employed to repel forces that threatened the country. We see this in festival of "The Victory of Horus"[39] in which several members of the priesthood would become ritually possessed by different Gods and Goddesses as they fought the forces of chaos.[40]

There are also multiple inscriptions found in the pyramid and coffin texts which clearly depict humans acting and speaking as if possessed. A good example of this can be found in Coffin Text Spells 331 and 332. These 'spells' begins by describing how the initiate should approach the Goddess Hathor in ritual, giving specific invocations to be recited. The texts then shift to the initiate speaking as the Goddess in the first person. A part of these read:

"I am Hathor who brings Her Horus,
I am Hathor who proclaims Her Horus.
My heart is that of the lion Neter,
My lips are those of the sytyw.
There is no limit to my vision,
There are none who can encircle my arms,
Every Neter honors me,
For I appear as Hathor,
The Primeval, The Lady of All who lives on Ma'at,
I am the Uraeus who lives on Ma'at,
She who lifts the faces of all the Neteru.
All the Neteru are beneath me.
I am she who displays beauty and assembles power."

This text continues on providing excellent insight into the nature of this Goddess in Her own words. There are several

39. If you are interested in learning more about the Ancient Egyptian festivals please see my earlier writings on the subject, especially *Pillar of Ra: Ancient Egyptian Festivals for Today.*

40. H.W. Fairman. *The Myth of Horus at Edfu*, 1942.

other similar texts found throughout Egypt, related to a variety of Gods and Goddesses.[41] Each of these follow a similar pattern, namely, the beginnings of a ritual invocation to a specific deity followed by the deity's own words written in the first person.

I think it is safe to say that while a major portion of Egyptian magic revolved around calling on, or evoking, otherworld beings in an effort to influence material affairs, there was a richer tradition as well. This was the invocation of the Gods *into a living person*. As we saw, the purposes surrounding such acts were complex. Yet the inscriptions appear to show that this was done primarily so that there could be direct interaction and communication between otherworld beings and humanity, as well as giving the deity direct access to objects and events in the material world.

In Hermetics, ritual invocation has become a vital part of the techniques used. Some esoteric groups have become quite adept at developing specific, highly effective procedures for calling different otherworld beings into themselves under very controlled circumstances. This is done through the use of various symbols, names and words of power, as well as what has come to be termed the astral assumption of 'God form' images. I would go so far as to say that, in the Hermetic system that I was trained, the assumption of 'God-forms', and thus the invocation of otherworld beings is one of the primary pillars of the Art which they practice.[42]

Of course, other forms of contemporary magical Arts outside of Hermetics also involve inviting possession

---

41. Several examples can be found in; El-Sabban, Sherif. *Temple Festival Calendars of Ancient Egypt*, 2000..

42. For those interested in learning more, I suggest carefully reading Osborne Phillips' work *Aurum Solis: Initiation Ceremonies and Inner Magical Techniques*, 2001. Keep in mind that this is a very technical book. It is best to start by reading Melita Denning & Osborne Phillips' five volume series *The Magical Philosophy*. Their series lays the foundation for understanding the techniques presented in Mr. Phillips' later work.

by otherworld beings. In particular those of Voudon, as well as different Shamanic practices that are alive and functioning around the globe, come to mind. However, unlike most Hermetic Magicians, the techniques used in these systems involve dance and various levels of trance to induce an almost ecstatic state of mind.[43] It is then that the individual's awareness steps aside, allowing the otherworld being to take over.

Spiritualism, too, with its use of mediumistic talents can technically be considered a form of invocation. However, seldom is it done with the view of drawing in a specific spirit. Rather, the medium generally opens herself to whatever spirits may be present at the time. For the most part, Spiritualism is limited to spirits of discarnate humans, as opposed to the more complex and, dare I say, more highly evolved beings whom we call Gods.

But what of the indigenous practice of Europe and the British Isles? Was invocation and possession part of their Art?

To understand this, we need to return to our discussion of the Mare from the beginning of the chapter. As noted, a frequent term used in Traditional Witchcraft is to "Ride the Mare". Oftentimes this referred to the fetch or spirit of a Witch possessing the 'second skin' or etheric substance of a more vital person or animal and using this as her vehicle. We examined this practice earlier in this book.

Yet, to Ride the Mare can also refer to *willfully allowing* another being to possess one.[44] To understand the significance of this, we need to turn to the myths inherent to European cultures. A number of Goddesses associated with horses also represented 'the Lady of the land' itself.

43. It should be noted that in Ogdoadic Hermetics dance and ritual movement is taught. Aleister Crowley also makes mention of dance during ritual, particularly in his classic work *Magick in Theory and Practice*.

44. I find it interesting that in Voudon when one becomes possessed by one of the Loa they are said to be 'ridden'.

For it was through Her that mortal kings were chosen. In a number of legends it was She who empowered them, giving them both the ability *and* authority to rule. Many of these Horse Goddess cults were vast extending across Europe and throughout the British Isles. Epona was so powerful that even a number of Roman soldiers adopted Her as their patron Goddess.

We had encountered one of these Goddesses in some of the writing presented earlier in the Geassa series. The crone who sleeps with the solar hero Niall, and then transforms into the beautiful maiden is none other than the Goddess Mongfind. According to Historian Sharon Paice MacLeod, this otherworld being's name means "White Mare". She was a Goddess of sovereignty in that it was through Her power that the kings of Ireland were chosen. To achieve this, the mortal man was tested by the Goddess. Then, only if She found him worthy as well as being someone who deserved Her attention, She would both support and empower him. This was done, in large part, through the act of sexual union.[45] Ms. MacLeod makes it very clear that there are numerous examples in Celtic myth surrounding this same theme. This always involved a Goddess of the Earth making the choice of who would be the king, and then supporting and empowering them through the act of sex. It needs to be noted that only very rarely were these Goddesses seen as a spouse to the would be king. And never was She seen as subservient. Rather, She was independent; an otherworld being bestowing Her support onto the mortal through this act.

The question becomes, "How was this achieved?" One has to wonder if, in fact, the legends represent an actual ritual act? After all anyone could claim that a Goddess had sex with them and because of this they were now entitled to be the king. Rather, a number of scholars have concluded

---

45. Paice MacLeod, Sharon. *Celtic Cosmology and the Otherworld*, p.91.

that these legends almost certainly do represented actual rituals involving living people. If so, we find ourselves facing a similar situation to that occurring in Egypt. In this case, a woman, probably of the druid class, and independent from the person aspiring to be king, would be the one who tested the person, chose the person, and then through ritual empowered this person to be king.

In his book, *The Magic Arts in Celtic Britain*, Lewis Spence comes to this conclusion while comparing this to other ancient cultures.[46] Ms. MacLeod points out that the Gaelic word 'feis' was used in connection to a number of rituals linking the king with the Land, including the rite involved in electing a new ruler. She explains that this word means "to spend the night together".[47]

For our discussion here, it seems obvious that if a ritual was to be performed, the druidess involved would almost certainly need to become possessed by the horse Goddess Herself. This, of course, is a classic example of the sacred marriage found in so many ancient cultures. Ms. MacLeod points out that the theme of the powerful woman as an otherworld being who empowers mortals through sexual union carried on. Some examples include the faery traditions surrounding Queen Mebh, as well as such folk ballads involving the Queen of Elphame. The ballad of Tam Lin is an excellent representation of this.

This doesn't mean that the magical use of invocation and possession were only reserved for rites of kingship and the divine marriage. There are multiple examples in European folk tradition of masks and costumes being worn with the view that the person was somehow transformed into the otherworld being portrayed. The story of *The Siege of Druim Damgarie* gives an account of the druid, Mug Roith, covering himself in the hide of bull and donning a feather

---

46. Spence, Lewis. *The Magic Arts in Celtic Britain*, p.118–119.

47. Paice MacLeod, Sharon. *Celtic Cosmology and the Otherworld*, p.127.

headdress as he begins his enchantments against invaders.[48] Documentation coming from the medieval era reports that frequently people would dress in animal masks during different festivals. A woodcarving from this time shows men and women dressed as a stag, hare and other animals.[49] These, of course, are some of the same animals discussed previously representing different types of familiar spirits called on in the Art.

The horse as vehicle of passion, power and prosperity makes her return later in history. In the annual festivals of Samhain and Beltane, a common feature in Ireland was the ritual of Lair Bhan. Dressed as a White Mare, people would go house to house while blowing horns and reciting verses meant to bring prosperity and joy in the coming season.[50] While in Cornwall, England, the custom of dressing as *Obby Oss*, a horse which dances through the streets bringing merriment and the promise of fertility continues to this day.[51]

While these are clearly examples of festive occasions, with the participants acting as much as entertainers as they are representations of the forces involved, the fact remains that in these roles these people are identifying with the beings portrayed. This is one of the first steps involved in ritual invocation.

Of course, we are still left with the question, does invocation and possession fit into the practices of the Traditional Witch today? In fact, it does in very real ways and for a variety of purposes.

---

48. Paice MacLeod, Sharon. *Celtic Cosmology and the Otherworld*, p.202.

49. Plate 11.1 page 197 Jones, Purdens & Nigel Pennick. *A History of Pagan Europe*, 1995.

50. Bord, Janet & Colin. *Earth Rites: Fertility Practices in Pre-Industrial Britain*, p.202.

51. Gemma Gary discusses the Mare in relation to the Obby Oss at length in her highly recommended book *Traditional Witchcraft: A Cornish Book of Ways*, 2008.

For example, as discussed earlier, in one of her many books Sybil Leek presents a photograph noted as "a rare picture of an initiation ceremony taken in England".[52] In this a woman is shown facing the new initiate. She is wearing what clearly appears to be a black mask through which her eyes can be seen. As part of this the black form of a crow or raven is depicted on the woman's forehead. Obviously the clear intent is that the woman represents the spirit of this totem itself. As such, an invocation of this familiar spirit, almost certainly representing the black spirits of the north road, or else any one of the many Raven Goddesses from British esoteric teachings, would have been conducted as part of the rite.

I am also aware of Traditional Witches who don full head coverings with masks as representations of the 'Horned One'. Often time this is done by the Mistress of the Coven. In doing so she is fulfilling a great Mystery that is echoed in Ancient Egyptian practices surrounding the ram headed God Atum as the 'Great He/She'. However, beyond these few words, this is not a topic I can elaborate on here.

In practical magic there are many reasons one would invoke a deity into oneself. This is usually done in order to gain a measure of their power for use in the rite itself. This is particularly so for the construction of specific talismans or magical tools. It can also be done to direct the being's power toward the achievement of specific goals. On other occasions a deity may be invoked in order to consult and interact with them directly, not unlike an oracle. In rites of initiation it is very common for those performing the rite to use invocation as a part of this.

There are also occasions when invocation is performed and the power is transferred into some food which is then consumed by the participants. This is done so that the essence of the being remains grounded as a part of the

---

52. Leek, Sybil. *The Complete Art of Witchcraft*, 1971.

Coven on a physical level.[53] While this practice is part of certain Christian rituals, it is far older, reaching into the magical teachings of cultures long before the current era.

For me though, there is a greater purpose for invoking a deity. True invocation brings with it a sharing or merging of consciousness with the being that simply can't be described. Keep in mind that most of these beings, assuming one is invoking a Goddess or God, are of a much more complex nature then we are. Many of them think and feel in very different ways then we. As such, during possession we only consciously grasp a small portion of the experience and expansiveness that is possible. Yet, true possession by such a being often brings with it a shear sense of ecstasy that is unmistakable. And long after the spirit has departed, this sense of immense pleasure or joy often remains for an extended time. Beyond this though, invocation helps to raise the Witch's awareness to new levels. With this too, the Witch finds that her ability to handle tasks normally associated with the deity come far more easily to her.

In the last chapter I discussed spirituality and opening one's awareness to the realms in which the Gods are more easily perceived. This was intentional, because the material presented thus far in this book was meant to carry the student to this point. It is one thing to reach a state in which one perceives the Gods; it is an altogether different level to actually share your body with them. Yet, if done carefully it can be one of the most moving experiences one can have in the practice of the Art.

There are important considerations though that one needs to take into account before attempting invocation. And, all of the steps required take time and preparation. First you need to ask yourself why you are doing this. What is your motivation? Almost certainly whomever you are intending to invoke is going to want to know this as well. You need

---

53. We saw a similar magical technique used in the last chapter involving the potion drunk from the cauldron.

to have a clear purpose in mind. Even if that purpose is simply to avail yourself to the deity for their own desires. You still need to be certain of why you want this to happen. Invocation is not an operation to be taken lightly.

My advice is to create a list, writing your answers carefully in a journal or your own grimoire. Doing so will help you to identify and then refine your motivation for this experience. This, in turn, will help you to choose who you will be inviting into your body. Invocation is a very personal, even intimate rite. Essentially you are letting another intelligence into your skin, into your mind and emotions. For that time they will have access to a large portion of who you are. Of course this only applies to those aspects of yourself that exist more or less in this realm. This would include your physical body and its sensation, as well as those of your Swt or fetch. On a psychological level the being will have direct access to your ego, your emotions and quite possibly even deeper portions of the subconscious. With time they will know your memories and thoughts as well.

Keep in mind that the more powerful and complex the being is, the more they will be able to see into, and control you during the rite. A strong Magician or Witch oftentimes can limit this access when working with less complex spirits, including discarnate humans. However, when working with beings on the level of the Gods this ability slips away, with the being have greater access should they desire this. Now bear in mind that there are different levels of possession and, with practice, the Witch can control the level as these unfold. Still, as the process continues, and deeper levels are reached much of this control evaporates.

It is for all of these reasons that one needs to carefully choose who you will be invoking. My suggestion is that once you have clearly defined your intentions look to a list of otherworld beings who can help you achieve your goal. Choose from those who are closely aligned with the system of the Art you work with best. The gender of the being matters little. I have had success with invocation of both female and male beings. In fact, even though I am male in this incarnation, some of the most moving experiences with invocation have come when calling in a Goddess whom I work with often.

In choosing the deity look to the character, legends and those qualities She or He embodies and governs. For your own safety you need to work with an otherworld being who will treat you well, having your best interest at heart and whose qualities are close to your own ethical code. Just because a being is a God or Goddess doesn't mean that their sense of right and wrong are similar to your own. Remember terms involving 'good' 'bad' or 'right and wrong' vary from person to person and certainly between the unique beings whom we call Gods.

Rather, you want to make sure that the being is someone you feel you can trust. In my opinion the arrangement should be more akin to a confidante, partner, friend, spouse or lover. Barring this, a deity may form a relationship that is similar to that of a parent or mentor. Each of these are valid depending on the reason you are invoking them in the first place.

My point is that you wouldn't let just anyone into your home simply because you can. This is a grave mistake that many people new to the Art make. In their excitement of making contact with a discarnate being they assume that somehow this entity must be morally and spiritually superior and thus someone to be trusted. Don't let yourself fall into this trap. Do your research. Set your protections. Know who it is that you are allowing into your body and set the rules from the beginning. You need to know that you can trust them to be respectful and not harm you or anyone around you in anyway.

It is also important to know that many times it isn't the Witch who chooses the deity, so much as the deity who chooses the Witch! It is very common for the Witch to find that specific symbols, images and events occur in their life that are directly linked to a specific otherworld being. At first these may seem spontaneous or coincidental. Yet the sheer frequency, as well as the impact that these have in one's life soon make it clear that a particular force has taken an interest in you.

When this occurs it is prudent to begin by examining your practices in the Art. Perhaps you had inadvertently aroused the attention of this being through ritual without realizing it. It may also be the case that someone else has evoked that being and is using its power to influence you. In either case the remedy is fairly easy. If the influence is unwelcomed reset your protections. This should be done as a matter of good psychic housekeeping at the equinoxes as a matter of habit.[54]

If you find that the influence was due to a mistake made in ritual, go back to your Roth Fail and call the being to the circle. Thank them for the attention they have shown and then ask them to return to their own realm. Keep in mind here that I am speaking of the influence of those beings whom we know as Gods or Goddesses. Lesser spirits and other entities need to be dealt with in a very different manner. My focus here is on the art of invocation of the Gods.

There are also those occasions when, of their own accord, deities may take an active interest in the Witch. This may happen because the Witch has visited a site once sacred to the being. Perhaps a shrine, temple, stone circle, or some other structure that is associated with the being. On the other hand, it may be that the deity is a local Goddess or God inherent in nature. Around the world there are specific places in nature where indigenous people have long known of the presence of such beings. Again, I believe that the entity whom I referred to earlier in this book is almost certainly the equivalent of a Goddess tied directly to this mountainous region of New England.

---

54. I will be discussing the methods we use for psychic self-defense as part of the third book in this series.

There are also those people who, for whatever reason, are naturally aligned with specific deities. I discussed this earlier in the chapter related to otherworld beings, but perhaps it bears repeating here. These cases are rare but important when they do occur. Such a member of the Art would do well to cultivate the relationship. For there is clearly a link that reaches across time and incarnations that needs to be explored and developed. In such cases the Goddess or God involved will prove to be vital as the Witch progresses and learns.

Once the decision has been made to move forward with invocation, there are three different approaches that one can take when invoking a deity. Oftentimes these can be combined. The first involves totally immersing oneself in all that is associated with the deity. This can include surrounding oneself with images, symbols, colors, scents, tools, and cult objects all associated with the being. Set up a small shrine dedicated to the deity. Each day a small offering consisting of food or other items favored by the being should be presented. With this one should spend time meditating, opening oneself to the being. If one is working with a being who has a specific place in nature that is associated with them, the Witch should spend time going to the site. There she will enter the state of *becoming* and then sit quietly inviting the being to her. Known as the devotional method of invocation this can be one of the most lasting and impactful methods. Yet, as can be seen, it also takes a considerable amount of time and patience.

Another method often used is that of ritually enacting a specific aspect of one of the myths involving the Goddess or God in question. Examples of this were shown earlier when I discussed some of the rites of Ancient Egypt. Both the "Victory of Horus" as well as the "Mysteries of Isis and Osiris" used this method to great advantage. This works well in group settings. However, for the solitary Witch it can be far more challenging. Having said this though, if you have a vivid imagination it would be possible to enact the scene in a private ritual setting. In such a case one would assume the role of the deity while envisioning the legend in one's mind. I have found that reading the legend in ritual can be very helpful.

The third method is that of a ritual of invocation. It is here that the solitary Witch, as well as those in very small groups, will probably have their greatest success. Like the other methods this requires patience and preparation. The Witch will need to consider the timing of the rite very carefully. For ritual invocation, the most powerful times are during the summer months and generally on the night of a Full Moon. Of course much will depend on the deity being invoked. If one is calling a solar spirit into oneself then by all means high noon would be the best time. Also, look to the dates of any festivals associated with the being. These will be excellent times for the rite. However, be certain that you calculate the date correctly. The calendar used in our current era has changed drastically from those used in ancient times. Do the research to ensure that you are performing this on the actual date of the festival as opposed to any that might now be mentioned on the Christianized calendar.

If circumstances permit, the rite should be done outdoors and in a location that corresponds to the nature of the being. Attempting the invocation of a woodland God in a city high rise apartment will not be nearly as effective as it would be in an actual forest. Having said this, if circumstances are such that one can't work outdoors one's hearth or private Roth Fail will also be effective.

In addition, you will need to prepare yourself for this over a series of days. Some guidelines that I have been taught include abstaining from sexual orgasm a minimum of three days prior to the rite. Do not eat any meat or dairy products during this time as well. If possible limit your diet to foods that are favored by the being whom you will be invoking. Be certain that you have similar foods and drink available for the ritual itself as once invoked the deity may very well want these.

In the hours leading up to the ritual ensure that all is ready for the rite. Like the devotional method you will want to have any cult objects, symbols, colors, scents, etc. present and incorporated into the rite itself.

An hour before performing the ritual you will want to take a relaxing bath. In the water be sure to include a handful of salt mixed with baking soda (sodium bicarbonate). Combined, these two ingredients have very similar qualities to Egyptian Natron which is a naturally occurring substance used in purification. To this also add any herbs or oils that are associated with the being.

While taking the bath let yourself slowly 'open' while gently focusing on the deity. Allow yourself to 'imagine' the spirit gently coming into you, merging with you. Don't force this. This is only the first step in the process. Rather, simply relax and enjoy the bath. During this you may want a small glass of wine or some other alcoholic drink known to be enjoyed by the deity. This should be kept to a minimum. You do not want to be intoxicated. Rather, this is meant to both help relax one while also making your body a welcome host to the being.

As for how to dress this depends on if you are in a group or working alone. In group workings it is best to use whatever is normal in ritual. When working alone this can vary. Some people prefer to have on hand either white clean clothing or a robe in the color associated with the deity. This, in my opinion, is entirely up to the Witch. I am certain that prior to the modern era the simple country Witch would not have had this luxury available. As such, she may find that the simplest method when alone is to perform the rite nude.

In practice I have found this to be the most effective for me. Once the rite begins one soon loses any sense of self-consciousness or inhibition. In fact, once the deity begins to transition into one's body your ego quickly disappears and you find that awareness of oneself changes. You become more of an 'active observer'. That is, unless or until full possession occurs, you are aware of your surroundings and the actions your body makes, yet it is as if you simply step aside. Having said this, if you would feel more comfortable clothed, by all means do so. However, be certain that the clothing isn't restrictive in any way. In particular you will want to ensure that the solar plexus is more or less unbound. This is why a shift, cloak or robe can work well in ritual.

After the bath proceed to the ritual area. Once there everything should be done with an unhurried calm. If outside, take several moments to merge with the Moon. Or if you have decided to perform the rite during the day, take some time to merge with the land, letting its energies fill you. If you goal was to call in a solar deity, now is the time to let the light of this star fill you.

As mentioned before, the ritual site itself will have been prepared in advance. Exactly how it is arranged will vary greatly depending on the being to be invoked. Despite this being an invocation of a deity, you will still want to perform this in a Roth Fail / circle. This is not done so much for protection as it is to link the worlds to this place and time.

No matter the being called, you should place the Stang in the north of the circle. Again, this is the traditional realm of the Gods. Ideally a lit candle should be placed between the horns. At the base of the Stang it is important to place a bone of some kind. Even if one is invoking a life affirming being, the bone represents the point of transition between worlds. At one time that bone was part of a living being here in the temporal realm, and yet the being has passed through the portal into other dimensions. The bone remains in the physical realm as link bridging the gulf between.

The bone is generally placed to the right side of the Stang. To the left a goblet or bowl filled with fresh well or spring water is set. Between these two items the Witch will have drawn the sigil of the deity. This can be drawn in the dirt or traced with flour and herbs. On the Hearthstone one will have placed any foods and drink that the being enjoys. The

Hearthstone should also be decorated with the colors and objects, images and incenses corresponding to the being.

At this point there are three key elements that will help draw the deity into one. The procedures presented throughout this book all now come to bear ensuring your success.

First, you need to have devised a vocal invocation calling the deity into you. While older invocations found in texts and grimoires can be very effective, the best are those that the Witch creates herself. That is, providing she has researched this completely, drawing on actual historical information related directly to the Goddess or God to be called. Make sure that you are accurate in your representation. So many times I have seen people write invocations that capture their own individual feelings but have no foundation in historical facts surrounding the deity they hope to invoke. Then they wonder why the ritual failed.

Don't worry too much about the prose or any rhyming involved. Rather, you want this to be something that is personal and moving to both you and the deity. This is your invitation to this force, welcoming Her or Him to you . . . into you! Keep it simple, direct, yet something that will stir your inner vision and heart. Be very clear in the intent and desire. It is this invocation which will form the basis of the ritual as you proceed.

Once the Roth Fail is sealed and the Watchers have been called, place an incense favored by the being on the coals. Then, with the Fe, move to the north where you will trace the sigil of the deity in the air, directly in front of the horns of the Stang. As you do, intone the name of the being. Feel the energy of the name rise within you as your voice carries out across the Worlds. In doing so you are creating a path, resonating with the intelligence called, getting their attention.

At this point it may be desirable to perform a version of the *Stirring of the Cauldron* noted earlier in the book. In doing so, you may want to use the invocation you had created. While circling the cauldron, begin to envision yourself moving into the realm associated with the God or Goddess you are invoking. See yourself walking up a spiral staircase in a tower climbing toward the world in which this being normally expresses itself. Keep the image of the sigil clearly in mind.

None of this should be done hastily. Rather, just relax and let the experience unfold. Let yourself go. Don't worry about what others may think. This is about stirring the energies, moving into different realms and opening the portal through which you and the deity can merge. Eventually you will sense the ritual area change. The entire feel of the space will be subtly yet perceptively different. As this builds, begin to slow your pace and then stop in front of the Hearthstone.

Facing the Stang, let yourself relax. If needed sit or lie down, though I prefer to stand. Then become aware of your Swt and Ka – your 'astral form'. Feel this forming. All those months of working with these bodies now come to this moment of climax. For here, in this circle, you become vital and alive. Far beyond anything your physical body can experience, your Ka body is present and thriving. Be aware in this moment as you then calmly, with the full force of your will and intention recite your invocation. Let it flow in passion, desire and yet keeping relaxed and calm. It is a delicate balance between 'enflaming yourself with prayer' as the old grimoires state and yet keeping a state of openness and receptivity. The key here is your desire and willingness to be that Mare for the deity.

As you do this begin to envision the deity coming to you, merging with your astral form. Let this build as the two of you become one. Feel your double changing form, shapeshifting into that of the being. In your mind envision the actual appearance of the Goddess or God as depicted in myth or in ancient carvings blending with your own Swt and Ka. See yourself change until you no longer identify with the image of your physical body, but rather with that of the deity. All the while continue the chant, repeating the invocation as many times as needed. Let the words flow from your being as the image of the deity overtakes you . . . fills you . . . merges with you.

Soon you may find yourself falling silent. Your awareness may shift to one in which you know you are there yet someone else is taking over. Just let it happen. Trust the process and your training. For now you have become a Mare, a receptacle of divine force. You may find that you move, perhaps drawn to the food and drink. Perhaps you find yourself speaking. Or you may begin performing some ritual act. Whatever occurs just let it come naturally.

You will find that the actions almost seem autonomous. This is not unlike breathing, chewing or any number of bodily functions. In those situations you have a level of control yet they come over you as natural and complete in themselves. The same happens in possession. You will be aware and can control the actions to some extent, and yet they have a life of their. Just let it happen and go with the experience. For it is the presence of the deity that is taking over now. At this time you will also probably find that images, symbols, concepts and ideas that words can't express will start to come through. Again, just be aware of these and let them flow. Later they will prove to be very valuable, assuming you can remember these.

As I noted earlier, there are different levels of possession. In the lightest stages one is fully aware, perhaps doubting that anything is happening at all. Yet there is a sense of merging or 'closeness' associated with the being. As this deepens the presence becomes stronger and you begin to 'feel' as if you are this otherworld being. Yet, there will still be a part of you that wonders if it is just your own imagination. Don't over analyze the situation. Just relax and let the experience unfold. I am convinced that the process of invocation is a natural, even normal ability. Because of your training and preparations, the setting of the ritual space and the type of being called, you are completely safe and protected. Step back and let yourself enjoy the experience.

It is at this point that the deity begins to take over. Yet you still have the ability to direct the actions. It is almost as if you both have formed a partnership within the single vehicle of the body. It is in this state, as the God or Goddess invoked, that you now can direct their energy toward your magic.

Eventually, as the state deepens, the role may reverse in that the deity assumes control, enjoying the sensations of being in physical form. As I noted above, frequently the being may dance, chant, eat and drink as well as speak directly to those present. At this point you may or may not be fully aware of what is happening. It may seem almost as if one is in dream. Eventually the being will withdraw and the Witch will return to normal consciousness. Depending on the extent of possession she may or may not recall what has happened.

You will find though that, except in rare occasions, you do have the ability to control the level at which the possession occurs, at least in the lighter levels. As one feels the other coming through, one can slow the process by still holding onto a sense of oneself. The only way to describe this is to compare it to the states experienced in meditation or hypnosis. In these one will feel oneself slipping deeper into these relaxed states. If desired, one welcomes the ever increase relaxation that accompanies this. Yet, just as easily one can pull oneself back simply by focusing on mundane concerns and thoughts. So too with possession. That is until the very deepest levels take over. At that point one needs to trust in one's Akh, true self and in the deity who has been called.

Now you understand why careful preparation and research into the force being invoked is essential. You need to trust that this being will treat you with the respect you deserve. After all, you have just allowed them access to your most precious physical possession, your body and mind.

Once the deity begins to depart, your consciousness will become more aware of mundane surroundings. Yet, almost always you will experience a sense of euphoria along with a feeling of connectedness to all in nature. Too, I have found that a profound sense of inner calm stays with me for days. You will almost certainly also find that you are left with a richer level of knowledge that is probably best described in abstract symbols and images. In time, you will be able to put these into words. This is one of the gifts from the Gods given to those who allow themselves to become vessels to them.

In finishing the rite, you will want to return to the Hearthstone. If any food and drink are left, hold these up as you thank the being for their presence. Let them know that you welcome them. Then consume the remaining food or share this with any Coven members who may have been present for the rite. If outside, remove all signs of the ritual, sweeping the sigil on the ground away with the Besom. Then retire to a meal and celebration or slip off to bed.

In the days that follow be very aware of your dreams as well as any impressions that may come to you in your waking life. Also, it is very common for 'coincidences' to happen, all revolving around the being invoked. Frequently you will have spontaneous information related to the deity come to you. You may find that books or other sources of information needed in your Art manifest. All of these and more are the otherworld being's way of continuing the conversation, while aiding you as you travel *the Willow Path*.

Conclusion

✦ A STAR IN THE WELL ✦

The first book in *The Geassa* series, *The Willow Path*, was meant to introduce the reader to the essential philosophy, fundamental symbolism, cosmology, ethics and basic ritual techniques of the Art as I have come to understand and practice these. As stated before, this is a synthesis of Traditional Witchcraft, Hermetics and Ancient Egyptian teachings. This second book, however, *The Horns of the Moon*, was written with a very different view in mind. While it is a continuation of the teachings discussed in the first, this book is intended to give one substantial techniques through which otherworlds and beings can be readily experienced. If performed regularly, they will increase the student's ability in the magical arts. In fact, over time these will form the foundation from which all other ritual activity will be built. In developing these skills, the seeds will have been planted which will, inevitably, germinate into the subtle nuances of all one's magical workings and skill going forward. It is in the third book, *The Art*, that all of this preparation and work will culminate for the student. For it is in that book that specific ritual procedures are given.

Yet the practice of the Art isn't solely about practical magic. Far from it. If anything, this current book *Horns of the Moon* exemplifies that at our core each of us is uniquely spiritual, reaching across all human understanding of time, space and dimension. The true purpose of the Art is in helping the Witch to not only understand this but to *experience* this in personal and profound ways. In doing so, she then becomes aware of her connection to all that is.

271

Like the star that reflects in the pool of the deepest well, so too does the individual spirit merge with all that one is in all realms and worlds. You are unique, and for those who seek it, the Art remains the means by which one can find this connection with the Gods. Perhaps a line from an invocation of the Great Queen expresses this well. In this the Lady states, "Come, take my hand, rise as a falcon that you may be as the Gods." She is there waiting for each of us if we only take the time to reach out to Her.

Table of Sigils

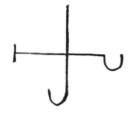

Opening the Worlds

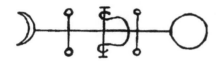

Transformative Power
of The Moon

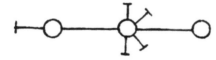

Lunar Sigil of Spirit
Summoning

"Witch Mark"
Sigil of the Mare

Sigils of the Sídh

Sigil of the Spirits of Air

Sigil of the Spirits of Fire

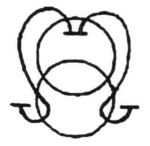

Sigil of the Spirits of Water

Sigil of the
Woodland Spirits

Sigil of the
Mountain Spirits

Bibliography

Arroyo, Stephen. *Astrology, Karma & Transformation: The Inner Dimensions of the Birth Chart*. 1978. CRCS Publications. Davis, California, U.S.A.

Assmann, Jann. *The Search for God in Ancient Egypt*. 2001. Cornell University Press. Ithaca, New York, U.S.A.

----------. *The Mind of Egypt: History and Meaning in the Time of the Pharaohs*. 2002. Metropolitan Books. New York, New York, U.S.A.

Bell, Lanny. "The New Kingdom 'Divine' Temple: The Example of Luxor". *Temples of Ancient Egypt*. Copyright 1997. 283 (note 10) Pages 127-184. Cornell University Press. Ithaca, New York, U.S.A.

Bleeker, C.J. *Hathor and Thoth: Two Key Figures of the Ancient Egyptian Religion*. Copyright 1973.48 E.J. Brill, Leiden, Netherlands.

Bord, Janet & Colin. *Earth Rites: Fertility Practices in Pre-Industrial Britain*. Copyright 1982.202 Granada Publishing, London, UK.

Cauville, Sylvie. *Dendera: Les Chapelles Osiriennes. Volumes I & II*. Copyright 1997. Institut Francais D'Archeologie Orientale.

Collier & Manley. *How to Read and Write Egyptian Hieroglyphs*. 1998. University of California Press. Berkeley, CA, U.S.A.

Crowley, Aleister. *Magick in the Theory and Practice*. 1929. Castle Books. New York, New York, U.S.A.

----------, *Moonchild*. 1929, 1997 edition sited. Samuel Weiser, Inc. York Beach, Maine, U.S.A.

Denning, Melita & Osborne Phillips. *The Magical Philosophy: Book I, Robe and Ring*. 1974. Llewellyn Publications. St. Paul, Minnesota, U.S.A.

----------. *The Magical Philosophy: Book II; The Apparel of High Magick*. 1975. Llewellyn Publications. St. Paul, Minnesota, U.S.A.

----------. *The Magical Philosophy: Book III; The Sword and the Serpent*. 1975. Llewellyn Publications. St. Paul, Minnesota, U.S.A.

----------. *The Magical Philosophy: Book IV; The Triumph of Light*. 1978. Llewellyn Publications. St. Paul, Minnesota, U.S.A.

----------. *The Magical Philosophy: Book V; Mysteria Magica*. 1975. Llewellyn Publications. St. Paul, Minnesota, U.S.A.

El-Sabban, Sherif. *Temple Festival Calendars of Ancient Egypt*. 2000. Liverpool University Press, Redwood Books. Trowbridge, Wiltshire, U.K.

Finkel, Michael. *The Stranger in the Woods*. 2018. Simon & Schuster, U.K.

Forrest, Steven. *Yesterday's Sky: Astrology and Reincarnation*. 2008. Seven Paw Press. Borrego Springs, California, U.S.A.

Gary, Gemma. *Traditional Witchcraft: A Cornish Book of Ways*. 2008. Troy Books Publishing. London, England.

Gray, William. *Western Inner Workings*. 1983. Samuel Weiser, Inc. York Beach, Maine, U.S.A.

Fairman, H.W. *The Myth of Horus at Edfu.* 1942

Fortune, Dion and Gareth Knight. *The Circuit of Force* 1998. Thoth Books, U.K.

Funk & Wagnalls Standard Dictionary of Folklore, Mythology and Legend. 1972.365 Funk & Wagnalls Publishing Company, U.S.A.

Harner, Michael. *The Way of the Shaman.* 1980. Bantam Books. New York, New York, U.S.A.

Hart, George. *A Dictionary of Egyptian Gods and Goddesses.* 1986. Routledge & Kegan Paul. London, England.

Holzer, Hans. *The Truth about Witchcraft.* 1971. Doubleday. New York, New York, U.S.A.

Hornung, Eric. *Conceptions of God in Ancient Egypt.* Copyright 1996. Cornell University Press. Ithaca, New York, U.S.A.

Howard, Michael. *Liber Nox: A Traditional Witch's Gramarye.* 2014.51. Skylight Press. U.K.

Huson, Paul. *Mastering Witchcraft: A Practical Guide for Witches, Warlocks & Covens.* 1970. G.P. Putnam's Sons. New York, New York, U.S.A.

Hunter, Jack. *Greening the Paranormal: Exploring the Ecology of Extraordinary Experience.* 2019 August Night Press

Illes, Judika. *Encyclopedia of Witchcraft.* 2005. HarperCollins Publishers. New York, New York, U.S.A.

Jones, Prudence & Nigel Pennick. *A History of Pagan Europe.* 1995. Barnes & Noble, Inc. U.S.A.

Kirk, Robert. *The Secret Commonwealth of Elves, Fauns & Fairies*. 1692. Reprint with commentary as *Robert Kirk: Walker Between the Worlds* edited and commentary by R.J. Stewart 2007.

Lecouteux, Claude. *The Tradition of Household Spirits*. 2000 & 2013. Inner Traditions, Rochester, Vermont, U.S.A.

Leek, Sybil. *Diary of a Witch*. 1968. Prentice-Hall, Inc. Englewood Cliffs, New Jersey, U.S.A.

----------. *Cast Your Own Spell*. 1970. Pinnacle Books. New York, New York, U.S.A.

---------- *The Complete Art of Witchcraft*. 1971. World Publishing Company. New York, New York, U.S.A.

---------- *ESP: The Magic Within You*. 1971. Abelard – Schuman. London, New York, Toronto.

---------- *Telepathy: The 'Respectable' Phenomenon*. The Macmillan Company. New York, New York, U.S.A.

---------- *Reincarnation: The Second Chance*. 1974. Stein and Day. New York, New York, U.S.A.

---------- *Driving Out the Devils: An Exorcist's Casebook*. 1975. G.P. Putnam's Sons. New York, New York, U.S.A.

Leland, Charles G. *Aradia, the Gospel of the Witches*. 1899.

Lurker, Manfred. *An Illustrated Dictionary of the Gods and Symbols of Ancient Egypt*. Copyright 1980. Thames & Hudson Ltd. London, England.

Macfarlane, Alan. *Cunning Folk and Wizards in Early Modern England*. 2010. University of Warwick, Rhode Island, U.S.A.

ID Number 0614383

MacGregor Mathers, S. Liddell. *The Key of Solomon (Clavicula Salomonis)*. 1888.1976 (edition used by author). Samuel Weiser, Inc. New York, New York, U.S.A.

Manniche, Lise. *Sexual Life in Ancient Egypt*. 1987. Kegan Paul International. London, England.

Morgan, Lee. *A Deed Without A Name: Unearthing the Legacy of Traditional Witchcraft*. 2012. Moon Books, U.K.

Moser, Robert. *Mental and Astral Projection*. 1974. Esoteric Publications. Sedona, Arizona U.S.A.

Naydler, Jeremy. *Temple of the Cosmos*. Copyright 1996. Inner Traditions. Rochester, Vermont, U.S.A.

Ó Tuathail, Seán. *Foclóir Draíochta*. 1993.

Paice MacLeod, Sharon. *Celtic Cosmology and the Otherworld*. 2018. McFarland & Company, Inc. Jefferson, North Carolina, U.S.A.

Pearson, Nigel. *Treading the Mill: Workings in Traditional Witchcraft*. 2016. Troy Books, London, England.

Phillips, Osborne. *Aurum Solis: Initiation Ceremonies and Inner Magical Techniques* 2001, Thoth Publications, U.K.

Pinch, Geraldine. *Votive Offerings to Hathor*. Copyright 1993. Griffith Institute. Oxford, England.

----------, *Magic in Ancient Egypt*. 1995. University of Texas. U.S.A.

Roberts, Alison. Hathor Rising: *The Power of the Goddess in Ancient Egypt*. Copyright 1997. Inner Traditions. Rochester, Vermont, U.S.A.

Schumann Antelme, Ruth and Stephane Rossini. Sacred *Sexuality in Ancient Egypt: The Erotic Secrets of the Forbidden Papyrus, A Look at the Unique Role of Hathor, the Goddess of Love*. 1999, 2001. Inner Traditions. Rochester, Vermont, U.S.A.

Scot, Reginald. *Discoverie of Witchcraft*. From the supplementary material added by an anonymous author to the edition in 1665.

Skinner, Stephen. *The Oracle of Geomancy*. 1977.34-37 Warner Books, New York, New York, U.S.A.

Spence, Lewis. *The Magic Arts in Celtic Britain*. 1993. Barnes & Noble, New York, U.S.A.

Tyson, Donald. *Three Books of Occult Philosophy written by Henry Cornelius Agrippa of Nettesheim*. 2006. Llewellyn Worldwide. St. Paul, Minnesota, U.S.A.

Warnock, Christopher. *The Mansions of the Moon – A Lunar Zodiac for Astrology & Magic*. 2006. Renaissance Astrology. U.S.A.

West, John Anthony. *The Traveler's Key to Ancient Egypt*. 1985. Alfred A. Knopf. New York, New York, U.S.A.

Wilkinson, Richard H. *Reading Egyptian Art*. 1992. Thames and Hudson Ltd. New York, New York, U.S.A.

Wisner, Kerry. *Pillar of Ra: Ancient Egyptian Festivals for Today*. 2004, 2020. Kephra Publications. Newport, New Hampshire, U.S.A.

Yale Egyptological Studies. *Religion and Philosophy in Ancient Egypt*, New Haven, Conn. 1989. By: James Allen, J.Assman, A. Lloyd, R. Ritner, D. Silverman. The article in question is by A. Lloyd: *Psychology and Society in the Ancient Egyptian Cult of the Dead* (ppgs.117-133).

CPSIA information can be obtained
at www.ICGtesting.com
Printed in the USA
JSHW021453281122
33788JS00004B/176